Parenting Children with
LEARNING DISABILITIES

LMS

Parenting Children with
LEARNING DISABILITIES

JANE UTLEY ADELIZZI AND DIANE B. GOSS

BERGIN & GARVEY
Westport, Connecticut • London

Library of Congress Cataloging-in-Publication Data

Adelizzi, Jane Utley
    Parenting children with learning disabilities / Jane Utley
Adelizzi and Diane B. Goss.
      p. cm.
    Includes bibliographical references.
    ISBN 0–89789–772–2 (alk. paper)
    1. Learning disabled children—Education—Parent participation—Handbooks,
manuals, etc. I. Goss, Diane B. II. Title.
LC4704.5.A34 2001
649′.15—dc21   00–064210

British Library Cataloguing in Publication Data is available.

Library of Congress Catalog Card Number: 00–064210
ISBN: 0–89789–772–2

First published in 2001

Bergin & Garvey, 88 Post Road West, Westport, CT 06881
An imprint of Greenwood Publishing Group, Inc.
www.greenwood.com

Printed in the United States of America

∞™

The paper used in this book complies with the
Permanent Paper Standard issued by the National
Information Standards Organization (Z39.48–1984).

10 9 8 7 6 5 4 3 2 1

CONTENTS

1

SATURDAY'S CHILD

Monday's child is fair of face,
Tuesday's child is full of grace.
Wednesday's child is full of woe,
Thursday's child has far to go.
Friday's child is loving and giving,
Saturday's child works hard for a living.
But the child who is born on the Sabbath day
Is good and kind in every way.
—Anonymous

You are probably familiar with this poem anonymously written to help children memorize the days of the week. Each line seems to hold such special meaning. When we realized that we were both born on Saturday, we laughed about what an apt description came with that day—"Saturday's child works hard for a living!" As we looked past our personal experiences in connection with the poem, we quickly recognized how well the description of Saturday's child fit the children, adolescents, and adults with learning disabilities who have become our collective life's work. They worked so very hard every day in order to keep up, measure up, and compete with their peers. Their goals are often to gain the respect and admiration of their teachers, parents, and friends. It sounds simple to most people, but to the 10 to 20 percent of the general population with learning disabilities (LD), attention deficit disorder (ADD), or dyslexia, it can be a monumental task that requires a great deal of energy, sweat, prayer, and support. We knew this guidebook was about Saturday's child.

As we researched the origin of Saturday, and moved past the Old Testament, we learned this was the name given to the seventh day of the week in honor of the Roman god Saturn. Saturn's Day seemed to represent what the Romans referred to as the "learning principles." This certainly seemed significant to us, as our chief concern was with those individuals who were often challenged in their learning. Saturday seemed to symbolize the last day, the day of rest in the week. For many of us Saturday means a day away from the grind of life, the challenge of learning, the stage upon which all mistakes are publicized. Saturday can be the day to watch cartoons, color in a favorite book, pretend your bicycle is a horse, have a tea party with your dog, build a castle, or look at the pictures and not read the words. Saturday could be the reward after all of the hard work! This felt hopeful.

As the poem tells us, "Saturday's child works hard for a living." The child who struggles to maintain a sense of equilibrium in her life when the sky is falling, when the headless horseman is chasing her, or when the mirror on the wall reflects a child who is dancing as fast as she can indeed works hard for a living. She works especially hard because she doesn't learn the same way that her brother, who earns As and Bs in school, learns. She has trouble reading, understanding her math, and like Alice in Wonderland, life around her looks and feels distorted and misshapen sometimes. She keeps bumping into things, both figuratively and literally. It's so difficult to explain to her mother why she feels this way. It's easier to just be quiet about it, and pray that things will become easier and clearer tomorrow. Her learning disability has been diagnosed for two years now. Her educational plan has been implemented in the eyes of special services at her elementary school, and still she feels dumb. Her mother feels frightened as she watches her daughter grow increasingly more quiet, isolated. She suspects that her daughter is depressed, but isn't sure that kids really can get depressed. Who should the mother talk to?

Saturday's child is also the boy who runs faster than his classmates on the playground, but makes mistakes when he plays checkers with his younger cousin. He's defeated every time! What a blow to the ego. His parents try hard to understand what might be "wrong" with him, because they have been conditioned to believe that whatever falls outside the perceived norm, must be wrong. The school sends home notes to his parents, using technical jargon that is meaningless to these parents who are desperately searching for whatever ray of light might illuminate their path to understanding. However, the idea that these impossible notes are sent to them at all is cause for worry, frustration, and eventually anger against a system that seems to hold all the power. They fret about what to do about their son. They call their friends. Some have suggestions that make sense, some have books to read, but no one is really able to sit down with them and explain the school's expectations for their son. They feel guilty because their child is struggling, and they feel inadequate because they don't understand what to do next.

These are parents who need a guide. As Saturday's children ourselves we hope to fill that role for you. Sometimes we will speak to you as parents in an instructive manner, trying to take you by the hand and lead you to some understanding about how the cognitive, socioemotional, neurobiological, cultural, and spiritual aspects of the self are all involved in the learning process and in family dynamics.

There will also be times when we will speak to you in the voice of Dr. Evah Nellsom. Dr. Nellsom is a composite of the most talented and caring learning specialists and educational therapists we know. She is the possessor of knowledge and experience, and she is the giver of much love and care. She is humorous, she is tender, and she too is an accomplished professional who doesn't waste any time in educating families about how to cope and adapt to a life that is full of obstacles. She too must be a Saturday's child.

TOPICS COVERED

In selecting the topics for this book, we kept in mind the many questions parents have asked us over the years. We definitely did not want to make this book a textbook on learning disabilities, covering all of the technical details, and spouting all of the current statistics. It's likely that that approach would give you more than you need or want to know. On the other hand, we are aware that most parents of children with learning difficulties are thirsty to understand some of that "specialized" knowledge that seems to be held by teachers and learning therapists. If you are reading this book, you are probably one of those parents. We hope that we will answer many of your questions and address most of your concerns, and we hope to do this without losing sight of the forest while focusing on the trees!

In covering each topic, we constantly asked ourselves, "What is it that parents need to know about this in order to help their children?" Some of you want "the big picture"—a general understanding of the topic. Others of you have specific areas in mind and want to understand them in greater depth. You want to get down to the "nitty-gritty details." Many of you want simply to find support, understanding, and emotional reassurance. We hope there is something here for each of you.

HOW TO READ THIS BOOK

Children with learning disabilities present their parents with a variety of questions, dilemmas, and puzzles. This book can help you to explore the current and most pressing issues you are facing. The term learning disabilities will be used interchangeably with the term learning differences, and LD/ADD/Dyslexia. We tried to include the terminology most commonly used in most parts of North America.

You will discover that there are many stories that help to illustrate the problems and joys that are faced by families who are dealing with LD/ADD/Dyslexia. Some of these stories include characters that are found in more than one chapter, such as our friend, Dr. Evah Nellsom. As a child psychologist, she visits the communities of many of the characters in order to enlighten them about issues concerning and influencing families that deal with learning disabilities. Dr. Nellsom is a dedicated professional. We wish she were a real person.

CHAPTER 1

This chapter introduces you to *Saturday's Child* as a means of understanding who the child with learning disabilities really is. The chapters of this guidebook are outlined for the reader, inviting discriminating choices in terms of material that is relevant for each person.

CHAPTER 2

Are You Saturday's Child? helps you to think about your own history, your classroom experiences, both good and bad, and your feelings about learning and about yourself as a learner. Parents are asked to reflect on their own educational histories, reaching back into their memories of both good and bad experiences in the classroom, on the playground, the streets, and at home. Knowing more about yourself will help you to understand your own reactions to your child's learning difficulties.

CHAPTER 3

Pieces of the Puzzle: Learning Deficits and Disabilities presents an explanation of what we mean by the term "learning disabilities." It explains the major terms used by professionals in defining various types of learning problems and describes the ways in which these problems can manifest themselves in your child's behaviors both inside and outside the classroom. This chapter will put into plain language and help you to make sense of the educational jargon you hear used in reference to your child.

CHAPTER 4

Diagnosis of Learning Disabilities takes you through the process by which specialists try to figure out whether your child has learning disabilities and what these learning disabilities may be. If you have a thick folder full of test results, educational plans, and progress reports, this chapter will help you sort the mountain of material contained in it! It will also help you to be sure your child has received an adequate and thorough assessment. It will even give you some suggestions on being a diagnostician yourself through careful observation of your child.

CHAPTER 5

Our Great Brain: Learning and Functioning offers you a description of the brain and its role in thinking, feeling, and learning through a story of a child who has experienced both physical and psychological trauma. It will help you understand the way we take in, process, remember, and put out information. It also discusses the way our thoughts, feelings, and behaviors are connected and work together in learning. This will give you a background for a better understanding of what happens when something goes wrong in the process as well as what happens when something goes right.

CHAPTER 6

The Socioemotional Impact of Learning Disabilities on the Child focuses on the connections between learning disabilities, feelings, and social relationships through several vignettes, and through the guidance of Dr. Evah Nellsom. If you yourself have struggled with learning or have tried to help your child to deal with learning problems, you know that this challenge brings out strong emotions—some of them painful—in almost everyone. You know also that difficulties in learning and functioning affect classroom performance, social relationships, and the quality of family life. Many children with learning disabilities struggle with depression, learned helplessness, frustration, anger, and low self-esteem. Many parents worry about their children's difficulties in social adjustment and in relationships and interactions with others. This chapter will help you to assist your child in coping with hurt feelings, isolation, missed social cues, and communication problems.

CHAPTER 7

The Helping Hand: What You Can Do to Help Your Child Learn offers general principles and guidelines for how to help your child in positive ways. It guides parents in avoiding the pitfall of providing too much support and fostering overdependency, as well as the danger of helping too little and leaving your child feeling frustrated and hopeless. It also tackles one of the most important jobs of all: getting organized. This chapter gives concrete and practical suggestions that can save hours of time and many tears.

CHAPTER 8

The Spoken Word: Listening, Speaking, and Silence explores both the receptive and expressive aspects of oral language. Some children with learning disabilities are not adept listeners and need to experiment with a variety of methods to accomplish this vital survival tool. This chapter offers parents some ways of developing their child's receptive language ability and helping their child to compensate for deficits in taking in and processing spoken language. It also looks at the expressive side of spoken language and gives suggestions on ways parents can help their children to translate their thoughts into clear, complete, well-organized, oral language. This chapter also explores the "silent voice" of the child.

CHAPTER 9

The Written Word: Reading and Writing explores both the receptive and expressive aspects of written language. It offers techniques for helping children to develop the reading and writing skills so central to school-based learning. It also suggests ways of dealing with the emotional impact of reading failure and of making the reading process less threatening for children with learning disabilities. It teaches parents how to encourage creative written expression, and how to help their children organize their written language clearly.

CHAPTER 10

The Language of Math addresses mathematics as a language in itself, and looks at how this concept is grossly underestimated as such by many professionals in education. Mathematics, with its world of symbols, formulas, and processes, can feel like a mine field for many children with various types of learning disabilities. This chapter explains various types of math-related learning disabilities and how they manifest themselves in a child's learning. It suggests strategies, games, activities, and materials parents can use to help their children develop math skills and concepts.

CHAPTER 11

Tools of the Trade: Using Technology to Enhance Learning gives suggestions on using some of the latest hardware and software available to help children with learning difficulties. These resources can open up a world of possibilities for learning. This chapter will introduce you to some of them and provide you with suggestions on using them effectively.

CHAPTER 12

Navigating the System provides a guide for parents as they try to work with school systems and other institutions that have so much power over the destinations of children with learning disabilities and, ultimately, their families. Through Dr. Evah Nellsom and the Horton family you will learn how to navigate the sometimes tumultuous journey in special education.

CHAPTER 13

The Holistic Approach: Crunchy Granola, Intellectualism, and Wisdom for the Family, a series of vignettes, offers examples of the many avenues that families can take in order to gain a sense of health and balance in their lives. This can be particularly important in a family struggling to cope with issues related to a child's learning difficulties. This chapter guides you in thinking about choosing the healing pathways that are consistent with your family philosophy and culture, mindful always of the emotional connection to learning.

Saturday's child walks parents through the forest, sometimes leaving a trail of breadcrumbs to a new pathway of understanding. We like to think we are walking you into the light, into the sunshine of hope that awaits you. Let us take you by the hand and guide you.

A WORD FOR FAMILIES

We have met many Saturday's children and their families. These families have come to us with their hands in the air, searching for hope, some concrete shred of meaning that will make everything look like it "fits" into place for their child, for their circle of caregivers and supporters. These parents and their children are seeking a sanctuary following a fast-paced week full of new things to learn and acceptable ways to behave in a society that often can't or won't take the time to allow for differences in learning and functioning.

Many hours have been spent in person, on the phone, and through the mail speaking with mothers, fathers, grandparents, and extended family members who care about the plight of these children. We have attended social functions where we enter the situation hoping to be lost in the crowd in order sit in a corner, quietly watching the people. More often than not, we are approached by someone who is eager to introduce us to a friend or relative as "someone who knows what your child is going through." The conversation begins, and before long the story of this child's struggles and aspirations unfolds to reveal a picture of a family, not just a child. This is because the child who lives with a learning disability does not exist in isolation. His life experience impacts the life experience of his parents, siblings, friends, and all of the other people in his life who interact with him.

The cause and effect becomes an all encompassing process, with family as the circle of survivors who hold each other up while one link in the circle falters, only to be brought to his feet again by the others who want to maintain the cohesiveness of the whole. Some children's circles are larger than others, and in fact some circles are very small, including just a few people that have to become even stronger links lest one should stumble to the ground. No matter what size the circle is, or in what way the family is configured or composed, the learning disability emerges as the core, and becomes the focal point of everyone's attention, energy, and hope for success, for victory. At times the learning disability is perceived as the enemy, making the circle tighter in its endeavor to overcome whatever obstacles impede the progress of the child with LD/ADD/Dyslexia, or less unified, leaving itself vulnerable.

We have walked with you in many places. Please let us again take this journey with you, reacquainting you with who you are, and who your children are. Let us be your guides to Saturday's child.

2

ARE YOU SATURDAY'S CHILD?

MIRROR, MIRROR . . .

Remember the movie *Snow White*? "Mirror, mirror on the wall, who's the fairest of them all?" This of course was spoken by the wicked stepmother in anticipation of an answer that would make her look like the best of everything, to everyone in the land. Who do you see when you look into the mirror, especially as a parent? Do you see someone who is yielding, compliant? Someone who is firm, authoritative? Do you see an adult who is intelligent, accomplished? Or do you see someone you are impatient with, and maybe disappointed in? And maybe you see the child you were, looking back at you.

Very often when we look at our children we are reminded of who we were as children, and who we are as adults, as parents. Looking at our children can be like looking in a mirror throughout each developmental phase of their lives. Their shining moments as human beings, as students, as siblings, as our sons and daughters, become our mirror images. We burst with pride. "This is me!" we shout to ourselves. "This is who I was. This is who I am!" Our egos are inflated. We strut, we cluck, we preen. Love that mirror!

On the other hand, when our children fail in school, disrupt our households, our personal and professional lives, and commit deeds that are appalling to us, the mirror image is disgraceful to us. We too are failures. We may act out our anger, our disappointment, and make sure that the perpetrator of this disgrace is brought to justice! Who does this person think she is neglecting her homework? Who is this boy who refuses to pay attention in his class? Are they like us, or is the universe paying us back for some misdeed in our past? More important, why is our pain so deep, so wide, when we are witnessing the pain of our children? Why do we feel so vulnerable when we witness our children's failures?

Often we search our mental files for notes on where we went wrong in our parenting histories in order for this child to bring such disappointment to herself and to her family. When children are sliding downhill in school, life becomes an upheaval of emotions and a disorganization in functioning within the family structure, especially in the child-parent relationship. Life begins to feel very different from what we once knew as a peaceful existence, or at least a manageable and routine lifestyle. We pray. We talk to our closest friends, maybe to our own parents, searching for some tried and true wisdom that will make sense of this situation, this dilemma, this very unfair and frightening experience of dealing with a child who learns and functions differently.

In desperation we search for books that can explain what learning disabilities are. What does all that jargon mean? What is inclusion, really? And, what in this world do the numbers and statistics mean? Parents just want to throw their hands up in desperation, in surrender, and say, "Just help me to understand this kid! Help me to help him!"

Maybe your child has been diagnosed with a learning disability by the school system or through a private educational diagnostician. And maybe your child has not been diagnosed with any specific kind of disorder or condition, but is behaving in ways that command your immediate attention. You've made more trips to the school to speak with the principal and teachers than you care to admit. You find it a mystery that your child never brings home his papers. You watch your daughter as she becomes physically ill every Monday morning, begging you to let her stay home. You stand there, ready for work, ready for your day, and she stands before you with pleading eyes, and an outstretched hand holding a thermometer she has just placed under a light bulb.

These children, these resilient, talented, and often wounded children are Saturday's children, and like the poem tells us, "they work hard for a living." What takes one child an hour to accomplish with homework, might take your child two or three hours, and might be accompanied by some prompting, some tutorial work in order for the concept, the expectations, and even the directions to be made understandable. For some parents this process is reminiscent of their own experiences in school.

LOOKING BACK

Sometimes it becomes important as parents to look back in time to our own experiences as children in the classroom. Although we are all aware how counterproductive it can be to keep reaching back into our pasts, it is only with a thorough understanding of who we are as a result of our personal and educational histories, that we can gain insight into who our children are. The fears and threats that often immobilize our children in their struggles to learn and function are often similar in nature to our own memories of ourselves as children.

For instance, reach back into the past for memories of kindergarten. Do you remember how you felt on that very first day of school? Were you frightened? Did you want your mother or whomever it was that brought you to school to leave, or to stay with you, at least within sight? What was your first impression of your kindergarten teacher? Was she scary? Did she immediately convey a sense of kindness and understanding to you? Try to respond to these questions with a sense of objectivity if that's possible. Do you think that your immediate responses to these questions might be similar to those of your children?

Do you remember your comfort level as you interacted with your peers during those very early stages in your educational history? Did you feel there were expectations beyond your capabilities for you to socialize appropriately, whatever that meant in your five-or six-year-old mind. Were you at ease and approachable? Or were you frozen with fear because someone might expect you to perform a task for which you were not prepared, or able to do?

When your teacher called out your name, were you proud, confident, and eager to get on with this kindergarten thing, or were you trembling, wishing the time away, just wanting to be at home and safe? Were the games you played in the schoolyard, in the classroom, or at home confusing to you, or were you the first person to raise your hand? Did you know how to count the spaces with your Monopoly figure?

The arenas in which our children must perform their understanding of concepts and directions are many. Life is full of these learning situations, and the child with learning disabilities may be proficient at some of these tasks, and often with many, although there is usually one area in which Saturday's child appears "stumped." As time passes the response to tasks that feel unmanageable to the child may become masked with coping and adapting mechanisms that deflect our attention away from the actual problem. After a period of trying to wrestle with the problem your child is experiencing, and ultimately you are experiencing, the problem may not look recognizable anymore, but the behaviors do. It is when these behaviors come to the forefront of life at home, at school, and in our relationships that our parenting skills are challenged, and the mirror is again held in front of our faces. Does this child look familiar?

Responses to the above questions can most often be traced back to a "reason." Those of us who shopped eagerly for our first day of kindergarten outfits, lunchboxes, and pencils weren't always aware of what awaited us within that room full of peers, tables, chairs, toys, and books. For some young children, the challenge of meeting this new experience was invigorating, much like some adults we observe as they meet each problem in daily life with gusto. For other children, the constant juggling act required in order to attend, listen, watch, and understand becomes a monumental undertaking. It's exhausting!

Some parents today had the advantage of attending preschool. However, that experience was not available to everyone, and it really depended upon where you lived, what economic bracket your parents were in, and whether it was an accepted part of your family culture. But for those parents who did attend preschool, they received at least a year's worth of experience in the socialization process—ready or not. For those who were ready, each day might have been a wonderful social and learning occasion, important stuff for survival within any stage of development.

For some parents who remember their experiences in preschool, it makes the ability to understand their own children's trouble in dealing with daily life in the classroom environment a little easier. Some parents remember the daily struggle of learning how to have friends, how to act with them, moving beyond the stage of parallel play to actually playing *with* each other, a true social interaction. Some parents are acutely aware of how painful it is to have to watch the child who moves with great trepidation through the process of learning how to interact in life with other people.

The struggle to fit into life's social structure may become an uphill struggle for the child with learning disabilities, an unfortunate term for those who learn and function differently. Those parents who themselves experienced challenges in their learning and functioning are sometimes attuned to the struggles of their children. As a result, these parents usually react in either of two ways: by demonstrating support that stems from deep empathy, or by pushing their children to perform in a manner that causes undue stress. The latter reason may be due to an insatiable need of the parent to rewrite history, to alter the script, to make life better. For the parents who know from experience what it's like to struggle in the classroom as far back as kindergarten, watching their children navigate through the same developmental struggles is like being in the moment again.

WHO ARE YOU?

Let's move this reflective journey back to who you were in elementary school, in high school, and then in adulthood. Can you recall who your favorite teachers were in elementary school? See if you can make a list of the attributes these teachers possessed. Is kindness an attribute on this list? Compassion? Patience? Did your favorite teachers have ways to make you feel worthwhile? Appreciated? Smart? What physical attributes did that individual possess?

Take a look at the teachers who stood out in your memories as being unkind. Why do you suppose that was? Were they impatient with your ability and speed of processing information? Did they demonstrate disgust or disappointment with your behaviors or performance? Did they make you feel threatened in any way? What physical attributes did that individual possess?

Please notice that I asked you to think about the physical attributes that both the favorite and least-liked teachers possessed. Often there is an imprint of an attribute embedded in our minds that acts as a trigger to automatic kinds of responses on our parts as parents. For instance, if a teacher who impacted your life in a very positive manner just happened to have red curly hair, you might find yourself responding in a most favorable way, at least initially, to another teacher with a similar attribute. We often hope for a repeat performance of that which was good for us in an earlier stage of our lives.

There is an awesome kind of power in the classroom, and often students do not share in this power, but may be the victims of power that is abused. If you were a child with a learning disability, you may have lived in fear of humiliation in many classroom situations. If your learning disability was diagnosed and acknowledged by your teachers, you may have received special attention, this may have been beneficial to you, or it may have proven an added burden to your growing list of worries as a child.

If your child also has a learning disability, you may find yourself watching her every move. You may listen to her accounts of her "mean teacher" and feel your blood boil with memories of your own fears and humiliations in the classroom. On the other hand, you may feel a sense of relief that your child is receiving better services and teaching methods than were available for you at that age. Each parent moves through this experience in a different way, and the feelings experienced as a result of watching your child with learning disabilities depend greatly upon your own experiences in similar circumstances.

Looking back to our experiences in elementary school brings us to reflect upon how the social development of our children keeps changing and becoming more complex in its sophistication. This means that as children move from kindergarten to elementary school, the stakes are higher. Friends are important. Socialization is vital. For parents who experienced difficulty in elementary school in social skills, these memories are most painful because the art of cultivating friendships is difficult enough without having the added challenge of being unable to read people. This difficulty plays out in the inability to interact appropriately with peers, and the inability to read the teacher, her expressions, her expectations, her feelings. The interpretation of nonverbal communication is a monumental task for some, an art for others, and always a concern for parents. Developing these skills is vital to survival, and they are carried with each child into adulthood.

If you are a parent who as a child experienced difficulty in the area of learning and functioning, you may or may not recognize your child's trouble in this arena. In your adult life you may still experience trouble reading people's expressions, the nuances in language, a good joke, and the psychic kinds of feelings we often receive from people as we interact, dialogue, smile, and love. There are no instructions in life in order to gain these skills. Some of these skills can be improved upon with intervention provided by professionals who are proficient in the diagnoses of nonverbal disabilities that impede communication. But for many children and their parents, the neurological wiring that gets in the way of effective communication is not rewireable. The effects of these difficulties permeate communication and relationships on many levels, both personally and professionally.

Another factor to reflect upon as a parent is the very real impact of humiliation in the classroom. Most parents can remember at least one experience in the classroom where they were embarrassed to tears. This may be experienced as a result of fears harbored over performing a specific task. As children, some parents may have been made to feel inadequate in the classroom by peers; taunting, bullying, and sarcasm leave many scars and deep-rooted anger that manifests itself in many ways, even into adulthood. Then there are those individuals who have suffered the pain of humiliation at the hands of a teacher who may have felt it necessary to parade individual inadequacies in front of the classroom. If you can recall some of these experiences, or were a witness to your friends' humiliations, think then about your own child, especially the child with learning disabilities, and remember how it felt to live in fear of humiliation. These are indignities that are very real, and although we prefer to think they occur less as time passes, the fact remains that they still exist.

This brings me to the high school experience and who you feel you were during this period in your life. Some parents can remember how it felt to be recognized by peers and teachers for outstanding ability in academic or athletic achievement. For those parents who were academically challenged, it was often a continuous search to find an arena in which achievement, recognition, and respect were possible. For some fortunate individuals, external motivation came from basking in the limelight as an athlete. For others, good looks, popularity, or an ability in the arts provided pathways to respect from others. Unfortunately for some individuals, anger toward a system filled with authority figures that felt like "the enemy" caused behaviors and attitudes that may have led to truancy, a self-esteem under constant threat, delinquency, and at the very least, low academic achievement.

Reflecting upon our own experiences as teenagers makes us look at our children, and again, especially those children with learning disabilities. What are the routes they have chosen in order to work out their joys, frustrations, and anger with themselves and others? What part do we play as parents? Do we help? Do we hinder? Do we ask ourselves these questions at all, or are most parents just so busy juggling the many aspects of life that they can't always stop to take stock of what is happening?

There are so many questions. But remember, we have to look at ourselves as parents, at our histories as learners, before we can presume to understand this child who "works hard for a living."

THE PSYCHOLOGICAL ASPECT

Another perspective that needs to be acknowledged as we look at who we are as parents is who we were as children as the result of the impact of psychological trauma on learning and functioning. Are our experiences much different from those of our children? Possibly the events are similar, although the players and stage design may change with the sociological demands of time. The consequential effects may manifest themselves in very similar ways, although each person's perception of the event(s) may differ as well as his or her abilities to cope and adapt.

Observing another's stress or trauma can be as painful as experiencing it yourself. Watching our children navigate life both in and out of the classroom environment often brings up memories that are impossible for us to look at in any other way than emotionally. Another important reason why it can be valuable to look back, or reflect, may be to learn from our experiences. Try as we do, it is not possible to rewrite the scripts of our lives. For children with learning disabilities, ongoing discussions about themselves, their experiences, and their perceptions in conjunction with their parents' reflections may bring greater clarity to what might appear or feel like confusion.

Let's look back again to the little girl who is holding out the thermometer to her mother, just minutes before the bus picks her up for school. From the child's perspective, her motives are clear and simple. If she can manipulate her mother successfully, she can stay home from school and possibly have her mother stay home with her. And the best part of all? She misses a test. She misses reading aloud to her peers, misses risking that same humiliation again. It doesn't matter that she still has to walk into that classroom on another day, look at her teacher, and face her peers and the expectations that have been imposed upon her by well-meaning educators. All that matters is that she misses the assault on her mind, her spirit, and her emotional survival for just one day. One blessed day.

Do you remember how that little girl felt? Possibly you were a child who bounded out of bed each morning, looking to the challenges of the day in school with a sense of excitement and joy. But maybe you were this little girl. Maybe you constantly felt so misunderstood and misjudged in the classroom that you would go to almost any length to avoid the experience. Often children who feel this way spend a great deal of time visiting the nurse's office at school; sometimes they become "regulars." Sometimes they get lucky and miss a dreaded test, math class, or a game that is particularly embarrassing because the directions are so hard to follow. The laughter from peers as a result of the mistakes can be painful and is often survived through some very artful coping mechanisms.

This little girl, this Saturday's child, might put endless extra hours of work into learning how to memorize a poem for her homework. Were you one of those children who used up all of his or her energy trying to listen carefully to the instructions before a test? Did the thought of the test reduce you to a mass of trembling limbs, make your stomach twist into knots? Did you feel nauseous at the thought of standing in front of the class to deliver a book report, describe your recent vacation, or ask a question that might shed some light on a new concept that was lost in the fog?

There are many reasons why Saturday's child works hard for a living. There are many reasons why he can't seem to grapple with his work, can't control it, can't succeed in ways that will offer him hope, peace of mind, and faith in himself as a learner and as a human being. For some children the business of surviving an unstable or threatening home life usurps all of the time and emotional energy he has. Saturday's child may experience panic attacks. Yes, even at this early age, human beings do respond in a most primitive way when their safety is under siege. The result of having to deal with such basic survival needs at a young age may be that the child's behavior and performance in school resemble that of a learning disability. For all intents and purposes, that's how it needs to be treated in order for that child to arrive at a level of safety at least within the classroom community. Yes, learning stops, is arrested, is impeded, and runs out of control when Saturday's child is not even able to work hard for a living.

Are you a Saturday's child?

3

PIECES OF THE PUZZLE: LEARNING DEFICITS AND DISABILITIES

Hannah remembers the tightness she felt in her chest the first time she heard the word learning disabilities used in reference to her ten-year-old daughter. At a routine parent-teacher conference, Rachel's teacher had confirmed something they had already noticed: their daughter's performance was uneven, puzzling, sometimes unpredictable. Though she seemed bright, she wasn't making progress in the key skills needed for reading. The words she copied into her workbooks were often indecipherable scribbles. Sometimes she was painfully frustrated in doing tasks most of the other children had mastered. Perhaps, the teacher suggested (oh so casually!), she should be tested for a learning disability.

The words hit Hannah with the suddenness of an ice cream headache. Rachel, her bright-eyed, dreamer. Rachel, the child who had talked early, noticed everything, and came out with comments that made everyone say she must be on her second time around! Rachel, only at the end of fourth grade, only at the beginning of a lifetime of educational opportunities. How could this be? Had they done something wrong? Did this mean the end of the dreams and hopes they had nurtured for their daughter from the moment she had charged prematurely into this world? And, of course, the universal question echoed in her heart too, "Why me? Why my child?"

After a few days spent alternating between denial ("That teacher doesn't know what she's talking about!") and fear ("She's never going to be able to succeed in school!"), Hannah and her husband began to pull themselves together. They would figure out exactly what they were dealing with and they would do something about it. They would get past this obstacle that had been thrown in their path. They believed in Rachel and knew that together they would find a way to help her.

Hannah and Ralph immersed themselves in research, clicking away on the Internet late into the night, coming home arms overflowing with books from their public library and local bookstore. But instead of finding clarity, they were overwhelmed by the information they found. It seemed as if they had opened a puzzle with no picture on the cover of the box. A pile of tiny pieces had spilled out, but they couldn't put them together into a clear image. Some of the pieces were unrecognizable. Lots of them didn't fit their daughter. But then, there were the bits that were familiar, that they recognized, that made them say, "That's Rachel!"

Like Hannah and Ralph, parents whose children are having difficulties of any kind are eager to "get the picture." They are willing, even desperate, to learn more about the thing that is causing problems for their children. When parents of children with learning disabilities seek answers, they meet with a bewildering array of definitions, classifications, and descriptions. If you're one of these parents, you probably know how hard it is to find your way through this confusing maze.

One of the first things you probably want to do is find out exactly what a learning disability is. However, even the experts disagree on some aspects of the definition. Learning disabilities are difficult to define because the term includes such a wide range of diverse learning problems, some of which are very hard to pin down. Coming up with a concise, neat definition that includes them all isn't easy.

WHAT A LEARNING DISABILITY IS NOT

It's a good idea to start with what a learning disability is not. Clearing up some common misunderstandings can allay many of the fears parents have when they first learn that their child has a learning disability. First and foremost, a learning disability does *not* mean that your child has a low level of general intelligence, so don't stop contributing to that college fund! Many brilliant people have had learning disabilities, and most children with learning disabilities have strengths that can help them overcome the problems they will encounter. A learning disability does not mean that your child cannot learn. It just means that he or she will learn differently.

Second, a learning disability is not an emotional or psychiatric problem. Though some children with learning disabilities do suffer from emotional difficulties like low self-esteem, anxiety, depression, rage, or withdrawal, these problems are not the cause of their learning difficulties. On the contrary, they may actually be effects of the failure and frustration they have experienced.

Third, a learning disability is not primarily caused by a sensory deficit (like hearing loss or poor vision) or by motor handicaps (like problems in controlling hand movements). A child with a learning disability may have 20/20 vision and still be unable to read the words on a page. Of course, sensory deficits do affect a child's ability to learn and to demonstrate his learning, but they are not in themselves considered to be learning disabilities.

Fourth, a learning disability is not the result of a lack of educational opportunity or competent instruction. This is an important distinction. If a child who is a visual learner is in an educational setting where most of the instruction is by "word of mouth," she may appear to have a learning disability when it may actually be simply a difference in learning style. Sometimes, because of an inadequate school system, a child doesn't have the opportunity to gain necessary skills. In other cases, the child may have missed some of the basics because of a childhood illness, moving to another school, or a family crisis that disrupted his ability to learn. Some children come to school inadequately prepared for learning because their families lacked the resources or knowledge to develop basic prelearning skills. While all of these children may struggle with learning, their problems are not classified as learning disabilities.

To make matters even more confusing, there is often more than one cause of a learning problem. Learning is an extremely complex and multifaceted activity. Many factors can positively or negatively influence a child's success in learning. A learning disability can coexist with one or more of the conditions described above. However, none of those conditions (mental retardation, psychiatric or emotional problems, sensory deficits, lack of appropriate learning opportunities) constitute a learning disability in itself.

DEFINITION OF A LEARNING DISABILITY

Many of the learning disability organizations as well as federal and state laws have defined learning disabilities for the purpose of identifying children who need services. Widely accepted definitions include those used by the federal government in the Individuals with Disabilities Education Act (1997), the National Joint Council on Learning Disabilities, the Interagency Committee on Learning Disabilities (1987), and the Learning Disabilities Association, among others. The definitions vary slightly, but all have some common elements. For example, all of the definitions recognize that the term learning disability must be broad enough to include a wide range of learning difficulties. By comparing and combining the various definitions, we can come up with some elements that are generally accepted by educators and other experts in the field.

Basically a learning disability is a disorder in one, or several, of the mental abilities involved in learning. The brain is not functioning properly in performing some of the neurological processes needed for effective learning. Learning is a very complicated task and involves the integration of many brain-based processes. These include processes for taking in information, interpreting it, organizing it in a meaningful way, and expressing the information or knowledge in a way that allows the learner to apply or convey his or her understanding to others. Learning also requires the learner to pay attention to the task and to monitor his or her own learning as it occurs. It is actually an extraordinary and miraculous process! It is no wonder that our brains may sometimes fail to perform every aspect of this process perfectly.

THE LEARNING PROCESS AND LEARNING DISABILITIES

PERCEPTUAL PROBLEMS

We take in information through our senses: seeing, listening, tasting, feeling, and smelling. The senses that are most important depend on the type of learning task. For example, no one ever learned to ride a bike just by watching someone else or by listening to someone else describe how to do it. Glitches in the way the brain takes in and interprets information from the senses are included in the definition of a learning disability. These problems are sometimes referred to as perceptual problems. A child who has problems in visual perception may not be able to recognize a particular shape as a triangle, identify a missing element in a picture, or see the difference between "b" and "d." A child who has deficits in auditory perception may have trouble discriminating between the sound of "bat" and "pat," may not be able to understand spoken directions, or may not notice sounds in his or her environment like the barking of the dog wanting to come in from the yard. Children with deficits in perception of tactile (touch) or kinesthetic (movement) information may have difficulty picking up the cues and feelings that would help them learn to pour a glass of milk without spilling it, or handle clay, paint, blocks, or a pencil in school.

INFORMATION PROCESSING PROBLEMS

Once we take in information (perceive it), we need to process it mentally, connect it to the network of information already stored in the brain, and find meaning in it. This might mean arranging the information in a linear sequence (one element after another in order) or organizing parts within larger wholes. It may involve recognizing relationships like cause and effect or comparing and contrasting the new information with previously gained knowledge. It may mean analyzing (picking it apart), synthesizing (putting it together), classifying (putting it into a category), or judging the validity of what is taken in. It can involve applying the knowledge to real life situations, drawing logical conclusions, or coming up with a creative insight.

Some children (and adults) have difficulty with these kinds of thinking tasks. Their minds can take in the ideas, but they can't make sense of them. Some have a rich and dense network of thoughts, but are overwhelmed by the number and complexity of their own ideas. Others don't process deeply enough and miss some of the connections between their ideas. They may have trouble drawing conclusions or moving from the specific and concrete (Fluffy) to the more general and abstract (feline).

MEMORY PROBLEMS

Another important aspect of mental processing involves holding the information temporarily in working memory or storing it for an extended period of time in long-term memory. Some children can't keep a telephone number in working memory long enough to dial it. Others will be able to solve an equation (even one with complicated steps) perfectly on Monday, but have no idea how to go about it on Friday.

Memories may be in the form of visual images, sounds, or tactile (touch) and kinesthetic (position or movement) sensations. Learning disabilities can involve specific aspects of memory. Some children can remember words, but not musical tunes. Others can recall pictures, but can't seem to remember how to tie their shoes. Some of you reading this book have surely lamented that your children can remember baseball scores or how to hit a ball with a bat, but can't master a list of the state capitals.

EXPRESSIVE PROBLEMS

Another phase of the learning process involves expressing or demonstrating what we think and know. In school, this expression is often in the form of talking and writing. However, creating a musical score or painting is also a form of expressive language. In fact, if we lived in a culture where these forms of expression were considered essential to learning, there would be many more of us classified as learning disabled! As it is, our educational system is very language-based, and it is children with difficulty in expressing themselves through speaking or writing who are considered to have an expressive language deficit.

Children with expressive disabilities experience the tremendous frustration of knowing more than they can communicate. Expressive disabilities may be in the area of language, for example, generating too little language or too much, being too specific or too general. But expressive problems can also be in other areas as well. The child may know what he wants to draw for his art assignment, but can't execute his ideas. He may have a great idea for a poster for his social studies presentation, but makes a mess of it—usually at 10:00 P.M. on the one piece of poster board you have in the house! This may be the child who studies hard, but fails the exam; the child who has lots of ideas for his papers, but never gets them done on time; the one who has gathered a pile of data for his science project, but can't put the pieces together.

ATTENTION AND SELF-MONITORING DEFICITS

Throughout the learning cycle, while we perform the tasks of taking in, processing, and putting out information, our brains are simultaneously busy with other important tasks. Specific areas of the brain are responsible for allowing us to focus on the tasks and maintain our attention on them. Other areas monitor or "watch" what we are doing, giving us feedback as to the success or lack of success we are achieving in our efforts. Executive functions like these direct our learning, help us to change pace, tell us when to try new strategies, let us know whether we understand what we are doing. Some children don't seem to be aware of what is happening as they learn. The process is a mystery to them, a mystery that often results in failed attempts and a child who is frustrated because he doesn't know why his efforts didn't pay off.

INTEGRATED LEARNING

The whole learning cycle, taking in information, interpreting and processing it, remembering it, and expressing what we have learned, is an obstacle course for children with learning disabilities. There are so many potential hurdles that must be jumped, so many subskills that must be mastered individually and then put together into a system that works well together. While your child may be great at a high pole vault, she may falter in climbing a low fence.

Children with learning disabilities have deficits in specific areas of the learning process. They often puzzle us because the contrast between their strengths and their weaknesses doesn't seem to make sense. Any attempt to understand your child's learning problems must look not only at specific areas of weakness, but also at his strengths and at the way the various areas of learning work together.

SPECIFIC TYPES AND SUBTYPES OF LEARNING DISABILITIES

To try to get a better handle on what is going on with specific children, learning specialists have broken down the catch-all term "learning disabilities" into a variety of subtypes. While there is no universal agreement over the way to organize and classify these various types of learning disabilities, being aware of some of the major categories can help you to understand the complicated world of learning disabilities.

As you try to make sense of these classifications, you should also be aware that children often have more than one type of learning disability and that these types may overlap in their effects. You will probably see your child in several of these subtype descriptions. Even learning specialists often have a hard time pinpointing the exact nature of a child's learning problems. Children (like all of us human beings) don't fit into neat categories!

LANGUAGE LEARNING DISABILITIES

One major group of learning disabilities can be classified as language learning disabilities. This umbrella term includes deficits in both receptive (taking in) and expressive (putting out) language and in both the spoken (oral) and written forms of language.

Disabilities Involving Spoken Language. Disabilities in the oral language area can involve deficits in listening (receptive) or speaking (expressive). Included among the oral receptive problems are auditory processing and memory deficits that make it difficult for a child to listen to, take in, and understand individual words, sentences, or longer oral presentations. These deficits can also make it hard for your child to follow instructions given orally, to get involved in class discussion, to take notes from lectures, to pick up cues from tone of voice, or to remember what his teacher told him to do for homework.

Oral expressive language disabilities, on the other hand, involve problems in putting ideas into spoken language. The term may be applied to the girl who says little, answers in incomplete or scrambled sentences, and leaves out essential details in her spoken communication. It may also, however, be applied to the girl whose language runs away with her, who generates lots of words, talks or writes "around the question," and has difficulty getting to the point.

Disabilities Involving Written Language. Written language disabilities include deficits in reading (receptive) and writing (expressive). One of the most common of the receptive written language disabilities is dyslexia or difficulty in reading. The term dyslexia includes a variety of deficits such as difficulty in discriminating between one letter and another, difficulty in discriminating between similar letter sounds and word sounds, difficulty in connecting letter combinations to the sounds they represent, and difficulty in understanding what is read. Since reading is such a complicated task, diagnosis of specific aspects of dyslexia is also very complicated. Working closely with the child, reading specialists attempt to figure out the patterns of the child's errors to determine the type of dyslexia she may have. For example, reading "dab" as "bad" or "flat" as "fat" is quite different from reading "to" as "for." Some children typically leave off endings, losing cues to the meaning of a sentence by reading "construction" as "construct" or "walked" as "walk." Other children blur the entire word into an unrecognizable hodgepodge of sounds. Some can read a line out loud perfectly, identifying each word correctly, but have no idea of what that series of words means. Their opposites can fail to identify half the words of a sentence, but somehow still know exactly what the author meant.

Disabilities in expressive written language include problems in translating one's thoughts into writing. Problems in spelling are a common component of written language disabilities and usually accompany dyslexia. In fact, the term dyslexia is usually used to include spelling problems. Children with spelling problems have trouble translating sounds into the symbols (letters) that represent them. They may reverse the order of letters, omit letters or entire syllables, or substitute incorrect letters for the correct ones. Spelling problems may be related to deficits in visual perception or visual memory as well as to deficits in auditory processing. The child who spells the word "nuclear" as "newkleer" is having difficulty with the visual representation of the word but is able to match sounds to symbols. The one who spells it "unclear" is having trouble with the sound-symbol relationships. Some children have trouble with both sight and sound and come up with some pretty creative spellings! Even spell checkers on computers are confounded by these spellers.

Also included among the written expressive language disabilities are difficulties in composition. A child with superb ideas may not be able to get these ideas onto the paper in a clear, organized, correct way. This may involve problems with the grammar rules that tell us how to put our words in order to make sense. Or it may be related instead to word-finding difficulties (dysnomia), problems in retrieving from memory the words that we need to express our ideas. It may also be related to a larger organizational problem resulting in a composition or report that resembles a ball of yarn after the kitten has gotten a hold of it. Expressive written language deficits may explain the child who labors to fill a half page in his composition notebook and spends hours trying to develop a sentence into a paragraph as well as the child who writes voluminously but can't get to the point. Children with written language disabilities may do poorly on tests, especially essay exams, because they may not answer the question completely, may give a disorganized response, or may not answer the question that was asked.

NONVERBAL LEARNING DISABILITIES

Another major group of learning disabilities can be classified as nonverbal learning disabilities—those that don't involve language. This umbrella includes visual perceptual deficits (discussed earlier in this chapter) that interfere with your child's ability to take in or process visual information. It also includes deficits in visual-motor (coordinating seeing and doing), visual-spatial (seeing how things are arranged in a space), psychomotor (being able to move self or other objects to achieve an objective), organizational, or problem-solving skills.

Children with visual-spatial-organizational deficits may be unable to copy a diagram from a science book, be frustrated at making a table of results for an experiment, be unable to see the pattern of main ideas and details in their textbooks, and brought to tears by a long-range, multitask assignment. They may lose their materials, forget to bring their notebook to class, operate on perpetual overload, and be late with every assignment. These are the kids most likely to use the time-honored excuse, the dog ate my homework! Organizational difficulties have an impact on every area of learning, especially as the child advances in grade. They often interfere with success even in areas where the child has strengths. For example, a child may be a good reader or writer, but never gets his act together enough to finish his book reports on time.

SOCIAL SKILLS DEFICITS

Many children with deficits in the nonverbal areas exhibit difficulties in social skills. They may miss the nonverbal cues that are important in much human interaction—the raised eyebrow, a shifting of someone's gaze, movement away from or toward another person. These are the children who unknowingly invade another's personal space or continue chattering when their listener is showing obvious signs of boredom.

Some children with language-based learning disabilities also have social skill problems. Their troubles with understanding spoken language, especially more subtle verbal cues like tone of voice, can cause them to miss or misinterpret signals from others. Their difficulties in expressing themselves verbally can result in others misunderstanding them. They are the ones who may "put their foot in their mouth," who may insult someone without meaning to, or whose silence is taken for snobbery. They may be the children who longingly follow the conversation at the cafeteria table, but don't know how to jump in.

Children with social skills deficits are the children who have difficulty making friends, who are the last ones chosen for the team, who aren't invited to the birthday party. They are the children who break a parent's heart as she stands by helplessly watching her child be hurt by rejection. These characteristics are not to be taken lightly and are just as, if not more, important than problems in reading, writing, and arithmetic. In adulthood, without support and intervention, people with social skills deficits rooted in verbal or nonverbal learning disabilities may have difficulty establishing lasting relationships and succeeding in the world of work.

DYSGRAPHIA

Dysgraphia (difficulty with handwriting) can involve problems in remembering how to form letters or mathematical symbols, as well as problems in the visual-motor skills needed to write these symbols. Children with dysgraphia may have mistakes in their handwriting (like letters written backward), may have illegible letter formations, may leave out parts of words they are writing, and/or may not be able to handwrite with the speed expected of them for their grade level. Children with dysgraphia often deliver assignments to their teachers that are messy and unreadable. In spite of the good ideas their papers may contain, their grades are often lowered because of the appearance of their work. They may also find it hard to complete in-class work on time since it takes them longer to write down their ideas. If your child has dysgraphia, he may avoid doing his written work, be embarrassed by the appearance of his written work, or become very frustrated in doing written assignments. Dysgraphia can be the result of problems in fine motor movement or in visual-motor integration (the way the eye and the hand work together). It can also be caused by memory problems—either in visual memory (making it hard for the child to remember what a letter looks like) or in kinesthetic memory (remembering how to make the hand movements that create the written symbol). Spatial problems can also contribute to dysgraphia, especially in cases in which the child crowds his letters together, has irregular spacing between words and letters, or can't adjust the size of his letters to fit a word in a given space.

DYSCALCULIA

Dyscalculia is a term used to describe a wide range of difficulties in understanding and using math. For some children, their math problems are mainly in computation. They can't accurately do the arithmetic operations and arrive at the right answer. They may add a column of figures five times and come up with five different answers.

Other children experience problems in understanding the concepts underlying mathematical operations. They don't see what they are really doing when they divide one number by another even though they may get the right answer. They may have no idea of what is meant by the area of a rectangle although they have memorized the formula and can apply it.

Still others have difficulty with the applications or uses of mathematics. Although they can divide, they do not realize that that is the operation they need to perform if they want to share 20 pieces of candy equally among 4 people.

Math disabilities may be related to problems in semantic memory that make it difficult for the child to remember the meaning of terms (like "area" or "average"). Math disabilities may also be related to visual and spatial deficits that prevent the child from seeing and understanding concepts like parallel lines, proportions, part-whole relationships (two-thirds of the money, 50 percent of the class), graphs, and other mathematical notions. Some children's math disabilities are related to procedural problems. These children may have trouble with the sequencing and logical problem-solving steps essential to many areas of math. These may be the children who can't remember the steps in long division, or in later grades, the order of operations for solving equations in algebra.

CAUSES OF LEARNING DISABILITIES

Many of the abilities we have as humans are hard-wired into the brain. That means that, although environmental opportunities and instruction are necessary to learn various skills, the ability to acquire them is inborn. Learning disabilities are caused by some flaw in the structure or wiring of the brain. Recent research using PET scans and functional magnetic resonance imaging (MRI) has shown differences in the brain activity of people with learning disabilities as compared to that of people without known learning disabilities.

When performing reading and other language-related tasks, brains of dyslexics are overactive in some areas and underactive in others. Since their brains can't handle certain tasks efficiently (like processing the relationship between a letter and its sound), dyslexic learners have to work harder to do what others find fairly simple. Other research has found differences in the shape or placement of certain cells in the brain, differences in the relative sizes of various parts of the brain, and differences in the electrical activity and brain chemicals of people with learning and attentional disabilities. The brain is still a new frontier in many ways with new discoveries being made daily that will continue to contribute to our understanding of how people learn and of what is going on when they don't.

A CHALLENGING COURSE

For now, since we don't have the scientific knowledge to pinpoint by medical tests the specific nature of an individual's learning disabilities, we use a variety of methods to try to put the puzzle together. Many of them involve looking for discrepancies. A child may have a large gap between her thinking ability (high IQ) and her actual achievement in school (low grades). Or she may have a big difference between her performance in various areas of achievement in school (a whiz kid at reading but failing in math). Or there may be significant variations among the child's mental abilities (for example, strong reasoning, weak memory).

Compare the learning process to driving a team of horses to a destination. The driver who has a team of horses that are wellmatched can move smoothly toward the destination, even if the horses are all fairly slow. They can work together efficiently and move at a steady pace. They will get there eventually.

The child who has a learning disability is driving a team of a different sort. Some of the horses are charging ahead like Kentucky Derby winners. Others are plodding behind finding it impossible to move ahead so quickly. Still others are trying to veer off the course to another direction entirely. The driver is struggling at every turn to control his team, urge them on, prevent the cart from overturning, and maintain his seating and composure. It's a rough ride, a challenging ride, and sometimes a painful one. But directing this uneven team can develop amazing strength, ingenuity, creativity, and stamina in the driver. If your child has a learning disability this is the team he is driving. He may not be able to choose a new team, but he can learn the strengths and weaknesses of the horses he has. He can learn how to use these to his advantage. He can run the course, and he can arrive at his destination.

4

DIAGNOSIS OF LEARNING DISABILITIES

Jennifer's posture was stiffly erect, her facial expression closed. She revealed little emotion other than a tense wariness. She kept her jacket on in spite of the warmth of the office and made no secret of staring boldly at the clock. It was the first meeting between Jennifer and her instructor in a college support program for students with learning disabilities. The semester was already in its third week. Repeated phone calls had failed to get Jennifer to come to the Learning Center to meet the instructor whose role was to provide her with support, guidance, and academic assistance as she adjusted to her first year in college. The instructor recognized the signs of resistance and had persisted in calling until Jennifer had finally showed up.

After making some small talk, the instructor described the support program and asked Jennifer if she had received any special support services in her high school. At this point, Jennifer's hazel eyes watered. Embarrassed, she lowered her head. "I was in some special classes," she admitted with shame, her face reddening. The instructor nodded reassuringly and pressed further, "Do you know why?"

"Something was wrong with me. With the way I learn. They thought I was stupid, I guess."

"And what did you think?"

"I didn't know," Jennifer said with a shrug, failing in her attempt to cover up the pain she felt.

THE NEED TO KNOW

Jennifer's story illustrates the reason parents and children need to know the difference between what a learning disability is and what it is not. It shows why it is important for both parents and children to understand the nature of the particular learning disability a child has. And it especially reveals the importance of focusing on the child's strengths as well as weaknesses.

Jennifer had a Wechsler Intelligence Scale Performance IQ of 121 reflecting superior visual-spatial and nonverbal reasoning abilities. In contrast she had a Verbal IQ of 95 with severe difficulty in expressive language. Though intelligent, she was unable to express her knowledge and understanding in spoken or written words. When her new instructor took out her testing and showed her a graph of her test results, she was surprised to see the many spikes into the above-average and superior range. No one had ever shown her her test results before. Though certain teachers and her parents had tried to assure her that she was intelligent, she hadn't really believed them. Her English papers, covered with bright red correction pen and her report cards with grades fluctuating wildly from As (only a few) to Ds and Fs were the proof.

The instructor began that day a process that should have happened many years before. When Jennifer left the office, there was a small glimmer in her eyes. The seeds of hope had been planted and would be nurtured over time as she came to know herself as a learner, strengths as well as weaknesses, and came to the self-acceptance that would let her be at peace with who she was.

DIAGNOSING LEARNING DIFFICULTIES

Most of us have a sixth sense that picks up on cues, spoken and unspoken, about ourselves and our place in the world. When children fail to learn as expected, the adults and other children around them respond with a variety of reactions: concern, support, puzzlement, frustration, sometimes anger and ridicule, and, worst of all, pity. Some of these reactions are subtle, some obvious. The child also observes herself and reacts in similar ways. A common response to learning problems is to ask, "What is the matter? What's going on here? Why can't I, or Johnny or Jenny learn?"

If you read the previous chapter, you know that by their nature learning disabilities are not easy to define and pin down. They involve a pattern of disparities and incongruities. One child's thinking ability is strong, but her academic performance is weak. Another's language skills are amazing, but her math skills are deplorable. A third can read a book in a few hours, but never gets the book report in on time. The patterns are many and varied. Each child is a puzzle. To make matters even worse, just when you think you have the pattern figured out, it falls apart like a design in a kaleidoscope, and emerges in a new way.

Figuring out the complex patterns involved in your child's learning requires detective work. As any fan of mystery novels or TV shows like *Diagnosis Murder* knows, this detective work usually involves gathering evidence, interviewing witnesses, checking on the suspect's background and history, and staking him out in a natural setting or in a fabricated situation created to observe his behaviors. Educational detective work, formally known as educational diagnosis and assessment, is no different.

Some parents are reluctant to have their child undergo such an assessment. If this is true of you, take a good look at why. You may be afraid of having your child labeled and having to bear the "stigma" of having a learning disability. You may be afraid the teachers will treat your child differently as a result. Perhaps you are afraid your child will be frightened or worried, or will be wounded in self-esteem by the testing process. Most of all, you may be afraid of what you will find out. All of these are definitely valid concerns. However, when conducted and interpreted properly, a diagnostic evaluation will be far more positive than negative. None of these negative results is a necessary effect of having an educational assessment. They are, instead, the result of a misuse of a potentially valuable process.

The alternative to assessment (not having the testing) is potentially much more harmful. Many children with learning disabilities are undiagnosed. This results in unnecessary frustration, reduced ability to benefit from learning opportunities, school failure, and damage to self-esteem. You may avoid pinning the label of a learning disability on your child only to replace it with others that are worse: lazy, dumb, unmotivated, stubborn, uncooperative, messy, careless. These are labels that it can take a child a lifetime to live down.

A comprehensive assessment is needed to pinpoint the causes of a child's learning problems. We need to find out the cause of a learning problem before we can treat it with the interventions, strategies, and support systems that will work. To go back to our detective analogy, a diagnostic evaluation involves rounding up the "usual suspects" and taking a close look at each one. We definitely don't want to convict the innocent and leave the guilty free to wreak havoc.

Unfortunately, when it comes to learning problems, there are a lot of suspects and the detective work is further complicated because some of them work together. Their MO is different depending on who their partners are at any given time. The previous chapter gave you an idea of the many skills and abilities that go into learning. A comprehensive assessment needs to look at most of them as well as at their interactions with one another. A child with strong vocabulary and good abstract verbal reasoning ability will show a different kind of math disability than one with weak vocabulary and good visual thinking ability, although both may be having problems learning algebra.

To complicate matters even further, other causes not considered to be learning disabilities can also be contributing to or even causing the child's learning problems. Psychiatric or emotional problems, sensory impairments, environmental or social conditions, family situations, physical illness, poor nutrition, immaturity, drugs and alcohol are only a few. The diagnostician needs to consider these possibilities as well, even if it's just to rule them out.

SHOULD YOU ARRANGE A DIAGNOSTIC ASSESSMENT FOR YOUR CHILD?

Not every learning problem warrants an extensive (and expensive) educational assessment. There are a few cues that, especially in combination, indicate whether you should consider this step. One of the clearest, of course, is that your child is not succeeding in school. She appears to be bright, but is not acquiring important basic skills (reading, writing, and 'rithmetic) and/or is not achieving decent grades in school subjects. Another indication is that your child is having trouble keeping up with her peers. Either in or out of school, academically or socially, her development seems to lag behind that of other children of the same age and grade. A third indicator of the need for a thorough assessment is that your child's attitude seems to be deteriorating. She resists going to school, may even become school phobic. She seems unmotivated and puts little effort into her school work. She seems depressed, discouraged, angry, overemotional, or anxious. She may be exhibiting behavior problems like aggression or withdrawal and isolation. Another sign may be a high level of disorganization. The child is late, books are misplaced or forgotten, her desk and room are in disarray, and her papers are messy.

Of course, all of these symptoms may appear from time to time in any child. The difference is in the severity and consistency with which they appear. If several of these signs are familiar to you, if you are saying, "Yes, that's Marisa," or "Sounds a lot like Christopher," then take a closer look. As a parent, you have that radar that gives you a "funny feeling" when all is not right with your beloved child. Listen to it. Talk it over with other observers (aunts, grandparents, babysitters) and with your child's teachers. Wait and watch for a while if you want to. We do not want to advocate turning molehills into mountains. But if things aren't getting better and indeed seem to be worsening for your child, then do something about it. A comprehensive educational diagnostic evaluation can be the first step in finding out what's happening and in giving you and your child the tools to deal with it effectively.

KINDS OF ASSESSMENT TOOLS

An educational evaluation may include a variety of tests, checklists, observations, and diagnostic interviews. The particular combination depends on the needs of the individual child. Becoming familiar with the various options that may be used will help you to know what the examiner is looking for. It will also help you to be sure your child is receiving a comprehensive evaluation.

Intelligence tests are a mainstay of educational diagnosis. These tests measure general mental ability and aptitude for learning. We can't tell whether a child is achieving at the level expected unless we have some measure of his potential or capacity for learning. These tests measure learning ability by looking at such things as the child's ability to think abstractly and logically, to solve problems, to process information, to connect ideas, to see relationships between parts and wholes, and to remember information both for a short time and over the long haul. Of course, no IQ test can be considered the be-all and end-all of a child's learning capacity. For one thing, these tests don't measure every aspect of a child's ability. What is measured depends on how we define intelligence, and our definition of that elusive quality is continually changing. In attempting to measure general aptitude for learning, most IQ tests today look at both verbal (language-related) and nonverbal (visual, spatial, sensorimotor) abilities. What they don't measure is also significant—things like musical talent, creativity, awareness of self, and the ability to understand others. A standardized IQ test might even miss the genius of a Mozart or Picasso. As they are, though, the standardized individual IQ tests administered in educational assessments do give us a picture of the kind of success in learning we might expect of a child in today's school settings.

Aptitude tests are a sort of specialized intelligence test. They measure capacity for learning in specific areas. An aptitude test can look at a single area (for example, mechanical ability) or can explore a variety of specific areas.

Achievement tests try to determine not what a child may be able to learn, but what he already has learned. These tests give us a measure of a child's current level of performance in specific knowledge areas. For example, an achievement test will yield a grade level in math, reading, spelling, or writing skills. These tests help identify specific areas we need to work on with a child. They also tell us, when compared with the IQ test results, if the child is learning as well as we might expect. Wide variations among various areas of achievement or big differences between the child's potential and his achievement in particular areas are indications of specific learning disabilities.

Diagnostic tests try to get at the source of specific learning problems. They give us a closer look at an area in which we might suspect difficulties. For example, if a child is not achieving at grade level in reading on his achievement test, we would administer a diagnostic reading test to find out more specifically what is going on. Is the problem in recognizing and remembering what a word looks like, sounding it out, hearing the difference between similar sounding words, knowing the meaning of the individual words, or understanding the meaning of words put together in sentences and paragraphs? Diagnostic tests may be administered in speech and language, sensory integration, motor skills, mathematics, and other areas. The results will give a learning specialist information on which to build an educational plan tailored to the child's specific areas of weakness.

Scales and checklists are observational instruments completed by teachers, parents, and students themselves. Sometimes these scales involve indicating how often or seldom a child engages in a particular behavior. At other times, they involve rating the child from poor to excellent in specific skill areas. Some simply involve checking off behaviors typical of the child. Such reports are, of course, subjective and may be colored by the perspective of the rater. For example, whether a child fidgets often, sometimes, or seldom may be more in the eye of the beholder than in any objective definition of "fidgitiness!" In spite of this, scales and checklists can provide valuable information to add to the total picture.

INTERPRETING THE TEST RESULTS

When the evaluation is completed and all the results are in, the task of figuring out what the results mean is just as much an art as it is a science. It takes an experienced practitioner to get an accurate picture of your child from the test results. And it takes an effective communicator to explain the results in ways that parents can understand. Many a parent has thrown up his hands in exasperation at the confusing array of numbers that are presented in the test report. The numbers are usually accompanied by an explanation of the test results that may or may not clear up the confusion. Parents who are experts in many other areas may not be familiar with the jargon of educational assessment. Many parents are afraid to question the examiner and don't want to admit ignorance of the various kinds of scores used to report results. Never let this fear stop you. Educational professionals recognize that their field has a language of its own that may not be familiar to you.

An understanding of some of the more common ways of reporting your child's performance will help to clear up some of the confusion you may feel. Test scores can be reported in a variety of ways, most of which involve comparing your child to other children of his age or grade.

Standardized tests use a large representative sample to establish norms to which your child can be compared. The raw score (usually the number of correct answers on a particular standardized test) is a useless measure unless it is converted. Whether a raw score of 15 is considered weak or strong depends on how other children of the same age or grade perform on the same test. A formula based on the average (called the mean) converts the raw score to a standard score. For example on the Wechsler Intelligence Scale for Children (WISC-III), a standard score of 10 represents the average score on each subtest, but the number needed for a child of a given age to achieve a score of 10 varies in the different subtests that make up the WISC-III.

Age norms are based on the median (middle) score of children at a particular age while grade norms are based on the median scores of children in a particular grade. Grade equivalent scores are expressed in years and tenths of a year. For example, a grade equivalent score of 4.8 would mean that your child performs at the median for children in fourth grade, eighth month.

Percentiles are another way of comparing children to others. A percentile score tells you what percentage of students scored at that level or below it. For example, if your child performs at the 75th percentile in reading, this means that 75 percent of children of his age or grade scored at or below the level of your child. Twenty-four percent scored above him (the highest possible percentile score is 99th, indicating that a child is in the top 1 percent of that population). A percentile of 50 percent is average with half of the population scoring below and half above that score. Percentile scores can be based on comparisons of your child with others in his grade (grade norms) or with others of the same age (age norms).

A stanine is a particular kind of standard score that uses a formula to divide the population into nine equal groups from lowest (1st stanine) to highest (9th stanine).

Standardized testing is far from being a foolproof method of measuring how well your child is doing. One of the most important considerations is whether the norm group for a particular test really is representative and is an appropriate comparison set for your child. Tests may be biased in favor of particular races or cultures. In a country as diverse as the United States, it is hard to find a test that can fairly compare every child or group of children to others. Tests that are "culture bound" are so influenced by a particular, dominant culture that they can't truly measure those who don't share that culture. We need to keep working toward greater awareness of racial, cultural, socioeconomic, and gender-based factors that influence test scores.

LIMITATIONS OF ASSESSMENT

This brings us to some of the other limitations of educational evaluations. A child is a whole person, not just a composite of pieces and numbers. The testing process takes his learning apart, but then we have to put it all together again to get a true picture. We have to remember to take into account the aspects of your child that cannot be measured by standardized tests or checklists.

A second grader, Nicky was severely dyslexic and brought with him to his new reading tutor a folder of diagnostic testing detailing his failings in reading and writing. Knowing he had become resistant to working on his reading, his tutor handed him a Polaroid camera and took him outside during his first tutoring session. She told him to take pictures of anything he saw that he liked. He gleefully charged around the yard snapping a variety of shots. When they returned to the house she had him paste the pictures into a notebook and asked him to give her a sentence about each picture so that she could print the words beneath it. His first picture was of a plane in the sky. "When I see a plane in the sky, I think of the wonders of man," he stated solemnly. The tutor had expected a much more limited use of language, something like "The plane is high in the sky." The rest of the lesson continued in the same way, uncovering strengths of expression and abstract thought that Nicky's testing had not revealed.

Standardized tests can't measure all aspects of intelligence. Howard Gardener's (1983) work on multiple intelligence reveals many forms of intelligence not often included in educational assessments. These include musical, interpersonal (understanding and relating to others), intrapersonal (understanding oneself), bodily-kinesthetic (controlling one's body and other objects), among others. The test scores of Greg Louganis probably reveal his dyslexia but don't measure the genius in bodily-kinesthetic intelligence that made him an Olympic gold medalist.

Standardized tests are also limited by their format. For example, in trying to get a measure of a child's vocabulary knowledge, a variety of formats may yield very different results. In some tests, the examiner presents a word orally and asks the child to define it orally in his own words. In others the child must read the word and choose from a group of possible definitions also in print. In some tests, the child is given a word orally and asked to select a picture or pictures that go with the word. In others, a child has to use a word in a sentence either orally or in writing. Some tests require a child to supply synonyms (same meaning) or antonyms (opposite meaning) for a word while others ask the child to choose a word that fits in a particular category like animals or colors. Obviously, a child's vocabulary performance on each of these measures can be affected by the format. Good diagnosticians will use a variety of measures and will use the variations among them to shed light on other aspects of the child's learning.

Another limitation of standardized testing is that it is administered in a carefully controlled environment. A child's performance in this setting may be better than his performance on similar tasks in the dynamic, sometimes hectic, settings of home and classroom. This can work both ways. Some children will perform better in comfortable, familiar settings with all the rich stimulation they provide. These children may feel uncomfortable in the impersonal, clinical setting interacting with an adult who is usually a stranger to them. The rapport established between the tester and the child is also critical. A child who feels anxious, intimidated, or uncomfortable with an examiner may not perform at her best level.

ALTERNATIVES TO STANDARDIZED ASSESSMENT TECHNIQUES

Other methods of looking at your child's learning profile should be used along with standardized testing to get a more complete picture. Collecting a portfolio of a child's work can be very valuable. These samples often reveal a child's approach and work habits as well as her knowledge and skills.

A method known as authentic assessment can also shine a brighter light on your child's learning. Instead of using the artificial tasks of standardized tests, authentic assessment involves giving a child tasks he actually has to perform at home and school. Observing the child as he completes these tasks is an excellent way to gain more insight and also has the advantage of being administered in the natural environment where conditions for learning are those the child will actually have to function within.

Diagnostic teaching is another way of involving the child in actual learning tasks. A learning specialist carefully and systematically observes the child's learning as she teaches him specific skills or works with him in learning how to handle particular subject matter. This will reveal his strengths and weaknesses in many components of learning such as the child's frustration tolerance, his ability to organize his learning process and materials, his use of language related to the task, his ability to abstract, transfer, or visualize concepts.

PREPARING YOUR CHILD FOR TESTING

In spite of their limitations, educational evaluations are crucial for understanding your child, obtaining needed support services, and identifying strengths as well as weaknesses. You want to do everything in your power to make the testing experience a positive one for your child.

Talk to your child ahead of time about the testing. Most children will be somewhat apprehensive and will have that little voice inside of them telling them that something is wrong with them. They will pick up on your anxieties, too. Try to defuse the situation with honesty, gentleness, and an optimistic manner. With little ones, you might say they will be doing lots of learning games to find out how they like to learn. With older children, you might explain that you are trying to figure out what they are good at and how they can use their strengths to learn better. If your child is aware of difficulties she is having in school, explain that the tests will help you to figure out the reason and find out how to help.

Talk to the examiner ahead of time and find out what to expect so you can prepare your child. If the testing session is long, ask if you can pack a juice box or crackers for your child to have during a break. Tell the examiner about any behavioral or emotional factors that may interfere with your child's performance. Be sure to complete any questionnaires or checklists that the examiner may give you to find out about your child's developmental and medical history. Search your memory for anything that might possibly be having an impact. That high fever and convulsions your child had as a baby could have some bearing on later learning. Let the examiner know about any medications your child may be taking currently.

You also want to be open about any physical or emotional trauma your child has experienced or about family problems that could affect your child's learning. This is, of course, a touchy area. If you don't feel comfortable sharing such information with a school-based evaluator, then consider having your child tested privately. These issues can have a tremendous influence on learning, and ignoring them is like walking around the elephant in the living room.

THE BOTTOM LINE

The bottom line of diagnosis and evaluation of learning difficulties is to help your child to learn. Giving your child a better chance at succeeding in learning is something dear to every parent's heart. A good educational assessment can go a long way toward this goal.

5

OUR GREAT BRAIN: LEARNING AND FUNCTIONING

THE STORY OF GEMMA

"It's all up here . . . everything you do and say, and everything we learn starts right there." Ms. Brown pointed to her head. Ms. Brown had just returned from a weekend seminar on whole brain teaching and learning, and felt empowered by what she perceived as cutting-edge research.

Eight-year-old Gemma frowned. She glanced around the classroom, watching the reactions of her peers. A few giggled, some looked awe-struck, and Gemma noticed a few foreheads wrinkled in confusion like her own. She carefully touched her small hand to her head, trying to be inconspicuous.

"What's Ms. Brown talking about anyway!" Gemma remembered hearing her grandparents refer to Ms. Brown as "radical," whatever that meant. Gemma thought they must have been referring to the different ways Ms. Brown approached learning, or at least different according to what was familiar or acceptable to them. They were very cautious about their grandchild's education. The small town in Oklahoma where Gemma grew up was where her mother grew up—in a one room school house—and where her grandparents grew up as well.

Ms. Brown strolled between the groups of desks, occasionally stopping to rest her hand on someone's shoulder, trying to make a connection with as many children as possible. She pointed to her head again. Ms. Brown was determined to help her students understand the many different ways in which our brains directed our lives both in and out of the classroom.

"What's up here," she began as she tapped the top of her head, "is central headquarters, the chief executive, the mother ship." There were a few more giggles. Gemma again touched her forehead. It felt the same as always. She thought that Ms. Brown was making this brain thing sound mysterious and a little scary. Gemma listened to the doctors talk about her brain, and always felt kind of left out of the conversation.

Ms. Brown walked to the large white board at the front of the room and began drawing with her fat colored markers. Gemma loved the way they smelled. They reminded her of her grandpa's truck. Gemma was quite unaware that the associations she made with her sense of smell were with the most primitive sense, and one that sometimes abruptly brought memories flooding back to her conscious mind. Ms. Brown was drawing a simplified version of the human brain from a bird's eye view, with two oval shapes representing the left and right hemispheres and what looked like shoelaces connecting the two larger shapes.

"This is your GREAT BRAIN." She wrote the heading in capital letters over the drawing. "It's the boss of all your organs, and only weighs a few pounds . . . yours isn't finished growing yet . . . but it decides everything! Everything! Isn't that awesome?" She smiled widely at the children. Some smiled back. Others waited for whatever surprise might come next. Ms. Brown was always full of surprises.

"Why don't you take out your crayons and draw along with me. Gemma, would you please pass out some paper? Thank you." Gemma immediately obeyed, rushing to complete the task as quickly as she could so that she wouldn't fall behind the others. She hated the feeling when she missed something, and everyone knew what they were doing except her. It threw her sense of organization way off and took her extra time to look around, making note of what everyone else was doing so that she could align herself with their efforts. Again, Gemma had no idea that she very naturally functioned in a way that demanded she pay close attention to the auditory stimuli, begging admittance to her very intricate and unique neurological system. She had no idea that her feeling of being off-task, or feeling as if her internal gyroscope had been tilted, was in any way related to the human brain (Adelizzi, 1996).

Ms. Brown began strolling around the room again, and this time stopped at the modest computer lab she had established in the corner. It boasted four updated computers and a printer. "Your brain, the boss of your organs, is like one of our computers." This time all the faces were solemn and attentive. One student rolled his eyes. "How would she explain this one!" he wondered.

"Remember last week we talked about our heart, our lungs, and other organs? Who can remember what the other organs were? Hands?" Two hands shot up. Gemma sighed. Same two who always answered everything first before anyone else had a chance to think! The two children who always answered first were the ones Gemma noticed whizzed through their reading and vocabulary at a much faster rate than the rest of the class. Ask them a question, and bam! the answer was immediate. As these two students were verbalizing their remembrance of a concept or fact learned previously, Gemma and some of her classmates were still scanning their mental filing systems in search of the information, the link, the connection. Why was that?

As the children began to draw with Ms. Brown, they copied the labels she placed on the shapes. They doodled in the margins. Ms. Brown encouraged it. They took out a second sheet of white drawing paper and began sketching the human body, just like last week. This was a repetitive task, but one in which they now engaged with some automaticity, quickly labeling the major organs of the body, and now adding the GREAT BRAIN to the picture. They reviewed the functions of the organs and what they had learned about the brain that day, adding yet another layer of knowledge to what had been learned already. Ms. Brown was carefully guiding them in constructing new knowledge, mindful that they remained aware they were connecting new information to their already existing fund of information and understanding. Some students moved through the visual and verbal task with ease while others still needed to hesitate from time to time, checking the work of others to make sure they were "doing it right." Checking with others was acceptable in Ms. Brown's class.

The afternoon passed quickly, and Gemma proudly rolled her drawings up and tucked them in her backpack. Ms. Brown said, "Now show your families your drawings, and see if they have questions for you. Tell them what you learned today about their brains. We'll share our stories tomorrow." Ms. Brown knew that it helped for students to become active in the process of making new information relevant to their lives outside of the classroom. If they went home and discussed the activities of the day, there might be questions by other family members that would hopefully lead to dialogue; Ms. Brown crossed her fingers.

On the bus ride home Gemma listened to her friends making up rhymes about the brain. She laughed along with them and felt empowered that she knew some things her family might not know.

> Ms. Brown is a clown,
> and she knows the brain.
> It's an organ in your head,
> the engine of the train.

"I bet my brain's bigger than yours," said a tall boy who seemed to lead the singing. They all looked at him. "I've grown more." Gemma's friend, Kylie, gave him a disgusted look.

"I don't think so! My mother said that boys are nowhere smart as girls, so your brain is probably tiny!" Ms. Brown desperately tried to point out to the children that girls often develop their language and vocabulary at a slightly earlier stage, but that boys looked at things differently, and tended to understand other kinds of information a little quicker than the girls. It seemed to work until she heard one girl, Leah, taunting one of the boys with her quick wit and sarcasm. He was hurt, humiliated, and didn't know how to verbally reciprocate. So he punched her. Ms. Brown felt the interaction epitomized developmental theory from her perspective as a teacher.

"My father doesn't have a spleen," said one little girl as the school bus rolled to a bumpy stop.

"Doesn't matter. Long as he has a brain," reported the tall boy very authoritatively. A few others nodded agreement. Ms. Brown discussed with her class the story of a boy in town who remained in a coma after six months. Several months ago he was removed from all life support systems, and still he lived on. He breathed on his own. His brain was keeping him alive, keeping his heart pumping blood, sustaining life in his tiny body that remained so still. Ms. Brown hoped that as the children learned more about the GREAT BRAIN they would begin making these connections to stories they had discussed and other new information they were adding to their bank of knowledge.

Gemma ran down the driveway to her grandparents' farm and into the kitchen. Her grandma was in the kitchen starting dinner. "Well, well, what did you do today in school Princess Gemma?" She loved it when they called her that. It made her feel important.

Gemma quickly unrolled her drawings and held them up for her grandma to see. The woman looked puzzled at first, but then pointed to the second drawing Gemma completed of the human body, and said, "Looks like one of those headache commercials." She took the other drawing in her hands, and asked, "And what's this now? Hmmmm. Looks like loaves of bread. Is it bread?" She peered over her glasses at her granddaughter.

"Nope. It's your brain, Grandma."

"Oh my. That Miss Brown is something, isn't she? My brain, huh? And are you gonna tell Grandpa and me about that tonight at supper?"

"Yup." Gemma couldn't stop smiling. "And look Grandma, I drew some other stuff too while Ms. Brown talked to us. Look at how I drew Casper." Casper was the family dog. Gemma drew him as she knew him best at home—with Grandpa in the barn.

"Now are you supposed to be doodling while your teacher is talking to you Gemma?"

"She said to doodle Grandma. She said to draw what we saw in our heads that made us smile. Casper makes me smile. He's so funny, and makes Grandpa happy. And Ms. Brown said to draw him on the right side of the brain . . . right here." Gemma pointed to the right hemisphere she had copied from the board. Gemma's grandmother looked from the drawing to Gemma, and back again. She shook her head.

"Now this'll be good supper conversation. Go get washed Gemma, and I'll put your new drawings up for Grandpa to see."

That evening at supper Gemma cleaned up the last of her broccoli, something her grandpa insisted on. "I grow it for you Gemma," he would say, "and it's your responsibility to eat it." Grandma made sounds of approval as she removed Gemma's empty plate, and replaced it with chocolate cake. The doctors had told Gemma's grandparents how vital a healthy diet was to Gemma's learning and functioning. Gemma was still recovering from a very long recuperative bout as a result of a head injury and a traumatic loss in her life.

"Now tell Grandpa about his brain, Gemma."

Grandpa pretended to be surprised.

Gemma stood beside the drawings Grandma had taped to the fridge and pointed to the hemispheres of the brain with a wooden spoon handed to her by her attentive audience. She informed her students that the left hemisphere was where her "words" were, and where she was able to figure out how to clean her room, her desk, and put everything into order. "It keeps things neat . . . in order," she reported. This, of course, was her eight-year-old interpretation. "And it's where I am on time for stuff, like doing my papers and homework—know what I mean?" They nodded. They well understood how Gemma had become rigid about her internal sense of organization. She was aware at her young age that if she didn't listen carefully and plan her time that she wouldn't finish anything she started. More than anything Gemma hated feeling fragmented, behind, and not able to keep up. That's what made her internal gyroscope tip dangerously, causing her to downshift (Hart, 1983), feel disoriented, and out of control in her learning and functioning.

Grandpa leaned over and pointed to what looked like the laces that connected the two hemispheres. "What's that for Gemma?"

"I can't say it. It's the c-o-r-p-u-s c-a-l-l-o-s-u-m. See, it keeps both sides talking to each other so one side knows what the other is doing. Something like that." She thought for a minute. "Ms. Brown said that's what keeps it whole. You know, like one brain." Her audience nodded politely.

Gemma then pointed to the right-hand shape on the paper. "This is the right side of the brain. See, it's another h-e-m-i-s-p-h-e-r-e." More polite nodding from the audience.

"This is where I draw—like the picture of Casper. And it's sometimes where I sing, but my words can be on the other side. I think it's where I cry too."

Grandma put her napkin to her mouth so Gemma wouldn't notice how emotional she felt at that moment. Grandpa's eyes filled with tears. Gemma looked at them. They were vaguely aware that their feelings were linked to their limbic systems, reasonably new information for them as they became more attuned to brain function.

"What's the matter?"

"Nothing, Princess. We're just so proud of you." Gemma beamed. She remembered that they looked this way when she sang hymns at church. They looked proud. When they looked that way at her she felt as if she could do anything, conquer the world, run a marathon, make the honor roll. Gemma was unaware that certain chemicals in her brain were responsible for making her feel this way, without the use of medication.

When Grandma was sure that Gemma was sound asleep that night, she closed the door to her bedroom so that she and Grandpa could have a private conversation.

"Jake, a lot of that stuff she was telling us tonight was some of what the doctors told us when Gemma was in a coma. Remember?" Jake nodded, remembering only too well the night they were called to the hospital in Oklahoma City two years ago. Their daughter and son-in-law were killed in an automobile accident. Gemma survived and remained in a coma for two days. Most of what the doctors told them became a blur in their minds, as verbal information often does during a time of extreme stress or psychological trauma. Little did they know that they were downshifting (Hart, 1983) a great deal of the time. Words and even visual impressions can become trapped somewhere in the brain and filed inappropriately so that understanding what is being said or what is occurring is nearly impossible. During those crucial weeks following the accident the words of other people sounded like static, like a bad connection on the telephone, like a foreign language.

Jake and Rowena Martin had lost their daughter in a tragic accident. They were robbed of their child. They were suffering from posttraumatic stress symptoms, although no one ever took the time to tell them what was happening to their thinking, their functioning, to the world as they once knew it. They didn't understand their constant state of confusion, their forgetfulness that lasted for months on end, and their feeling that life had come to a stop. Why was everything and everybody else still moving? There wasn't time to find out why they experienced odd aches, pains, headaches, and disruptive sleep patterns in the months that followed. There was only time to take care of Gemma, to nurse her back to health. Concentrating on Gemma's survival became their anchor, their reason for moving from day to day. Gemma's well-being kept them from focusing on their own sense of traumatic loss.

Gemma came to live with her grandparents on their farm following the accident. There was plenty of room to play, and her mother's old school was only a few miles up the road. Neighbors and extended family members hovered around, unsure of what to do or how to help. They suffered with Jake and Rowena, and mourned Gemma's loss with her. They watched helplessly as three people whom they loved struggled with the daily grind of life, not to mention the challenge of following doctors' orders, new diets, and trips to the hospital. The demands were relentless and left them exhausted.

A few months following the accident, Gemma seemed to regain some of her old spirit. She put on a couple of pounds—her grandparents were vigilant about her diet, and were reminded faithfully by the Oklahoma City doctors how important Gemma's physiological well-being was to her full recuperation. They brought her to school and were gravely disappointed when the principal called after the first week to inform them that "Gemma just wasn't ready." They suggested some psychotherapy, accompanied by home tutorials. Jake and Rowena were puzzled by all this, but mechanically moved ahead with the school's requests. Fortunately, the Martins were referred to an enlightened and sensitive therapist who administered educational diagnostic testing to Gemma.

During one of their initial appointments, Dr. Lite held a chart up for the Martins, and explained Gemma's scores. "Gemma has never been tested before so I don't really have anything to compare this to. I only know that she was a good student prior to the accident according to your recollections, and to the reports I received from her school before the accident." He chose his words carefully. "Gemma appears to have the profile of a child who is dyslexic. In other words, she seems to experience trouble with short-term memory . . . and trouble with language. However, this may be due to the accident, to the coma . . . we don't really know for sure. But whatever the reason is, we will treat this as a learning disability because that's the way it's presenting itself for Gemma. At least right now. We'll keep a sharp eye on it, and keep in touch with Oklahoma City as well." The Martins nodded.

Dr. Lite was thoughtful again. "Gemma has some difficulty with left hemispheric related tasks. Be patient with her general organization at home. Give her smaller chores at first that require order, step-by-step procedures . . . stated simply for her. Then build onto these skills as she appears to master them in isolation or as multitasks." His words began to sound jumbled to them, a familiar experience since the accident. It was a verbal overload, and they couldn't find a way to tell people this. He looked at their faces.

"I'm so sorry. This has been incredibly difficult for both of you. I'm giving you a verbal overload, inviting you to shut down in your thinking and feeling. Forgive me." He paused in thought again, trying to assess whether he should take this moment to talk about brain function.

"Since the accident I'm sure that you have experienced many moments when you feel as if your systems just want to shut down, like you want the world to stop for while so you can catch your breath. There is a term that is often used when we become so scared, or so traumatized or overloaded that we can't think, plan, or comprehend much of anything. It's called downshifting (Hart, 1983). The brain will very kindly take a rest when the outside world is assaulting you with too many demands, some of which are unkind to our systems. I'll write some of this down for you to take home, and I'm also going to recommend a couple of books for you. Our office will order them for you. No hurry. Don't rush to read them. They're for your own understanding of how the brain functions." The Martins were grateful for Dr. Lite's understanding of what was proving to be both mentally and physically exhausting to them.

On the way home Rowena read the piece of paper Dr. Lite handed her. She read aloud, "*The Amazing Brain* by Robert Ornstein and Richard F. Thompson. Hmmm. Think it sounds good, Jake? And another one, *Learning and Memory* by Marilee Sprenger." She waited for a reaction from her husband. He kept driving in silence.

"Well," she went on, "at least his secretary will order them for us, and we won't have to worry." Again, she waited for a reaction.

"Jake, you OK with all this? Talk to me."

"I'm OK. Just as Dr. Lite said. I'm overloaded. I'm scared we're going to make mistakes. I'm scared for Gemma. I'm scared for us. So what part of my brain is that, huh?"

The following year was filled with doctors' appointments, therapy for Gemma, for Jake and Rowena, and endless meetings with the school. Finally, the principal and special education director felt that "Gemma is ready to try school again."

With great caution Jake and Rowena encouraged Gemma to make friends, bring guests home, and gradually resume a life that resembled what they perceived as being normal. Dr. Lite was right. Small tasks with simple directions needed to come first. Step-by-step directions. It got better. They took it one day at a time, until they felt that her memory and sequential skills had somewhat improved. Her teachers and tutors were very supportive of the Martins, and eventually life began to unfold as a comfortable routine. Keeping simple schedules, refining daily tasks to step-by-step processes proved to be helpful for Gemma, and for her grandparents as well. It helped everyone develop a routine that in turn kept the family feeling organized, or as Gemma put it, "in the left side of the brain."

Jake and Rowena sat in silence while Gemma slept peacefully. They were grateful for her academic progress, and grateful that her emotional healing had continued. It would never be healed completely, but her tragic experiences might become integrated into how she viewed her world and her life.

CONNECTING THEORY TO REAL LIVES

The story of Gemma offers a framework or a hat rack for understanding brain theory, or at least a tiny slice of theory. Sometimes it's easier to understand brain function when we talk about it within the context of real people and real events.

Ms. Brown was obviously what many parents and professionals refer to as an enlightened teacher. She intuitively knew that a comfortable and nonthreatening atmosphere would enhance her students' opportunities for learning. She researched various teaching methods, and eventually learned about Caine and Caine's brain-based learning (1994). As she added new strategies to her repertoire of teaching skills, she began to witness the difference between traditional teaching methods and approaches that engaged her students more actively in the learning process. Making the children aware of how they learned and functioned became a challenge she accepted with a sense of commitment and pride.

When Gemma first arrived in Ms. Brown's classroom she was still recovering from a major physical and emotional trauma in her life. Ms. Brown immediately consulted with not only the special education department at her own school, but also made it a point to communicate with Gemma's teacher from the previous year. This meant extra phone calls and research after school hours, but she felt it worth her while in order to better understand this child who appeared to be struggling with gaining a sense of equilibrium physically, mentally, and emotionally. Ms. Brown, Gemma's grandparents, the school, and other professionals in Gemma's life maintained a collaborative relationship, one that is often identified as educational therapy.

As Ms. Brown observed Gemma's progress each week, she became acutely aware of the child's inability to stay on task for long periods of time. Ms. Brown gently pressured Gemma about trying to persevere, and the child seemed to eventually grow stronger in her efforts to gain a sense of control over whatever activity she was engaged in at the time. Just as Gemma's grandparents concentrated on giving her clear and simple directions and tasks to perform, Ms. Brown did likewise. She asked Gemma to collect the papers, pass out the papers, run errands to the office, help a classmate find her place in their reading. The other students didn't seem to mind. It was as if they understood that this was part of a healing process, and they were serving as guides on some occasions. By the end of the school year Gemma had gained a sense of what she could take on in terms of cognitive tasks. She had also learned that when she felt overloaded her system would give her distinct physiological signals.

When Gemma felt threatened by a particular task, she felt vulnerable to humiliation in front of her peers. This of course is difficult to articulate for a seven- or eight-year-old child. Gemma became aware that when she felt frightened, her physiological well-being was under seige. She experienced sweaty palms, nausea, and a general feeling that she must "exit" or escape that which she perceived as a threatening situation. Leslie Hart wrote extensively about such phenomena as he explored the idea of "downshifting" (1983). Dr. Paul D. McLean's (1975) triune brain concept offers us a peek at how Ms. Brown will probably plan her next lesson on brain functioning. His work has been deeply respected since the 1970s and is still referred to by many professionals interested in how human beings learn and function.

The human brain can be looked at as being a threefold process in learning and functioning. The oldest and most primitive part of the brain, the reptilian brain, is where our need for survival is situated. Earlier in the developmental history of human beings this part of the brain was extremely active and kept people literally running up trees in order to prevent being eaten for lunch by a predator. Today this part of the brain may be relied upon less, but still kicks into action when we are feeling threatened beyond what cognitive rationalization can provide for us. When we're "scared stiff" we might want to vomit, or just run away. This feeling may be accompanied by various other physiological symptoms and may reoccur each time we are placed in a similar situation that evokes the same feelings of fear or threat to our survival.

The mid-brain, or the old mammalian brain, concerns itself with emotions and is associated with what we refer to today as the limbic system. It regulates or tempers emotional responses in us depending upon the situation or circumstances with which we are presented. The newest brain, the neocortex, is the thinking part of the brain, and was relied upon less during the earlier development of human beings. Today we often rely on this part of our brains for decision making, conceptualization, and strategizing in a variety of situations.

As children and as adults we are occasionally faced with situations that throw us into the survival mode. We begin to operate from a more primitive level, sometimes losing our ability to understand what is being said to us, and maybe being driven to silence. Generating language in order to answer a question or articulate a need becomes an impossible feat. A child in a classroom who is experiencing downshifting may either flee the site or become completely immobilized. They may reply "I don't know" to virtually every question asked, and that is of course if they can generate any language while their integrities are under seige.

Gemma and her grandparents most certainly experienced frequent bouts of emotional memory as a result of their traumatic loss. There is a tiny, almond-shaped part of the brain called the amygdala that is a ware-house for emotional memories. Ms. Brown will probably not introduce this part of the brain in her lessons, as the complexity of this part of our human functioning can be best addressed with her students in discussions of hemispheric relationships and the triune brain theory. The amygdala, like the old mammalian brain we spoke of earlier, will grasp information that is emotionally charged and decide how the body will respond. Will there be a plan? Or will the body respond in a more primitive manner?

All of these theories have implications for learning, and most definitely for the child with LD/ADD/Dyslexia. Whether the learning profile emerges as a result of genetics, or as a result of significant trauma such as Gemma's and her grandparents', the same kinds of operations occur in the brain. However, children with learning differences and specific disabilities are more vulnerable to threat in the classroom and are more likely to experience downshifting as a result of their frequent humbling and humiliating episodes. Sometimes children develop coping mechanisms that allow them to downshift less as a result of desensitization, but more often than not, each new insult, humiliation, or imposed threat acts as a reminder to the sophisticated systems that scan stimuli for our two-legged predators.

Our Great Brain. We know so little. We feel so much.

THE SOCIOEMOTIONAL IMPACT OF LEARNING DISABILITIES ON THE CHILD

WHOSE TEARS ARE THEY?

Kiley Cove was a picturesque little town on the New England coast. The neighborhoods were neat, well trimmed, and aligned with the marketing that kept the town's tourist industry booming from one year to the next. There was no room, let alone tolerance in Kiley Cove for sloppy neighborhoods, messy yards, and youth hanging on street corners. The town boasted up and down the coast of its streamlined efforts in education. There were two regional elementary schools that accommodated three coastal communities, one very large regional middle school, and two regional high schools, one offering a college prep track of varying levels, and another school that was geared to students who were perceived by the school system as not being equipped for college. The alternate high school offered an agricultural program along with other smaller, more trade school–oriented programs. The cultural boundaries and expectations were clear even to the most unenlightened students and parents.

This particular spring day Paulie was walking ever so slowly toward his house. Several yards ahead of him walked a few of his buddies who every now and then turned to look at Paulie, puzzled by his chosen isolation. They knew that sometimes Paulie wanted to be alone, away from his friends, and alone with his thoughts. Their nine-year-old minds struggled to understand what made him do this sometimes. They knew after years of being Paulie's friend that this happened when he experienced a particularly bad day at school. He would brood, sometimes for days, and then eventually work his way back to the little group of friends he had played with since preschool.

Paulie kicked pebbles angrily toward the street, appearing as if he were aiming for parked cars. Once or twice a small rock hit a car, nicked it, and ricocheted against a tree or the sidewalk. It felt good to hit something, damage it in some small way. He wanted to yell at his friends to stop turning around to stare at him.

"Just keep walking, and mind your own stupid business!" he wanted to shout. But he didn't. He hoped his silence was message enough to be left alone in his misery.

When no one was noticing, Paulie ducked down a driveway lined with freshly painted white pickets, around the little garage, and into his own backyard. His dog, Jack, greeted him with great yelps and whines, dancing nervously in hopes of a good game of fetch. Paulie paused for only a moment to pat his dog, bury his face in Jack's neck, and croon approval to his very best and most loyal friend.

Paulie's mother, Anne, was watching from the kitchen window. She knew the signs. Her heart sank, and she could feel her stomach turn into knots. She knew from past experience that this would be a tough afternoon and evening with Paulie. She hoped it wouldn't spread into days of bleak despair for the household as it had in the past. That part always felt unpredictable to her.

Eventually Paulie made his way up the back stairs and into the kitchen with Jack by his side. Paulie stood silent, glaring at his mother.

"Well, it happened again, and you said it wouldn't!" he shouted as he slammed his books on the table with such force that they knocked the sugar bowl onto the floor, spilling the contents conveniently for Jack to slurp. Anne tried desperately to maintain a sense of calm. She pulled a chair out from the table.

"Let's sit down so you can tell me what happened today, honey."

"I don't want to sit down! I've been stuck to a chair all day!" He paced restlessly around the table, stepping unconsciously over Jack. His face was red with anger, and Anne was afraid he would explode again.

"Paulie, how about if we call that doctor Auntie Carol mentioned to us. She said he can help sometimes when you feel like this."

"No, I don't need a doctor! There's nothing wrong with me! It's them, it's them, it's them! I hate them, I hate them, hate 'em, hate 'em!" he wailed as he ran from the kitchen and up the stairs to his bedroom. Anne heard the stereo blaring and knew that he was burying himself in the music, in the noise, drowning out his own misery. Or was he becoming one with the rhythm, with the words? She could never tell. She only knew that she had to sit and endure. Sit and wait. This was the vigil.

Out of desperation she dialed her friend Callie's number.

"Hi Callie. Sorry to bother you again. Can I talk to Joey?" She tried to keep her voice to a whisper.

"I knew you were going to call, Anne. Joey said Paulie wouldn't walk with them today. . . . that he had a bad day." Her friend hesitated. "Anne, this makes Joey really uncomfortable, talking to you about Paulie. He feels some kind of disloyalty to his friend. Can you understand that?"

Anne sobbed uncontrollably into the phone. Her friend waited patiently for her to continue. "I'm sorry Callie. I hate doing this, but I'm so desperate. I don't want to drag him to the doctor. I don't know what to do anymore . . . the school looks at me as if I've lost my mind . . . my husband thinks a good spanking will cure Paulie . . . and I just want to protect him, but know I can't." She cried again and kept apologizing for her tears.

Anne had watched her son slowly deteriorating academically, socially, and emotionally over the past two years. Each time she approached the school about what she was observing, she felt brushed aside. Every new teacher pretended to know about how each student learned differently, but they couldn't seem to understand how that transferred to family life. They looked at her blankly. She felt like a whining parent who couldn't control her kid. Anne couldn't understand how Paulie's academic problems could be placed neatly in a compartment of an egg carton, sitting next to, but segregated from another compartment that held Paulie's social relationships and his emotions as they impacted virtually every area of his life and learning.

"Anne, just sit tight for now. After supper I'll come over and pick you up. I think I know someone who can help." Anne whimpered a thank you to her friend. She hated being this vulnerable and dependent and feeling so inadequate as a mother.

"My God," she thought to herself, "I'm calling Paulie's friends for help, and now my friends are telling me that my behaviors are intrusive and inappropriate! What is happening to me! What is happening to my son . . . to my family!"

Upstairs she noticed the volume had been turned down on the stereo. Now might be her chance to at least initiate a conversation. She poured a glass of ginger ale for Paulie and loaded a plate with cookies. On her way up the stairs she wondered if the cookies were for her or for Paulie.

She tapped on the door loud enough for him to hear above the droning of the guitars and the steady beat beat beat of the drums. Paulie opened the door, eyes red and swollen, looking much as his mother did. His lip began to tremble again.

"Can we talk?" she asked meekly. He walked away from her, but left the door open which was usually her signal to enter, but with caution.

She sat cross-legged on his bed and began munching on the cookies. She held the ginger ale out to him, much like a peace offering. He took the glass and sipped slowly, watching his mother over the rim. As he began crunching the ice cubes, he sat down on the bed with his back to her. At least it was a step closer.

"Was it Mr. Williams again?" Paulie shook his head and continued to sip and crunch. Anne knew it would be a guessing game, that Paulie could not articulate to her, or to anybody, exactly what had happened. His expressive language always frustrated him so. This was Paulie's second year in the third grade, a deep humiliation for him, and one that occurred after valiant efforts with summer school, private tutorials, and a great deal of encouragement and support from his family.

Anne wanted the problem to be Mr. Williams, the social studies teacher. He was an impatient man, getting ready to retire, and fed up with kids. She wanted Mr. Williams to be the perpetrator of Paulie's trouble so that her son would not be blamed for anything. It was helpful for Anne to be able to place blame on someone or something other than her son's behavior, attitude, and academic challenges. Putting the blame on Paulie was putting the blame on her.

Anne was on her third cookie now. "Was it gym class?" Again, he shook his head, but would not face her. She dared to reach her hand out and stroke his head. He didn't leap off the bed. This was a good sign.

Gym class would be easy to blame as well, so Anne was disappointed. Paulie loved some sports, but had difficulty in gym when he was made to follow quick, verbal directions. Invariably, he marched the wrong way, used the wrong hand, fell behind the others. His gym teacher called Paulie the "wise guy" in the group. Paulie's mistakes often made the other boys laugh, and when Paulie was having a good day he was willing to be regarded as the class clown. It took the pressure off sometimes. The role of clown, however, was becoming increasingly more tiresome, because Paulie just didn't feel very funny anymore.

Suddenly Anne thought she had it. Last night Paulie struggled so hard with the project that was due today. It was a brief presentation on a book of his choosing. She worked tirelessly with him as they read together, organized his talk, and prepared his note cards. They made up questions his classmates or the teacher might ask. She really thought he'd be OK, and he seemed more confident than usual.

Casually, and with a small silent prayer, she asked, "So, how was your presentation today?"

The glass sailed by her face so quickly she wasn't immediately aware of what happened. It smashed violently against the wall, and fell into a million glittering pieces on the rug, casting tiny rays of light all over the ceiling. Anne found herself staring at the kaleidoscope on the ceiling and continued to chew her cookie. Why wasn't she reacting, she wondered. She watched her son's face. He sat facing her, his serious face pale in the sunlight that poured through his window. Outside she noticed the view of the harbor, the sparkling cobalt blue of the water, and wondered why everything in this room felt so wrong when everything outside looked so beautiful and normal. The world felt strangely incongruous to Anne.

She had vague memories about the diagnostic testing Paulie had received two years ago. The brief feedback she did receive from the examiner left her with the feeling that Paulie's difficulties might reach into other areas of his life in the future. It was unclear as to how exactly his profile explained what Anne was observing in Paulie's schoolwork and at home. Everything felt vague, risky, and out-of-focus. She felt like Chicken Little and wanted to warn Paulie that the sky was falling, as if he didn't know.

Taking an enormous chance, Anne reached over and pulled Paulie to her, hugging him as hard as she could. His body was limp. He didn't resist, and eventually she felt him begin to cry. They cried together, sometimes great wracking sobs. In her grief for him she knew she would find a solution, she would find a way for her son to be at peace with himself. She would find a way for him to survive in school, to survive life.

That evening Anne's friend Callie picked her up.

"How did the afternoon go Anne?"

"It was awful at first, but once we talked through what happened in school it got a little better." She sighed deeply. Her eyes filled with tears again. "Now he's just very quiet. He's in bed watching TV with Jack beside him. He wouldn't eat tonight, but promised he would tomorrow."

Callie pulled away from the curb and headed toward the next town.

"Where are we going anyway?"

"Well, I guess I'm kidnapping you. I told your husband where I was taking you, and he seemed hopeful that you'd be pleased." Callie looked a little guilty. Anne looked suspicious.

A half hour later Callie pulled into the driveway of a well-known private school. She shut the engine off and turned to her friend.

"Anne, this is a meeting for parents of kids with learning disorders. Or disabilities. I'm not really sure what all this means exactly. But I know you told me that Paulie was tested a couple of years ago. It sounds as if the school is not giving you the information you need, and it sounds as if they don't really understand who Paulie is. Anne . . . I'm just worried about you. You're so worried about Paulie . . . you're so wrapped up in his misery, that we never see you anymore. All your time is devoted to keeping him in some kind of balanced state so that he doesn't isolate himself. But now you're isolating yourself, too."

Anne still looked suspicious.

"C'mon. Let's just go in and have some coffee. If you don't like the people we can leave and go shopping. Is that a deal?"

Anne smiled feebly. She knew that everything her friend said was true. Together they walked into the brick building, past the sign that pointed the way to the parents' support group.

People were milling around a long table, helping themselves to coffee and cookies. Anne looked around at the others. There were a few couples, but mostly women who Anne guessed to be mothers, and a few fathers who were there alone as well. Some people looked as if they might be grandparents. She turned when she heard Callie strike up a conversation with two other women.

A woman about Anne's age was saying, "I just didn't know what I'd do next—someone gave me the name of the person who runs these seminars. My daughter, Terry, moons around all day, says she feels sick every morning, and is now refusing to go to school at all. The school is fed up, mostly with me I'm afraid. I must be a pain. I keep telling them that she's so humiliated by her constant attempts to succeed when she only experiences failure time after time." The woman looked like she wanted to cry. Anne felt her own eyes fill up and turned away, unable to bear witness to this woman's pain. Her own wounds were still fresh after today's episode with Paulie.

Anne thought, this is really a family experience, not just the child's.

The polite tinkling of a bell could be heard as a small, elderly woman invited everyone to be seated. She introduced herself as Vera Price, the headmistress of the Donnegal School. Miss Price explained briefly the history and mission of the school, and then introduced the guest speaker.

"I am proud to have with us this evening for the first in a series of eight seminars, Dr. Evah Nellsom. Evah is visiting with us from Maine where she does a great deal of work with children with learning disabilities and their families. She is here this evening to discuss how learning disabilities can contribute to childhood depression and to the dynamics of the entire family involved in the life of the child." Everyone applauded. Anne felt hot tears run slowly down her face. Her friend Callie squeezed her hand.

"This is gonna be great Anne. Just great!"

BULLY, BULLY, FOR YOU

Rachel hid between two bushes at the end of the school's driveway. She didn't take the bus home today because she preferred walking the mile and a half home, rather than subjecting herself to the newest arch enemies in her life, Joye and Esther. She would make up a story to her mother.

From her hiding spot, she watched her bus pull out of the school's driveway. There they were at the back of the bus looking out, their blonde heads bouncing with each bump in the path. Rachel slipped deeper into the bushes, her heart beating wildly. "What if they stopped the bus, and told the driver to look for her?" she thought to herself.

Rachel started feeling sick to her stomach again, just as she had so much of the time lately. She pressed her hand to her chest and felt her heart pounding. Remembering her experiences that morning, she bent down to examine her shin. A purple and red bruise was beginning to show itself on an almond-sized lump, although the blood was finally beginning to clot where the skin was scraped. She'd tell her mother she decided to walk home because she was gaining weight and needed the exercise. Then she'd say that she tripped because she was reading her homework assignment while she was walking. The rest should be obvious, Rachel thought. Besides, it would look like she was at least doing her homework. That would keep her mother off her back, at least until tomorrow.

Cautiously, Rachel stepped out onto the sidewalk, choosing the tree-lined side of the street rather than the ocean side. This way she was better hidden from oncoming traffic. Being alone was becoming preferable to Rachel. Less risky. She began to hum a favorite tune, slowly feeling her stomach return to normal. The pain in her shin, however, was a constant reminder of what she needed to face again the next day.

This morning in Mrs. Crow's class Rachel was called upon to read aloud. She thought she had escaped the nightmare this time. All of the passages had been read aloud; there were none left. Rachel breathed a deep sigh of relief, noting that there was only another hour of this misery to endure before lunch. Her stomach rumbled, but she was not sure if it was from hunger or fear.

"Rachel Woods! Please read the first paragraph in the next chapter." Mrs. Crow peered at Rachel over her glasses. Rachel froze. All heads turned. Joye on her left and Esther on her right both snickered. Rachel couldn't understand what happened. They weren't supposed to start the next chapter until tomorrow. Not today!

"C'mon dummy. Read!" hissed Joye. Esther giggled, pleased with the power she felt over her less able classmate. Rachel's silence continued. She felt her hands sweat, and her heart beat accelerate. The nausea swept over her again, and she gripped the sides of her desk with white knuckles. She felt like a hunted animal.

"C'mon dummy. I said READ!" Joye spewed, poking Rachel in the leg with her pencil. Rachel didn't even feel it. The silence continued. The snickers continued. Finally, the bell rang. Rachel exhaled loudly.

"Rachel Woods. Remain in your seat. Everyone else, file orderly into the hallway please." Rachel could hear Mrs. Crow's heels clicking on the tile floor as she approached her. She sat down in the now empty seat in front of Rachel.

"Rachel, what is it? You've been getting extra help for the reading. Aren't you paying attention? I know you can read Rachel!"

What Mrs. Crow didn't know was that although Rachel's teachers encouraged her to read aloud, the child was even more frightened of her classmates' perception of her halting speech, her mistakes, her rhythmless reading. The bullying she was subjected to by two peers in particular had become yet another layer of worry, humiliation, rejection. She felt powerless and victimized and had no language or framework of thought to articulate these feelings. Rachel was experiencing classroom trauma as a result of her learning disability and bullying from her peers. What was once fear of humiliation had intensified to a terror so great that she found herself experiencing panic attacks. She was downshifting (Hart, 1983), her brain sliding from rational, cognitive processing to a more primitive mode of operation. Indeed, she was like a hunted animal.

Rachel was still frozen to the spot, unable to explain how she felt, what she feared, what she dreaded. Words swirled in her head, disjointed, disconnected. Nothing made sense. She felt beads of perspiration on her lip and looked blankly into Mrs. Crow's face.

"Can I go to the bathroom Mrs. Crow?" With a sigh of disgust, Mrs. Crow nodded.

Rachel tripped her way up the aisle, bumping into chairs, knocking over books. Mrs. Crow frowned, not knowing what to do next with this child. She wondered if she should request that Rachel be placed in special services for a greater portion of the day. Mrs. Crow remembered that Dr. Evah Nellsom was coming to the school for an inservice next month. Maybe she should ask about Rachel. This was holding up the class. Mrs. Crow was unaware of the symptoms of downshifting and ignorant of Rachel's raw fear. Rachel's internal gyroscope was tipped (Adelizzi, 1996), and she was experiencing a sense of disequilibrium, both internally and externally.

Just in time Rachel reached the stall in the girls' bathroom. She vomited, feeling her body tremble with weakness. She wished she would die. She wondered if other ten-year-old girls felt like this. She hated school so much, hated Joye and Esther, hated Mrs. Crow. Why couldn't someone figure out how scared she was? She started to cry, tears of frustration, fear, embarrassment, because she didn't know how to take control of the situation. The line outside in the hallway was moving to the lunchroom. She knew she couldn't eat and would do anything to avoid more abuse from Joye and Esther.

Cautiously, Rachel peeked around the corner. The coast looked clear. Just as she headed for the stairs, she tripped and fell against the metal edge of a step. Down she went onto her knees, one of her legs bearing most of the weight. She could immediately feel the burning pain. But what was more frightening was the giggling she heard. Joye and Esther were behind her. She couldn't figure out where her predators came from, but knew they had tripped her and caused the fall.

"Get up dummy!" Esther doubled over with laughter.

Joye shoved a book under Rachel's nose. "Read dummy!" Both Joye and Esther laughed uncontrollably. Rachel rubbed her shin and sobbed.

"Why can't you leave me alone! Just leave me alone!"

Just then Mrs. Crow came up the stairs. "Joye, Esther, what are you doing here? Why aren't you in the lunchroom?" She bent down and looked at Rachel's leg.

"Rachel, you are so clumsy. How did this happen?" Joye and Esther glared at Rachel, clearly conveying their intent should Rachel decide to disclose the truth about her fall.

"I'm just clumsy, like you said," she sniffed. Joye smiled.

As Rachel continued her walk home from school she tried to erase the memories of the day from her mind. She did this daily. At least this year she did. This was the year that Joye and Esther decided to pick on her and call her dummy all the time. Sometimes the other kids chimed in with them, and sometimes one or two of her friends would try to defend her. This was not an easy task however. Both Joye and Esther were bright, articulate, and well liked by their teachers. More importantly, they were feared to some degree by their classmates. They were a little bigger and more aggressive than the others, to the point where most of the boys avoided conflict with them as well.

Rachel's parents were waiting for her on the back porch. Rachel loved her house. She thought it was the prettiest of the prettiest in Kiley Cove. It was white with deep blue shutters, and her parents always kept their yard perfect. Suddenly Rachel frowned, wondering why she wasn't as perfect as the house she loved. And her brother, look at him! The baby, and the smart one too! "I hate him too," she thought.

Carl Woods stood up from his wicker chair. "Rach, we have to talk. Come over here and sit down."

Rachel felt a lump in her throat. "Not them too," she thought in dismay. She felt friendless and totally miserable. She hung her head, and climbed the steps slowly to the porch. Her mother grabbed her by the waist, and pulled her down on her lap.

"We know what happened today, Rach," her father began. "Mrs. Crow called. She said it took her a while to figure it all out, but once she did she was worried sick how you were after school. She said things would change for you . . . or at least she would try to make things change. She told us about a Dr. Nellsom who was coming to the area to talk to parents." Carl Woods wrung his hands. Rachel's mother rocked her.

"Rach, Mom and I are going to attend some meetings to find out what more we can do for you . . . for all of us. This is not just your problem. It's our problem. We're all in this." He looked with troubled eyes at his daughter. Rachel's little brother, Sam, hugged Rachel's legs. She winced in pain.

"Finally!" Rachel thought with relief. "Finally, they'll know."

IT'S ALL ABOUT ME!

"Me, me, me! That's all he thinks about!"

Kristen Rideout scrubbed her counter angrily. Her eleven-year-old son had just come home and demanded that she drop everything to take him to the mall. Robert hung in the doorway, watching his mother clean the kitchen. He knew that his mother was having company to-night, but his project was due tomorrow. He needed more poster board. He needed it now. He stood in the doorway, waiting for her to stop what she was doing.

"Rob, why didn't you tell me this yesterday? Why?" He shrugged.

"You don't know?" Kristen rolled her eyes, imploring the heavens to grant her some understanding. She threw the sponge in the sink, grabbed her car keys, and stomped out the back door. Her perfect view of the harbor greeted her, the smell of salt air, the toot of the ferry whis-tle.

"God, my life stinks. At least the view is great!"

On the ride to the mall Rob went on to issue his mother a list of things he needed in order to complete the visuals for his project, the Taj Mahal. "I need new markers, some colored paper, glitter, glue, cotton, and some of that shiny blue stuff you wrap around Easter baskets." His mother glared at him. He looked back at her, genuinely puzzled by her obvious hostility.

"How long have you known about this? Answer me this time. Don't shrug. Just answer me!" Rob was deep in thought.

"Answer me I said!"

Rob snapped back to attention. "Umm, I think in March. I forget exactly."

"March? This is May, Rob! May! Do you hear me? May!" Again, Rob seemed perplexed by his mother's frustration with him.

"I've been busy, ya know," he whined. "I tried out for baseball, for the big part in the play, and I have other stuff to do at school." He be-came lost in thought again, concentrating on the scenery outside, the traffic, the buses, the boats, the people, the quiet music his mother al-ways played on the radio. He began to pick at his hands. Kristen noticed how red and raw his wrists were.

"You're busy? You're busy . . . I don't believe it! Rob, I work hard for you and your sisters. I'm always busy! And, you come home and give me orders according to what you need, what you want . . . what about me?"

"I dunno Mom. What about me?" She just stared at him in disbelief.

In the mall she handed Rob a twenty dollar bill. He was always good with money, with numbers, to a fault sometimes Kristen felt. He obsessed about them actually. His sisters teased him good naturedly about it.

"Rob, check your watch. Be back here in a half hour. I'll wait right here." They synchronized their watches. Rob loved it when they did that. It felt like a spy movie. Kristen watched her son conscientiously set his watch. She felt remorse at the way she spoke with him earlier in the car. She attempted to give him a hug, but he backed away stiffly. Most mothers would have suspected he backed away because he was eleven years old, and his friends might see him hugging his mother. But Kristen knew it was much more than that.

On many occasions she complained to the pediatrician that Rob didn't like to be hugged, kissed, or touched. He didn't like any physical contact and avoided it when at all possible. Kristen felt the doctor regarded her concern too lightly. It wasn't to the degree where he refused to let the doctor touch him. It wasn't an obvious, in-your-face kind of thing. It seemed subtle to Kristen, or at least she thought so. But the older Rob got, the more she noticed it. She watched Rob move down the corridor of the mall, a spring in his rather military-like step, his head on a swivel, taking in the sights, the smells, the sounds. He bumped into a younger child, but just kept walking. He walked right past the store he was headed for!

Kristen power-walked her way down the corridor after him, hoping she wouldn't bump into any friends. She whispered hoarsely, "Rob! Rob! Turn around. Rob!" He didn't hear her. Finally she caught up with him and touched him lightly on the shoulder, careful not to alarm him. He spun around, losing his balance, tripping over his feet. He hated to feel off balance in any way. He hated it when she surprised him like that.

"What!" he yelled at his mother. She had clearly frightened him, caught him off guard.

"I'm sorry I scared you Rob. But you walked past the store. C'mon, it's back there. I'll walk you there and then go back to the spot where I told you I'd wait." He looked puzzled for a moment. He was trying to reorient himself. Rob was clearly in a state of disequilibrium.

"OK," he said. She walked with him to the paper store and ushered him inside.

"I'm here now. You can leave." She tried to smile as he stared stonily into her face. Lately, she couldn't tell if he was developing a dry sense of humor or if his speech was just plain flat. She noticed he didn't smile back.

As she headed for the spot where she was supposed to wait, she reflected back on the past few years. Being a single mother hadn't been easy, especially with three kids. The girls never gave her much trouble, but Rob—she was never sure if she was doing the right thing with him. He wasn't a bad kid. He always obeyed rules, unless he just "forgot," which did happen fairly often. He just didn't seem to be on the same wave length with everybody else. Kristen thought at first that maybe it was just at home, but then two years ago the teacher called her.

"Mrs. Rideout, would you mind coming in so that we could talk about Robert?"

"What's wrong?" Kristen didn't believe in beating around any tactful bushes.

"Well, maybe nothing. But let's talk, OK?"

Rob's teacher, Mr. Onge, a new teacher from New York, began by telling Kristen how bright Rob was in math.

"He really understands the mechanics of English, too, Mrs. Rideout. As a matter of fact, he understands the mechanics, or the concrete aspects of most things. It's when we travel down abstract and uncharted territory with Rob that I feel I've lost him."

Kristen asked for examples. As she listened to Mr. Onge, she nodded, understanding how Rob could quickly calculate in his head, hold facts and numbers, retrieve them, spit them out, give the right answer—always. She also understood how he just couldn't "see" other things, like expressions on people's faces, nuances in conversation, humor, body language. She listened to all this while silently praying that it would get better with the next stage of development.

The baseball team loved Rob. He knew what to do and was skilled to a point. He understood the rules of the game and could recite them. Rob could run, rather stiffly, but he could run. He knew his right from his left, unlike some of the other kids Kristen watched at games. But he hated it when someone bumped into him or if he inadvertently got caught up in a scuffle. It upset him much more than Kristen thought it should. She tried to explain this to the pediatrician again, but he just shrugged. The pediatrician's response to her concerns reminded her of Rob's reaction to most things.

Mr. Onge suggested that Rob receive educational diagnostic testing to determine if there was any kind of a learning disorder. Kristen was hesitant. She didn't want to look for trouble. The other side of it was that she really wanted to know what she was dealing with.

Two weeks after the testing was completed, the examiner called Kristen to come in for a consultation.

"So, what is it? What's wrong with Rob?" she asked impatiently.

The examiner began by telling her the same things Mr. Onge had already said.

"I know all that. Skip to what's wrong, please. Don't make me go over what I already know." She could feel her frustration building. She drummed her fingers on the table. The examiner took a deep breath and let it out slowly in a soft whistling sound.

"Well, Rob appears to have what some professionals refer to as a nonverbal learning disability, although I think it's marginal. You know, not severe. There is a significant discrepancy between the verbal and performance modes of intelligence on his Wechsler testing, the performance being much lower."

"And what's a nonverbal learning disability? I know what a plain old learning disability is. I've been reading about it . . . you know . . . trying to figure out what's going on here . . . and it doesn't seem to be what Rob has." She continued to drum her fingers on the table.

"Well, uh, Rob doesn't seem to read people well, catch the hidden meanings embedded in language, in conversation. It would help even further if I could observe him in a social situation. The testing situation is so stilted, so "pretend." Rob is smart. He knows this. We talked a little about it." The man hesitated. "Have you noticed that Rob's hands and wrists are very rough and red? They look sore. Does Rob seem to wash his hands more than your other children?"

Kristen's face colored. "Well, he is a very fastidious boy. He is forever cleaning his hands and nails—he hates to be dirty. He always hated it, even when he was a small child. So I give him lots of lotions to use on his skin, and try to explain that he really doesn't need to wash so often." She thought for a moment. "Actually, some days or weeks are better than others. I used to think it was the weather or the season, but I can't really predict when it's better or worse or why."

The examiner nodded understanding. "Back to the social situation, Mrs. Rideout. I would really like to be able to watch Rob interact with other people, maybe some kids his own age."

"And?"

"And, could I spend some more time with him in some group situations? Would you mind? I really think it would help Rob, and you as well."

Kristen stood up and turned to the door. She could feel herself losing control. She felt very blamed in some way.

"How is this going to help me, mister? How is this gonna help me cope with him? I can't get through to him. I can't hug him. He hates me to hug him! I can't make him stop being so hung up on being neat and clean. No one listens to me. How is this gonna help me, Kristen Rideout!" She turned on her heel and walked with a purpose down the hallway, out the front door, and onto the Main Street. The tears nearly blinded her as she walked to the parking lot. When she was safely inside her car, she sobbed for ten minutes.

As Kristen sat in the mall waiting for Rob, she thought with regret that she should have listened to the examiner. Maybe Rob should have been in a group. Maybe this would have helped to determine how and why he behaved as he did. He had what she considered to be a quirky kind of learning disability. She loved him so much and felt so much frustration in her efforts to understand and cope with him. She desperately wanted to believe that this wasn't her fault, that there was another reason why Rob was the way he was.

Finally, forty-five minutes later, Rob ambled down to where his mother sat waiting. "Want an ice cream Rob?"

"You said you had to get right home, remember?" He fished through his bag of purchases looking for something.

"I know, but we need to have a little talk. OK?"

"Yup, it's OK." Rob pulled a red eraser in the shape of a dolphin out of the bag and handed it to his mother.

"Here. You're always complaining that I steal your erasers." One end of his mouth curled up in an effort of a smile.

"Thank you, Rob. Can I have a hug?"

"No. Let's get an ice cream, Mom." He walked ahead of her toward the ice cream parlor, a destination he rarely walked past while lost in thought.

Kristen thought to herself, "I'm going to call that examiner when I get home. I have to do something."

BROKEN HEARTS

Dr. Evah Nellsom looked over her audience as Miss Price was introducing her. She thought they looked like a frightened group of people, much like the other groups with whom she had worked.

"Poor people," she thought. "They've been through the mill with their kids. They look as if they're all running on empty tanks." Dr.

Nellsom remembered the last group she spoke with in Oklahoma, and the desperate looks on the faces of Rowena and Jake Martin, Gemma's grandparents. She hoped that in some small way she was able to assist them in their journey to understanding and to healing as a family.

Kristen Rideout sat in the front row, jiggling her keys and tapping her left foot in time to some internal rhythm. With an eyebrow raised she gave Dr. Nellsom an initial critical assessment, noticing how her suit matched her shoes. Kristen felt self-conscious in her jeans and sweater and started to look around to see how everyone else was dressed.

Rachel Woods's parents sat two rows behind Kristen Rideout. They held hands and looked extremely nervous. Dr. Nellsom knew they would be the kind of people who might not raise their hands during the group process, but might call her office tomorrow, or seek her out privately following the seminar, if no one else was around.

Dr. Nellsom stretched her neck a little to look at the small cluster of people sitting in the back, near the exit and the refreshment table. She saw Anne, Paulie's mother, dabbing at her eyes with a tissue. Her friend, Callie, kept leaning over and reassuring her.

When the applause ceased Dr. Nellsom smiled warmly at her audience.

"Thank you for letting me visit with you this evening. I hope that I'm able to answer some of your questions and explain some things that have probably felt very mysterious to you about learning disabilities, about depression, and possibly assist you in seeing how coexisting disorders really 'connect.' Each of our seminars will deal with another aspect of this octopus—this emotional octopus you are wrestling with. Each seminar will give us all something new to take home and think about and to teach to others who need our help."

The room was quiet. Dr. Nellsom removed her jacket and placed it over a chair. She faced her audience and waited a moment before she began.

"Tonight we'll begin by talking about broken hearts. Most of you are here to learn more about your children who have learning disabilities, and that means that you are aware of either an old or new diagnosis of dyslexia, attention deficit disorder, or a nonverbal learning disability. Within these categories lie many subtypes, disorders, and many faces and combinations of LD/ADD/Dyslexia. Because you have been valiantly coping with the effects of learning disabilities at home, in your families, and in your relationships with your children, you probably have felt now and then as if your heart has been broken. And I know that you have watched your children struggle, and that you have witnessed their broken hearts. It feels like an endless cycle, doesn't it?" She paused and watched her audience.

Kristen Rideout wiped her nose with a calico handkerchief. Mr. and Mrs. Woods squeezed each other's hands and leaned closer together, drawing strength from their closeness. Anne started to get up from her chair, but her friend Callie pulled her back down and put an arm around her.

Dr. Nellsom continued. "Keep your broken hearts and those of your children at the forefront of your mind, but be aware also that this room is full of people who understand how you feel, the great lengths you go to each day to maintain balance in your home life, to keep your child with LD afloat so to speak. It's not easy work. And if you weren't conscientious about what you're doing as parents, as caring human beings, you wouldn't be here tonight."

"Many of you have children who have language-based learning disabilities. For some, the diagnosis of dyslexia has been included in a formal evaluation that has been completed by a psychologist or learning specialist either within your school system or through private agencies. Language based LD affects your child's ability to read, understand what he or she has read, and then articulate this understanding in writing. The idea of receptive and expressive language sounds simple, but it's actually very complex. Simplistically, what I have just described is the full cycle of literacy, and according to some adults who have lived with a language-based LD all their lives, being deprived of language in the fullest sense is like being robbed of something valuable in life. One adult said to me 'If you can read, you have everything!' I knew he meant that from the bottom of his heart because he still carried the pain of his educational history with him.

"Books for these folks are not to be enjoyed, they are to be feared, avoided, and sometimes truly hated. Reading out loud in a classroom is a form of torture for some kids, and good for at least a panic attack or two each time the situation presents itself. The emotional impact of a language-based learning disability, or dyslexia, as you will hear it referred to often, is enormous. The emotional fallout seeps into virtually every area of a child's life. The fears can be overpowering, depending upon the resiliency of each child. Humiliation leaves scars as deeply as a wound that requires stitches.

"Attention deficit disorder is being diagnosed in large numbers. I'm not really sure if all of these children and adults are really suffering from ADD/ADHD or if their symptoms are part of yet another kind of disorder. Whatever the case, children and adults with ADD often suffer from depression as well. If the right combination of medications isn't administered, and this often takes some time to experiment with, then the system is thrown into a neurological upheaval. The brains of people with ADD actually need to be stimulated more, not less. Their medication keeps them stimulated so that their systems are not working overtime in order to maintain a feeling of equilibrium." Dr. Nellsom scanned her audience again. Some parents shifted uneasily in their seats.

"According to some professionals, nonverbal learning disabilities put a child more at emotional risk than do language-based disabilities. Kids who make it through school with dyslexia, into college or the workplace, and eventually into their adult lives, can often do so with the assistance of rich relationships, laughter, humor . . . and of course the appropriate academic support. They are usually able to experience and reciprocate with a full range of human emotions. For the child with nonverbal learning disabilities, these taken-for-granted expressions of love, humor, appreciation, and just small talk become monumental tasks in daily life. Sometimes these disabilities coexist with a psychiatric disorder, like obsessive-compulsive disorder for instance, a double whammy for some kids as well as for the families who love them."

Kristin Rideout conjured up a picture of Rob in her mind, standing at the bus stop about two yards away from the other kids who were laughing, telling stories, sharing books. He was shifting uncomfortably from one foot to the other, stepping out of his space now and then to peer down the road. He always looked so ill at ease. Kristin was always aware of this, but found a different excuse every month to explain Rob's behaviors, his isolation, and what appeared to be his own, private, broken heart.

Dr. Nellsom continued. "Some of these kids are aware that the nuances in conversation, expressions on people's faces, and the general environment can challenge their ability to cope, adapt, and interact appropriately with other people in a variety of situations. They may make the same social mistakes consistently, not remembering or being able to connect what went wrong last time to the next situation that exhibits the same set of circumstances. Many of these kids will isolate themselves as they get older and realize that socializing is a skill for them that seems just beyond their reach. They've suffered the consequences. They know the pain. They are intelligent people and know that they're not liked by some of their peers or teachers. Often they're aware that they disappoint and frustrate their families, and they don't know how to rectify this. Their broken hearts become yours." Dr. Nellsom's audience was solemn.

"Many children with learning disabilities have been subjected to classroom trauma. Let me define that for you. Classroom trauma is a significantly unpleasant (or horrific) external event or stressor that occurs within the confines of an educational environment—for example this means a traditional or nontraditional classroom, a small group, or a one-to-one tutorial. This type of trauma, which is a psychological trauma, may leave the student with diminishing self-esteem and in a state of fear, humiliation, or learned helplessness to the degree where similar situations will be avoided by the student in the future. The specific and original cause may be a person, such as a teacher, or even a peer. Although with each repetition or trigger, the perpetrator is not necessary to induce fear or humiliation. A situation that is just reminiscent of the original classroom trauma is sufficient to resurrect feelings of fear or humiliation, which may impede learning and functioning. This type of trauma may occur repetitively, especially in students with learning disabilities" (Adelizzi, 1996).

"Now for some kids, classroom trauma is part of daily life. These kids sit in their seats literally sweating bullets, dreading being called upon by their teachers, trying to control their emotions so that they can appear undaunted, untouched by the next wave of humiliation. Every child has different triggers. For some it's reading. For others, it's speaking in front of others, articulating their thoughts. For a lot of kids, it's the constant bullying or teasing they receive from peers, and in some cases from siblings and other family members. Some kids become desensitized. Some don't. Some are resilient. Some are not. Sometimes we don't know why one of our kids is resilient, flexible, positive about life and the many lumps and bumps it has to offer, and why another child in the family simply cannot endure emotional pain, even in the tiniest doses." Dr. Nellsom strolled back and forth in front of her audience.

"The drama plays out at home as well—I don't have to tell you that. You're the experts. Many of these kids save up their anger and frustration for you, for the family. This is safe. In most cases kids can take the chance that you will still love them no matter how badly they behave, no matter how angry they are. Also, they're waiting for you to guess what's wrong sometimes because it's so difficult to explain, either because the words don't come, or they're too embarrassed by their emotions. Sometimes when they shrug and say 'I don't know!' they really mean it. They truly don't know why they behave as they do.

"And many of these kids are angry. Real angry. If a kid is lucky enough to become involved in sports or an activity that allows them to work off some real issues and frustrations, or just the events of the day, then they might be a little easier to live with at home. Their risk for depression might be a little less if they experience success and skill in another area of life . . . outside the classroom.

"However, there are too many kids who feel so beaten down by their LD that they begin to lose interest in outside activities, in their favorite foods, their friends. Often they are lost in TV, their music, or just the isolation of their rooms. Some kids eat their way through their depression. Others don't eat at all and need to be coaxed and bribed to eat. This of course feels to parents as if it's their failure somehow, that they have caused this, that they're not doing enough. Then we begin to see a family in depression, a family that feels hopeless and helpless."

Dr. Nellsom paused for a moment and scrutinized her audience. Her gaze scanned the room. "Don't ever let anyone tell you that kids can't be depressed. And don't ever let anyone tell you that learning disabilities, attention deficit disorder, and any other coexisting disorder don't put your child at a greater risk for depression. Don't ever let anyone minimize your fears and your concerns. Don't be shoved aside, made to feel as if you're overreacting." She raised her hands to the ceiling, and looked up as if she were praying.

"Be pushy, even at the risk of a teacher thinking you're overstepping your bounds. Remember, your child's depression becomes your depression. Your child's broken heart is your broken heart."

THE HELPING HAND: WHAT YOU CAN DO TO HELP YOUR CHILD LEARN

Dom breathed a contented sigh as he sank into the recliner. Mike Wallace was just finishing his introduction and the *Sixty Minutes* clock ticked along on the TV. He'd retrieved the sports section from the Boston Sunday *Globe* and had it spread out on his lap. A ribbon of steam rose from his after-dinner mug of coffee.

It had been a good weekend. They'd spent it at the beach house on Cape Cod. It was the first weekend the family had gotten away since school had started. Dom felt good about the time he'd been able to spend with his son, thirteen-year-old Anthony. They'd tossed a football back and forth on the beach in the golden October sun, while Robin and six-year-old Rosie scoured the beach for shells. Later, comfortably full after grilled burgers and corn on the cob, they'd actually had a decent conversation about Tony's high school plans. Dom was in favor of St. Regis, where he thought the religious brothers could give Tony the structure and discipline his hyperactive son needed. Tony was lobbying for the local public high school where most of his buddies were headed. Dom had tried to listen for a change. There'd been too much tension between them. With the onset of adolescence and the ongoing challenges posed by Tony's attention deficit, it seemed like they were at each other all the time lately. He didn't want to lose his son. He wanted to have a better relationship with Tony than he had had with his own father. And Tony was maturing; maybe he could be trusted with a little more freedom and responsibility for himself. He envisioned a new closeness between them. Dom promised himself that he'd be more patient, less critical of Tony, more open.

His resolution lasted all of two minutes. Before the first segment of *Sixty Minutes* had even begun, he heard Tony rooting around in the hall closet amid the jumble of boots, jackets, toys, and assorted junk that had collected there. "What are you looking for?" Dom asked.

"Just some stuff I need for my history project," Tony responded. His tone had that edge that warned Dom to back off. Dom knew the warning signs. When Tony responded in that voice, it meant he was probably feeling guilty and would go to great lengths to deny his culpability for whatever situation he had gotten into.

Still, Dom couldn't help pursuing the question. "What do you mean, history project? I thought you told me Friday that you didn't have any work you had to bring to the Cape?" Dom could hear the note of accusation creeping into his voice. He knew Tony could too.

Defenses up, Tony replied. "It's just a map of the thirteen original colonies. It'll only take me ten minutes." He started off in a voice that said the assignment was no big deal, then he finished with a whining complaint, "But I can't find any poster board. We never have anything we need around here!"

Dom could feel his contented mood slipping away like the steam from his coffee cup. Acid indigestion replaced the comfortable feeling in his gut. He tried to control his tone as well as his words.

"Can't you just draw it on regular paper. There's a package of computer paper on the kitchen counter."

"Of course not," Tony responded, his tone bordering on insolent now and implying that his father's suggestion was the height of stupidity. "I have to do a presentation in front of the class with it. It has to look good. I need to color all the states in different colors. I'm going to make labels for them on the computer."

The last part was the straw that broke the camel's proverbial back. They'd only just purchased the computer and it wasn't even hooked up yet. Dom exploded, "Can't you ever do anything the right way? Why does everything have to be last minute with you? No wonder you're doing so poorly in school. If you weren't so lazy, you would have gotten the map done on Friday afternoon before we left for the Cape. When are you going to wise up? I've just about had it with you!"

Tony stormed past the den, and Dom heard the door of his bedroom slam shut. He kept telling himself to keep out of it, let Tony learn a lesson. He tried to concentrate on the sports page. He stared blankly at the TV screen. He hoped Robin would step in to help, but she was busy downstairs with the laundry getting everything ready for the busy week ahead. After a half hour of feeling like a failure as a father as he listened to his son angrily banging around in his room, Dom let out a sigh of resignation and headed out to the twenty-four-hour drug store looking for poster board and neon markers. It would be a long night.

THE DAILY DILEMMAS OF PARENTING CHILDREN WITH LEARNING DISABILITIES

Dom is certainly not alone in his frustration. His story is one many parents can identify with, perhaps especially those who have children with attention deficits and learning disabilities. Parents of these children are often caught in a difficult dilemma. How can they be supportive and helpful to their children and at the same time hold their children to standards they have the right to expect of them? How can they be understanding and sympathetic while also challenging their children to grow and accept responsibilities? How can they balance their child's needs with their own needs and the needs of other family members? While the bad news may be that you often find yourself in Dom's shoes, the good news is that it doesn't have to be that way.

If you are reading this book, you are a caring parent who wants to do the best you can for your child. There is no question of caring or not caring here. Instead, the question is whether you will direct your care in ways that will *enable* your child or in ways that will *disable* him. The *American Heritage Dictionary* defines "enabling" as supplying "the means, knowledge, or opportunity to be or do something." But the self-help literature and literature on addiction uses the term in a different way that is applicable to understanding the dilemmas involved in helping a child with learning disabilities. Enabling in this sense can mean becoming a *co*dependent with your child, collaborating with him in fostering learned helplessness, rescuing your child from his own choices. Each time you do this, you are reinforcing the very behaviors you want your child to overcome. The cumulative effect of this reinforcement is the development in your child of a deep-seated sense of incompetence and a life-long habit of reliance on others for what he believes he cannot do for himself. Such *co*dependency does not result in a closer parent-child relationship. On the contrary, it often fosters resentment and anger on both sides of the relationship.

Before you feel too guilty about typing that paper for your daughter last week, or getting those books out of the library for your son, take a look at why you did it. Parents who find themselves in the role of rescuer certainly do not intend to cripple their children and rob them of self-efficacy. They rescue their child when they are worn out, when they don't know what else to do, when they are just plain at the end of their rope, and when they can't bear to see their child struggling any longer. They can't simply resolve not to jump in and take over learning tasks that rightly belong to their child. They have to take specific and concrete steps that will allow this to happen and will allow them to enable their children in the positive sense of the word: give them what they need in order to do it themselves. So, where do you begin?

GIVE UNCONDITIONAL ACCEPTANCE

When a teacher in a college learning disabilities support program asked Elizabeth, one of her students, what was the single most important thing the teacher could do to help her succeed during the upcoming semester, Elizabeth replied without hesitation, "Continue to give me your unconditional acceptance." The student had encapsulated a world of wisdom in her words. Acceptance is often the crack in the door. Our children and adolescents won't let us in enough to help them unless they first know that we accept them, and that we accept them with all their failures and deficits. Until we give them that complete acceptance, they will be forced to defend their fragile egos with denials, deceptions, and defiance.

Acceptance doesn't mean approval of the destructive behaviors your child may exhibit. But it does mean acceptance of the child, in spite of mistakes, missed deadlines, poor report cards. You have to continually reassure your child that, though you may disapprove of her way of handling a particular situation, you do not love her less. Don't be sure your child knows this. Take the time to tell her.

You also have to be sure your child knows that you accept her limitations, including those related to her learning disability. The best approach to this is to constantly remind her (and yourself!) that the human condition is not perfect. We all have strengths and weaknesses. It's what we do with what we have that counts. Many older children with learning disabilities say they feel they have been a disappointment to their parents. This is especially true of children from high-achieving families. Parents may be unaware of the subtle clues the child uses to come to this conclusion. You need to counteract this perception explicitly by assuring your child of your pride in the person she is, not in the one she can become, and especially, not in the one she feels she can never become.

An important part of conveying acceptance is avoiding the hurt words. These include the judgmental words and phrases that assign blame without really looking at the root of the problem. They include a long list of offenders from "You're lazy and unmotivated" to "How could you have been so stupid!" and include a whole parade of ugly things you wished you never said in between.

ACKNOWLEDGE YOUR CHILD'S FEELINGS

Paula was turning off the hall light and checking the locks on the front door when she heard a muffled sound coming from Jovita's room. She was startled, realizing immediately that Jovita was crying. It had been a long time since she had heard her daughter cry. Now fourteen, Jovita had built a defensive shell around herself and didn't express much emotion. Over the past two years she had changed from being an open child with a sunny disposition to a distant, closed adolescent that Paula barely recognized. Her grades had plummeted with her attitude. Paula was at her wit's end. She had warned Jovita that she wouldn't put up with it any more. She'd better start bringing home better grades or she'd be grounded permanently.

Paula rapped gently on her daughter's door. When there was no answer, she opened it a crack and peered in. Jovita was huddled on her bed, struggling to regain her composure. She wiped her face on the sleeve of her oversized sweat shirt and tried to hide her tear-stained face from her mother.

"What is it, baby? What's the matter?" Paula tried to hug her but she pulled away.

Her algebra book lay open beneath her, one of its pages damp and wrinkled.

"Honey, you can talk to me. I'm your mother. I love you. There's nothing I won't understand."

"No, I can't talk to you. Everytime I try to talk to you about it you just get mad!" Jovita shouted between sobs. "I'm failing math. Are you satisfied? I can't do it! So punish me and just get it over with!" She flung the book across the room.

Paula was stunned by her daughter's fury. But even more, she was stunned by the pain she knew her daughter was feeling. She had had no idea that Jovita was so upset. In fact, she had believed that her daughter didn't care about how she was doing in school.

She gathered Jovita into her warm bosom and rocked her gently. Just as she had comforted her when she was a baby, she whispered softly, "OK Sweetheart, OK. Mama's here. It's going to be all right. I know. I know."

When a child has failed to perform as he or she is expected to, one of the best ways of avoiding the hurt words is to acknowledge the child's feelings. You may not always be aware of the way your child feels about her schoolwork. It's important to open up opportunities for her to tell you. Timing is important here. Asking your child how she feels about a mistake may be counterproductive at the moment the mistake has been discovered. But later, after the dust has settled, the report has been written, the test has been taken, at a time when both you and she are relaxed, try to get your child to look back and talk about her feelings. This step takes a lot of sensitivity and the realization that your child has the right to her feelings, however misguided they may seem to you. You aren't judging whether the feelings are right or wrong. You are simply trying to understand them. Once you realize that your child, while avoiding her assignment until it was too late to do it, was feeling very anxious, overwhelmed, or hopeless about her ability to do it, then you can start to come up with some solutions.

Sometimes acknowledgment of feelings can best be expressed without words. A simple touch on the shoulder can convey wordless understanding to a child who is sitting miserably at the kitchen table, blinking back tears as he struggles with a difficult assignment. A cup of hot chocolate quietly placed on the table may speak volumes about your empathy and can release a child who is staring paralyzed at his work like a deer in the headlights, unable to move forward. Sometimes, just a few words like, "I know it's frustrating, honey," can go a long way for the child who's about to give up on his algebra.

EMPHASIZE COMPETENCE

Burt's eyes shone as he saw his mother take out the vase he had made for her at the ceramics studio. It had a neat shape with a fat, bulbous base and a long, skinny neck. The colors were cool too, deep purples and greens that made him think of an underwater scene. Tonight his

Aunt Liddy and Uncle Mort were coming over for dinner. He was glad his Mom had chosen his vase for the table. He knew they'd admire it.

One of the most important things you can do as a parent is to be sure that your child becomes aware of his own competence. Robert Brooks, a psychologist who works with children who have learning disabilities, warns that you can't just tell your child that you believe in him and value his abilities. Words aren't enough. You have to give him opportunities to experience success.

Unfortunately, because of their deficits, we spend a lot of time with our learning disabled children focusing on what they cannot do well, providing them with help and support for their weaknesses. We have to be sure to build in opportunities for them to demonstrate and develop their competence as well. This can be through sports, community service, taking care of a pet, cooking, babysitting, creating music or art, planting flowers, building models, or any number of other specific and concrete chances for them to show that they are "able." This can help raise self-esteem and also create a more optimistic attitude in your children. They can see that their efforts do pay off, that they can succeed. Later when they are struggling to believe in themselves as they tackle a difficult academic challenge, you can give them the gift of proof of their efficacy. When your son tells you he'll never be able to pass his history test, so why should he bother to study, you can remind him of the effort he put into earning his scout badge. Children need to learn from experience and be reminded often that effort does pay off.

Take stock of how many times in a day you give your child negative feedback. Resolve to give him twice as much positive feedback. Look for opportunities to "catch" your child doing the right thing and immediately offer a word of praise. Simple phrases like, "good job," "thanks for picking that up," or "it was really nice the way you shared the candy with your sister," will accumulate in your child's consciousness and help to create a self-image that defines him as a responsible, kind, or competent person. Compliment your child on his schoolwork whenever possible. Praise his ideas, creativity, understanding of a concept. Applaud effort, "Wow, you worked hard on that essay!" as well as achievement. If there are only two right math answers, start with these when you go over your child's fraction homework. Point out what he did right on those problems before you tackle the mistakes in the others. Use those problems as models. When you read an essay, point out the interesting ideas or phrases before you help your child correct his grammar or spelling. Always read an essay through completely, commenting positively as you read, before putting a single mark on the paper.

KNOW YOUR OWN LIMITS

While everyone would like to be the perfect parent, no one really is. If you have been under the erroneous opinion that you can be SuperMom or SuperDad and can make up for all your child's learning problems, it should come as a great relief to you to know that you don't have to do it all! Knowing and accepting our own limits is one of the keys to success in helping our children deal with theirs. If your own fear and anger rises when you try to help your child with his math homework, then you aren't the one to do it. Arrange with your child's school for additional in-school and after-school support. Check out local colleges for college students who might want to do some tutoring. Find community agencies like the YMCA, Jewish Community Centers, and Boys and Girls Clubs that have volunteer tutors. Get professional help for your child if he needs the specialized services of a language or learning therapist. Send your child to a private learning center or after-school program that helps with homework. Consider enrolling your child in a different school more able to meet his needs. If you come home after a long day at work and have to face several hours of torment (for both you and your child) helping your child with homework, something has to give. Sharing the job with someone else can give you the chance to spend time with your child that is more enjoyable and, in the long run, more productive.

Get support for yourself if you are experiencing frustration, guilt, shame, or inadequacy about your ability to parent your learning disabled child effectively. Having a child who is struggling with a learning disability can often bring out unresolved issues in oneself. The chance to talk about these feelings and issues with a counselor can be a great relief and will help you as well as your entire family. Joining an organization like LDA, CHADD, or other parents' group can provide you with ideas, suggestions, information, and most of all, support. The Internet also opens up opportunities for you to feel connected to others who understand and care, many of whom may be going through exactly the same things you are. Without support, you may suffer the exhaustion and burn-out common to many parents who have to cope with a child's special needs. Just knowing that others may also feel the same pain you feel for your child, the same disappointment, or the same stress may give you strength.

NEVER DO FOR YOUR CHILD WHAT SHE SHOULD DO FOR HERSELF

This is a tough one because, of course, you can do a fraction problem or write a paragraph faster than your fourth-grader. You can stop by the library or get on the Internet at work and find the information your son needs for his report on the presidential elections. You can build a model for your daughter's science project while she is at gymnastics. The temptation is there because we're juggling so many demands and many parents are stretched to their limits. Working with a child who has a learning disability and providing the support so the child can do it herself is time consuming and often frustrating work. It takes huge amounts of patience, patience that may be in short supply at the end of the workday. However, getting into the habit of doing work for your child will only compound the problem. You need to ask yourself, "Whose work is it?"

If your child truly can't do the work, even though you have set up a structure and support system for her, then it's time to talk to the teacher. Perhaps arrangements can be made for more school-based support in the resource room, transfer to another level or type of class, modifications to the amount or kind of homework. It's important for the teacher to know if your child is putting in extraordinary amounts of time or experiencing extreme frustration in completing assignments. Together you can come to a positive solution.

DON'T OVERLOAD YOUR CHILD

With so many opportunities for a life full of exciting, beneficial, and enjoyable activities, many families find themselves on perpetual overload. The calendar hanging on the kitchen bulletin board looks like one for the Joint Chiefs of Staff! After school, evening, and weekend hours are chock full of sports and scouts; dancing, art, and music lessons; food and clothes shopping; church, mosque, or synagogue services; doctor, dentist, and haircutting appointments; clubs and other leisure activities; household chores, visiting Grandma, and babysitting. The list goes on and on. While some children can handle and even thrive on such an abundance of activity, children with learning disabilities are often overwhelmed by it. Many become overstimulated and unable to focus on school assignments. It's always easy to find something else they "have to" do. Others are exhausted by it and have little energy left to devote to homework. Often there is just no time left for working on the science project or preparing for the upcoming math test.

Of course, all of these activities in themselves are positive and many are even necessary. They contribute to your child's growth and development, allow your child to learn experientially, and provide opportunities for your child to demonstrate the competence so essential to feeling "able." However, children with learning disabilities find it difficult to negotiate in many arenas of life, not just in school. Each activity presents new demands that they may have to struggle to meet. Many tasks take longer for them than for other children. When your child is functioning on overload, stress and anxiety can build with resulting negative behaviors. The key is to find the right balance. School is one of your child's most important jobs in life, and tasks related to it shouldn't be crammed into the leftover minutes of your child's life.

Take a good look at your child's (and the whole family's) weekly schedule. You may want to make a chart for each week with a column for each day and a row for each family member. Enter the activities for the day in the blocks. Honestly assess the level of busyness. Talk with each family member about whether he or she is feeling comfortable with the number of demands on his or her time. When a four-year-old recently confided to her parents that she longed to have a Saturday where she could "kick back" and relax without having to be somewhere, it was a signal to her parents that her young life was overbooked! Help your children to prioritize their activities and select those they value the most. Teach them to balance pleasure with responsibility (there are life lessons here!). Though homework may not be high on your children's pleasure index, they may discover that it's not nearly as unpleasant as they thought if they have plenty of time to do it and aren't feeling tired and stressed.

Be sure to build in time for your children to do absolutely nothing. It is during the quiet hours that your child can reflect on his life, sort out confusion and conflicts, find reserves of peace inside, and maybe even write in a personal journal. It is when he slows down that he can enjoy the creative luxury of daydreaming. It is when there is "nothing to do" that he can activate his imagination and turn the backyard into a magic island or build a castle with long-forgotten blocks.

Taking an honest look at your lifestyle will benefit the entire family. It's not surprising that the movement to restore sanity and simplify our lives is taking root across the United States. Our consumer culture encourages frenetic activity, praises those who "do so much" with their time, and offers us an endless array of choices. Many people are beginning to question the "perpetual motion merry-go-round" that our lives have become. Creating an oasis of sanity in your home will benefit every member of your family, not just the child with learning disabilities.

HELP YOUR CHILD FIND TIME-MANAGEMENT STRATEGIES THAT WORK

Finding the right time-management strategies is a challenge not only for children with learning disabilities, but for everyone. We have only to check out the multitude of calendars, planners, and electronic schedulers available at any office supply store to see that people are searching for the answer to this perennial challenge. Business and self-help sections in bookstores offer volumes of advice. Magazines carry regular articles.

There are many reasons why a structured time-management system is especially important for children with learning disabilities. The child with dyslexia may require twice as long to complete reading assignments. The one with visual-motor integration problems may have to work more slowly and painstakingly to record readable answers. The student who has difficulty with part-whole relationships may need extra time to figure out what is involved and how to go about completing a multistep assignment. The one with expressive language problems may spend agonizing hours trying to retrieve the right words for the ideas she wants to communicate.

Telling your child to organize his time on his own is like tossing him into the swimming pool before he's learned to swim. There will be a lot of thrashing around, an overload of anxiety, and in the end, you'll have to dive in to rescue him anyway. When you warn your child, "Don't leave that vacation book report until the last week of summer," or "Make sure you start your research paper early enough," your advice is valid and your child's intentions may be good. The problem is in the large gap between valid advice and good intentions and the realities involved in implementing a workable time management plan. It's not that your child doesn't want to do it. It's that he doesn't know how.

Step one in setting up a time-management system is getting the right planner/calendar. Which one is right depends on your child's age, grade, and preferences. Though there are many features that may make a particular planner better than others, the best planner of all is the one your child actually uses. Be sure to involve your child in the choice. The one with the *South Park* or *Far Side* illustrations may not be the one you prefer, but may be the only one "cool enough" for your tenth-grader to take out in class when the teacher gives the assignment.

Apart from considerations of "coolness," one of the best types of assignment book/planners for junior high, high school, and college students is a teacher's plan book available at educational supply stores and often at college bookstores. These planners show a week at a time on two facing pages. There is a column for each day of the week and six or seven horizontal rows for the various subjects your child is taking. Opening these plan books to any given week reveals everything due in every subject. The rows and columns keep each day's assignments in each subject in their own squares, eliminating much of the confusion common among learning disabled students. Hopefully, it also eliminates the phone calls your child must make in the middle of homework time to ask friends what the teacher assigned or when an assignment is due.

These plan books can be used for long-range planning as well as for short-range. All assignments are entered in advance on the page for their due dates. Students should color-code major assignments with highlighters to make upcoming tests, projects, papers, and reports stand out from the daily homework assignments. When a long-range assignment is given, sit down with your child and help her to generate a list of all the subtasks that need to be done to complete the assignment before the due date. Let your child come up with as many as she can, and then suggest others she might have forgotten. Help your child to set target dates for each of the subtasks and enter these in the planner. Be very specific. Do not take it for granted that your child will know that she has to buy poster board or other materials for a presentation. If there's a book report due in three weeks, set target dates by which each chapter will be read. If it's a task that involves collecting information, set dates for going to the library, gathering data on the Internet, reading and taking notes on the material, and writing small sections of the report. Once she has done this, your child can see a dreaded, overwhelming project as a series of small, doable steps that she can take one at a time.

Most children and adolescents need help in this process; however, you want to give your child as much control over the process as possible. This will increase the likelihood that she will follow the plan since she has some ownership of it. It is easier to make a commitment to something we have chosen for ourselves than to something others have imposed on us. For example, you may think that Friday night is a good time to go to the library, but your child may need a break after a challenging school week and prefer to go on Saturday morning. Discuss the pros and cons of each choice but let your child decide and learn to live with her choices on Saturday morning.

Each week, at a regular prearranged time, take a look at the planner and review progress toward long-range goals. If the system has broken down and the subgoals aren't being met by their target dates, engage your child in some problem analysis. Again, this is sometimes difficult to do without being judgmental. It's easier to say, "You're spending too much time horsing around," than to ask, "Why do you think you are having trouble getting your work on this project done on time?" The latter question will yield better cooperation and will help move your child to acquiring self-regulatory behaviors he needs as he grows older. Also, because it tackles specific behaviors and parts of assignments rather than generalizing, it is more diagnostic. It may result in identification of problems and solutions you hadn't thought of previously.

The assignment book/planner is not an appointment book. It's basically a way of keeping track of assignments and progress made toward their completion. So you will also need some method for keeping track of daily, weekly, and monthly schedules. Some families like a big wall calendar. You can use different colored markers for each person. Some children find a big desktop calendar in their own room works well. You may have to experiment to find out what works well. Evaluate your method. If it's not working, try something else.

Daily time should be specifically scheduled for homework on immediate and long-range assignments. The more consistency in this schedule, the better for your child. Children with learning disabilities need more structure and predictability than others. They may also be more likely to avoid the unpleasantness of school-related tasks and put off assignments until they are tired and cranky, making for even greater unpleasantness—a self-fulfilling prophecy! Experiment with the schedule to find the best time in the day for your child to do homework. While it might be nice if your child could do his homework right after school, many children come home from school stressed or fatigued and need a break for play or even a nap before tackling a potentially troublesome task. The after-dinner hours are best for some children while early mornings work better for others. It may take some time to figure out what is best for your child in your household. Don't be afraid to test and reevaluate your options.

CREATE A LEARNING SPACE THAT PROVIDES A SETTING FOR SUCCESS

The question of where your child's learning space should be is another one that depends on the individual child, the family, and the physical structure of the house. Small children in the primary grades may do better at the kitchen table where they have the comforting presence of others within range of eye and ear. Even some older children who need more human contact may feel banished if sent to their rooms for study. By junior high and high school, however, most students should have a separate space where they can focus on the more extensive assignments they receive and can develop the independence that is an important developmental task for their age.

Wherever the child works, you want to minimize distraction and create a calm, relaxed environment. This is the way the brain functions best on cognitive tasks. While the sounds of Dad doing dishes at the sink may be soothing, the debate between Mom and the older child over curfews should take place out of earshot of the child who is doing math homework.

The TV should be inaudible. You may even want to shut it off entirely for at least a few hours on school nights. If you want to allow your child one or two special weekday shows, tape them and let him watch them after he has completed his homework. Even the adults may be surprised at how much they accomplish when the TV is silenced.

Many children and even some research reports (there's debate on this) say that background music aids learning. If this seems to be the case with your child, choose something without words (like classical, new age, or instrumental jazz) that contributes to the relaxed, calm atmosphere needed for optimal study. If music makes the time spent on homework more pleasant for your child, then let him have it. Homework can be painful drudgery for children with learning disabilities, so if you can do something to make it more enjoyable, why not?

The best place for study may also depend on the assignment. Your daughter may want to be cozily wrapped in her quilt on her bed or in a big easy chair as she reads her novel for English class. However, when she is writing the answers to questions about it, she will probably be better off at the computer, her desk, or the kitchen table. Some families are lucky to have a home office, which can be a perfect place for homework. Others create a work space in the child's room or in the family room. Wherever the child works, be sure she has an adequate work surface, comfortable seating, good lighting, and freedom from distractions. Involve your child in setting up her workspace and let her add a few decorations to make it visually appealing.

Get rid of clutter in the work area and help your child to get into the habit of putting learning materials where they belong after using them. Shelving, stacked drawers, file cabinets, storage boxes or crates, and other materials can be a big help in organizing the area. Organization is a major challenge for children (and parents!) that don't have a natural gift in this area. You may want to seek help from an organized friend or relative to get started. You may also need to set a specific time each week to restore order to the study area. There's nothing wrong with admitting that you have trouble meeting the organization challenge. It's just one more example of the fact that we all have different gifts and different needs.

GATHER MATERIALS THAT FACILITATE SUCCESS

Having the essential materials on hand can save time and tears. Make a list of all the equipment your child has needed for school work and create a survival kit. If he has a desk and shelves in his study area, that may be the best place to keep it. If not, a big plastic underbed storage box is great. Just make sure it is all together so he's not wasting time digging through the kitchen drawers looking for scissors!

Some of the essential tools include a three-hole punch, stapler, calculator, tape, glue, markers and highlighters, pens and pencils, ruler, scissors, paper clips, a variety of papers (construction, lined loose-leaf, poster board), loose-leaf binders and dividers with tabs, plastic sleeves for papers, stencils for lettering, index cards, spiral notebooks, pocket folders, and report covers. Some children need a cooking timer you can set at various intervals so they can pace themselves while doing assignments. Watch for sales at office supply stores and stock up in advance. Bring your child with you so he can have a hand in creating his tool kit. Let him add a few fun things like stickers to get him interested. Most children enjoy putting the kit together and love having such great "stuff" at their fingertips. They can use their survival kit for play, too. The only rule should be to take care of the materials and put everything back where it belongs.

Speaking of putting everything where it belongs, your child should end each homework session by putting anything he needs for school the next day in his backpack or book bag. Placing the bag near the door the night before can increase the chance that, in the midst of the morning rush, your child will remember to take it with him.

One more thing that might be needed in your child's survival kit is a duplicate set of schoolbooks. If your child (in spite of repeated efforts) forgets and loses his books, it's worth it to purchase a duplicate set for home. This also allows your child to use markers to highlight important information.

MONITOR THE STUDY/HOMEWORK SESSION

So Johnny or Jennie is comfortably ensconced in a well-stocked, well-lighted, comfortable workspace. Everything is ready and available. Your job is over! Or is it? Most children with learning disabilities will need some supervision during their homework sessions. This does not mean that you have to be sitting beside them for the duration. On the contrary, such intensive intervention may foster an unhealthy dependency. The trick is to find the optimal amount of support and supervision your child needs during any given study session and give just that amount. Think of this as building a sort of scaffold to help your child.

Start the session by taking a look at the evening's assignments as well as any of the subtasks for long-range goals that your child should be making progress on. Go over the assignments to determine what needs to be done and help your child to estimate the time needed for each assignment, the difficulty level, and the need for assistance. This will teach your child to analyze her learning tasks, an invaluable lesson. Help your child to consider the order in which she will tackle the various assignments and make a schedule for the evening, putting down estimated start and finish times for each. Be sure your child understands the directions for each assignment. Many hours have been wasted by students who did a great job, but not the one the teacher assigned.

When your child identifies an assignment she will need your help with, again provide her with only the support she truly needs. Whenever possible, ask leading questions instead of telling her what or how to do her work. For example, if she can't get started on a composition, don't just tell her how to start it. Ask a series of questions ranging from what the teacher told them about the composition to what your child knows about the topic. Start broadly and generally and then narrow the discussion down to the specifics by asking successively more detailed questions. Use a brainstorming method that doesn't judge or organize the responses, but simply generates lots of ideas. Create a map with the main idea in the center and branches extending from it representing the various subtopics. If it's a math assignment, help your child create a model like a flow chart or visual diagram of the steps and ask her to explain the process in her own words. Stay with her while she tries a few problems, guiding her in identifying and correcting any errors she may make. Once she knows what she is doing, leave her alone to work independently. Check her work at the end again asking her to explain her process when you see errors. Praise right and partially right answers before pointing out errors: "Oh, I see you knew how to set up the equation. That's great. Now, what did you do here?"

Check on your child's progress at regular intervals during the homework session. That way you can see if she is spending too long on one assignment, is getting too frustrated, or needs a break. Sometimes a child may be like a sculptor trying to carve a human body out of a huge block of marble, chiseling away for hours at a single eye while time runs out and the rest of the body has yet to emerge from the block. Or maybe your child is going from one assignment to the next like the bumble bee flitting from flower to flower, sampling each but not finishing any.

Regular monitoring can help you to move your child to more productive behaviors before it is too late to get the assignments finished. It will also let you know when your child needs a break. Some need more breaks than others. Generally younger children have shorter attention spans than older children, but children with attention deficits and those who have tactile/kinesthetic learning styles will also have trouble sitting at a desk or table for long periods of time. Breaks should involve stretching and other physical activity since movement can get the circulation flowing and activate areas of the brain's large motor system that have been relatively inactive. A healthy snack of fruit, raw veggies, or juice can help your child return to his work refreshed.

Checking in at regular intervals can also allow you to make suggestions as to effective strategies your child can use in particular learning tasks. Build on your child's preferred learning styles. If your child is a tactile/kinesthetic learner, he needs to get physically involved in his learning. Provide him with manipulatives like real or play money, fraction circles, or pattern blocks (available in educational supply stores) and encourage him to role play or use gestures as he tries to memorize material for a test. Get your visual learner to color code her textbook and to draw pictures, symbols, maps, and diagrams or make mental images of ideas she is studying. If your child is strong in musical intelligence, have him create rhythmic patterns as he recites his learning out loud. Ask your verbal learner to talk to you about what she has learned. Use your child's spatial strengths by getting him to create a chart that organizes the information in a chapter. Combine all these strategies for a multisensory approach that will help any child. You'll find that your own repertoire of strategies will build as you become more actively involved in your child's learning.

For all children, encourage them to apply their reasoning abilities to whatever they are doing. Discourage rote learning (it doesn't last!) and mindless recitation. Help your children to connect their learning to past learning and to their own experience. Ask them to apply abstract concepts to real life situations. Encourage them to compare and contrast various elements in their learning. If they are preparing for a quiz or exam, teach them to predict possible questions and engage them in self-testing so they can get feedback for themselves about what they need to continue to work on.

TAKE PREVENTIVE MEASURES

"An ounce of prevention is worth a pound of cure" when it comes to helping your child to succeed in school. There are many steps you can take to avoid the predictable crises that seem to occur with astonishing regularity in the lives of children and adolescents with learning disabilities. These steps involve creating a context within which children can function at their best. You can't control the fact that your child was born with dyslexia or spatial deficits, but we can give that child his best shot at becoming a successful learner.

Creating a context for successful learning means organizing time, space, and materials to construct the basic infrastructure every child needs. These three things are like a three-legged stool, which can support your child. If one leg is missing, it's practically impossible for him to maintain his balance.

Creating a context also means forming an emotional climate in which your child feels comfortable, safe, appreciated, and capable. Years of work with students who have learning disabilities has taught us that, when children are refusing to do their schoolwork, it's usually about the feelings, not the phonics. The personal, emotional support you provide at home will have a powerful effect on your child's learning.

8

THE SPOKEN WORD: LISTENING, SPEAKING, AND SILENCE

"Wake-up, Scottie!" Shannon snapped. She was impatient to find out whether she could take the car next Saturday, and her stepmom was trying to coordinate everyone's schedule. Scottie was tipped back from the table, balancing precariously on two legs of his chair. His blank eyes said that he hadn't heard a thing they'd been talking about.

"Get with the program, Scottie!" Shannon muttered with barely veiled contempt. She had no tolerance for Scottie and was sick and tired of his mom making excuses for him.

"That's enough, Shannon," Cora said wearily. She was tired, too. Tired of dealing with the strain of trying to create harmony in her new blended family. When it had just been Scottie and herself, she had found it easy to be patient with him and had gotten in the habit of repeating everything several times to accommodate his auditory processing problems. Now there were others to consider as well. Phil, her husband of six months, and his daughter Shannon were both type-A personalities, quick to react, and not used to making allowances for a child with a learning disability. They said she needed to be more demanding of Scottie. They accused her of being overprotective. Sometimes she thought they might be right, but at other times she felt he was doing the best he could with the cards he had been dealt.

Turning to Scottie, she touched his arm gently and asked again, "What time is your soccer practice on Saturday?" But now Scottie was busy trying to give Shannon a retaliatory poke with his fork. Leaning too far to the right, he lost his balance and tipped over his milk glass. Shannon jumped up and left the table in a rage, wiping milk from her sleeve and shrieking, "If you ruined this blouse you're going to pay for it out of your allowance!" Cora watched her storm out of the room and heard echoes of her father's voice in her threat. She wondered wearily whether they would all be able to work things out.

She turned back to Scottie, the edge of exasperation creeping into her own voice now. "For the third time, Scottie, what time is your soccer practice on Saturday?"

This time he answered, but still didn't provide the information she needed. "I dunno. Coach didn't say." Handing her his empty plate, he added, "More!"

"Scott, I think you can ask more politely than that," his Mom prompted.

"More, please," he replied, stretching out the last syllable.

Cora sighed and refilled his plate with spaghetti. Sometimes she didn't know whether she should let things go or whether it was worth a struggle. Scottie had been diagnosed at age seven with a learning disability that affected both his receptive and expressive oral language. The diagnosis had been a relief in some ways because it explained some of his more aggravating behaviors: misinterpreting what others were saying, tuning out when you were talking to him, not following directions, forgetting what he'd been told to do. In the two years since he'd been tested, Cora had tried to use the strategies suggested by Dr. Evah Nellsom, the learning specialist they had consulted. Scottie made progress for a while, but had slipped again in the six months since she had married Phil and they had joined their families together. The issue of how to handle his language problems was a source of friction in their new family, and she wasn't sure what to do about it.

Cora had gotten used to repeating things for him. She had learned to touch him lightly to get his attention before telling him anything important, to write down things he needed to remember if he ran into the convenience store for her. She didn't get upset if he still forgot the milk or bread. It had gotten to be a natural part of their communication patterns, but it drove her new husband and his daughter crazy. Scottie's one-word answers or even simply grunts of acknowledgment were all she expected when she asked him questions, though she did try to use subtle probing as Dr. Nellsom had suggested to encourage him to elaborate more.

Scottie had been slow to talk as a baby. Even now, though he was nine, he mispronounced a lot of words, often saying "pah-sketti" for "spaghetti" or "min-o-le-um" for "linoleum." Getting information out of him was like pulling teeth. He gave partial answers or misunderstood what you were asking and answered a different question instead. His teacher said this was beginning to present a problem on tests in school. Even worse, it was now interfering in his relationships with the other kids in his class. Cora had noticed that he never brought any kids home to play and was spending a lot of time in front of the TV. She was worried.

Cora had hoped Scottie would outgrow his learning disability even though Dr. Nellsom had told her he wouldn't. She had explained that he would overcome certain challenges only to be faced with new ones at different stages of his language development. She knew now that Dr. Nellsom was right. It would be a continuous battle and now that he was getting older, she needed new weapons in her arsenal.

THE IMPORTANCE OF SPOKEN LANGUAGE IN HUMAN COMMUNICATION

The importance of language in human communication can't be overestimated. Of course, there are lots of ways in which human beings communicate. We use music, images, scents, and gestures. We even use our intuitions to "read between the lines" and understand things not transmitted through sensory data. We perceive and interpret the flashing red traffic light, the screech of the tea kettle's whistle, the pungent odor that tells us our dog has tangled with a skunk, the touch of our child's hand in ours seeking reassurance. We tell others how we feel by a caress, the slam of a door, or a raised eyebrow.

These are all important ways of communicating, but none of them have the same potential for the rich and varied expression of ideas that language has. The ability to use and understand language is central to human communication and to human learning. Language gives us a medium for representing and manipulating abstract ideas and is therefore essential to our thinking as well. It also widens our world because it allows us to hear and speak about things that are not in our direct experience.

The language cycle includes both oral and written forms, and both receptive and expressive components. Each part of the cycle (speaking, listening, reading, writing) affects the other parts in an ongoing interactive web of knowledge and abilities. Some parts may be more highly developed than others, but all are interdependent. Oral or spoken language (including both listening and speaking) comes first and is the base on which written language is built, so we will start there. The next chapter will deal with written language (reading and writing).

Listening is the receptive side of the spoken language coin and speaking is the expressive side. We take language in by listening and put it out by speaking. Listening comes before speaking in the normal sequence of language development.

We know now that language has a biological basis—humans are born with brain structures and neurological wiring that allow them to acquire and use it. But it is only through our interactions with our environment that the connections can be made in the brain to "turn on" the amazing capacities we have for language. Nature and nurture have to go hand in hand for language to develop.

Even before birth, your child was hearing the sounds that would some day make sense to him. From the moment he was born, the words and sounds around him were part of his experience of the world and were turning on tiny neurons (cells) in his brain, building connections from one nerve cell to another, spurring his brain's development.

Later he began to be aware that there was meaningfulness in the soft babbling voices and high pitched exclamations telling him, "Yes, you're my big, beautiful baby boy!" He began to respond with a wide toothless smile, an outstretched hand. He imitated in his own cooing and babbling the speech of the adults around him and eventually became able to say "real" words that communicated to others in a language shared by those in his culture.

At every stage, key developmental tasks were being achieved, and this development, of course, doesn't end in infancy. It continues as the child grows, first speaking in single words, then phrases, and finally in full sentences; building a larger and larger set of vocabulary words to use; learning how to put the words together in a socially determined order. "Go!" becomes "Me go!" and becomes "I go" and later, "I want to go to the playground!" (Unfortunately, only too soon, the last phrase turns into "I want to take the car to go to the rock concert!") And the process continues as the child learns to manipulate the language to understand and create more complex constructions. It's a process that never ends since even as adults we have the potential to further improve our language abilities, though it is in childhood that the most dramatic growth is seen.

At each stage, there is potential for the natural pace of development to be delayed or to be enhanced. When it is delayed, you need to figure out the nature of the problem before you can address it effectively. After all, you wouldn't give your child cough syrup for a stomach ache! However, since language is so multifaceted, getting a handle on what's going on isn't always easy.

MAKING SENSE OF THE SUBTYPES OF SPOKEN-LANGUAGE DISABILITIES

A comprehensive assessment needs to look at all aspects of language development to find out the specific areas that seem to be problematic for your child. Often there is overlap, with more than one type of language disability present.

To make matters even more confusing, language problems can sometimes be confused with other conditions. Attention deficits have some of the same symptoms as receptive language disabilities and sometimes these two different conditions *co*exist. Hearing problems (deficits in the sensory reception of sound) can also be the source of the problem for children who don't seem to be processing what you are saying to them. As with attention deficit, a hearing loss is not considered to be a learning disability in itself. On the expressive language side of the coin, it's important to note that when we are referring to expressive spoken language disabilities, we aren't talking about the inability of the child to control his muscles and produce the proper speech sounds. Problems with physical production of speech are not considered learning disabilities per se. These are articulation problems and are usually treated by a speech pathologist rather than a learning specialist. There is, again, some overlap in these conditions, and children may have both speech problems and language-based learning disabilities.

A thorough evaluation is the first step in sorting out the actual causes of language learning problems from the red herrings. Since the roots of the different problems vary, effective treatments will, too. For example, a hearing aid will not compensate for a receptive language problem, and a spoken cue that may assist the language-disabled child will not work for the hearing-impaired child.

So what is included in the range of disorders known as receptive and/or expressive spoken language disabilities? One way to classify language-based learning disabilities is by looking at the aspects of language that are affected. Whether your child's language learning disabilities involve receptive language or expressive language (or both), they can affect his ability to handle the sounds of language (phonology), the meaning of language (semantics), the grammatical aspects of language (syntax), or the practical uses of language in social interactions (pragmatics).

LANGUAGE-BASED LEARNING DISABILITIES INVOLVING THE SOUNDS OF SPOKEN LANGUAGE

One group of spoken language disabilities involves problems with the sounds or phonological elements of language. Though most obvious in the early years, phonological difficulties persist and appear in different guises as the child grows. A young child (in spite of having normal hearing) may not have the auditory discrimination needed to distinguish between similar sounding words like "tap" and "tab." A second-grader may be unable to identify rhyming words. An older child may find it hard to identify and separate the various syllables that make up words, pronouncing "indivisible" as "invisible." Others may find it hard to make distinctions between similar sounding words. Betsey, a sixteen-year-old, elicited peals of laughter from her friends when she came out with her frequent malapropisms. She called a Doberman pinscher a Doberman pinto and said her college-aged sister had an internment instead of an internship. Though she laughed along with her friends when she made these mistakes, she wondered why her brain got these words confused.

LANGUAGE-BASED LEARNING DISABILITIES INVOLVING THE MEANING OF SPOKEN LANGUAGE

Betsey was experiencing problems with both sounds and meanings of words. The word "semantics" is used to refer to the meanings of individual words as well as groups of words in sentences and paragraphs. Difficulties in semantics represent another type of language learning disability.

Some children with receptive spoken language disabilities have trouble acquiring new vocabulary and retaining it in long-term memory. They may also have difficulty understanding words that can have more than one meaning depending on the context. For example, it may take them longer to puzzle out what an expression like "Take a stand" means. They can't easily switch gears in their minds, automatically distinguishing the word's meaning in that context from its meaning when used in "hot dog stand," "stand up," or "I can't stand it!"

Children with semantic difficulties will frequently find it hard to understand subtle distinctions between words they learn. For example, they may not grasp the difference in connotation between "thrifty" and "tight." High school and college students with semantic difficulties often complain about the technical terms used in many subjects instead of more common everyday terms. "Why do they have to make it so complicated!" is a plaintive refrain we often hear from them. They are often unaware of the precision more technical terms provide. Some have particular difficulty with the more abstract terms and thus experience more academic difficulty in the higher grades than they did in the lower grades.

Children with semantic difficulties often rely on approximations or more general terms instead of using a more specific and appropriate word in a particular context. They will frequently resort to using "thing" (for almost anything) or a more limited but still not specific word like "tool" for a particular implement like "screwdriver." Sometimes they will rely on gestures—a twisting of the wrist to distinguish screwdriver from hammer. They will also often have difficulty finding appropriate synonyms for words they commonly use so their speech may lack variety and richness.

Semantic aspects of receptive and expressive spoken language involve not only individual words, but the grouping of words in particular ways to convey meaning. A quickly spoken sentence or group of sentences may be received as a confusing hail of words. The child may be left with a general impression of what was meant or with a misinterpretation of the message. They may hone in on the beginning or ending of a statement, but lose the rest, resulting in a partial understanding of the thought. These children often have a confused expression when listening to oral explanations, their eyes reflecting their feeling of being lost. Some of them will stare intently at a speaker, even narrowing their eyes and leaning forward, perhaps in an effort to "see" what they can't "hear." Others get frustrated and even belligerent. "I can't understand a thing you're saying! I don't know what you're talking about!" was a frequent, exasperated refrain from one eighth-grade girl as she worked with her tutor. Her outbursts had earned her the reputation of being an angry, belligerent child with a short fuse until she was finally diagnosed with a severe receptive language problem.

Language-Based Learning Disabilities Involving Syntax

Yoshiaki paced back and forth, peering out the window every few minutes. He checked his watch for the tenth time. Mikio was twenty minutes late. He should have been home from school and getting ready to go to the dentist by now. Yoshiaki had reminded him that morning, "After you come home from school, you'll have to go straight to the dentist." His thoughts were angry. "A seventh-grader should be able to remember these things," he fumed.

Lately he'd been wondering if he should have brought his family to the United States after all. If they had stayed in Japan, he thought, Mikio would have been more obedient, less rebellious. But the international electronics firm he worked for had given Yoshiaki an opportunity for advancement, a higher salary, more prestige if he would move to their New Jersey office. They were living in Ridgewood and had many Japanese friends there, but his son had both American and Japanese companions. His American friends called him Mike instead of Mikio. And he was picking up some of their bad habits. Yoshiaki's wife, Chiyo, defended her son. "He's a good boy," she'd say. "Of course, he's becoming Americanized. What did you think? He's lived here more than half of his life. You can't stop it."

Chiyo also defended Mikio's poor school grades, which were an embarrassment to Yoshiaki who had come from a high-achieving family. In Yoshiaki's family, children were expected to study for long hours each day after school and to bring home good grades. He believed that the two Ds Mikio had received were the first ever earned by any member of his family. He never told his parents who were still living in Tokyo about his son's school troubles.

The teacher had said Mikio had a language learning disability. It was not caused by his having to learn English when he came to America at five years old, she had said, although this may have made that transition more difficult. It was a neurological condition. His brain didn't process language well so he had trouble taking in information and was often confused by verbal directions.

But that was no justification for disrespecting his father's wishes. This time the boy would be punished. He would stay home on the weekend and help clean the garage instead of going off with his friends. Mikio would learn that Yoshiaki would not allow disobedience and would not accept excuses. It was time to call the dentist and cancel the appointment. There was no way they could make it there on time now. "Family Dental Associates," the receptionist answered with a lilt. "Oh, hi Mr. Tanaka," she responded when he identified himself. "Mikio is in with Dr. Samuels now. He should be finished in about twenty minutes."

Surprised, Yoshiaki recovered enough to say, "Let him know I'll pick him up. I should be there by the time he is finished with the dentist." As he replaced the receiver, Yoshiaki realized that Mikio had misinterpreted his early morning reminder. Instead of realizing he had to go to the dentist after coming home from school, he had gone straight there from school. The dentist's office was a long walk from the school and it was raining heavily. And Yoshiaki knew his son would have been carrying his heavy backpack too. He sheepishly faced the fact that he had misjudged his son. Mikio wasn't being disobedient. He was doing what he thought he had been told to do.

Mikio's misinterpretation was a sign of his problems in processing syntax. He applied the words, "you'll have to go straight to the dentist" to the phrase "after school" instead of to the clause, "after you come home from school." Syntax refers to the way our language is organized so that we can clearly communicate meanings. Grammar rules guide us in doing this. Although we are born with the ability to acquire and use grammatical structures, we have to learn the particular patterns agreed upon in our language and culture. We learn them first by listening to others around us and then imitating them. We further develop our understanding of syntax from models in the books we read. During the school years, we also have formal instruction in the rules that govern syntax. While all of these pathways are easy for some children to negotiate, children with language-based learning disabilities often find syntax perplexing.

Syntax difficulties can have a negative impact on receptive aspects of spoken language. Some children, like Mikio, are confused about what words various sentence parts refer to. Children and adolescents with syntax problems often have trouble recognizing two statements arranged in a different order but having the same meaning. Conversely, they will also have trouble distinguishing between two statements arranged in a similar order but having different meanings. "Jackie and Dad will meet you at the mall," may be interpreted to mean the same thing as "Jackie will meet you and Dad at the mall." On the other hand, "When you get to the mall, you will meet Jackie and Dad" may not be seen as being closer in meaning to the first sentence. If your brain is able to make these distinctions automatically, you may think your child is simply not paying attention or is deliberately ignoring instructions.

In the upper grades, where much of the subject matter is taught through spoken language without the use of supporting visuals, the child with syntax difficulties is at a great disadvantage. The content being taught may be lost and assignments given may be misunderstood. It's painful to watch a student put hours into an assignment and receive a bad grade because that wasn't what the teacher wanted. Brittany, a college student taking a teacher education course, spent hours writing five separate lesson plans for an assignment. In fact, she was supposed to have created only one lesson plan with a couple of activities that would get the children using all five senses. Instead, she wasted a lot of time writing five whole lesson plans, one for each of the senses. And the worst part was, after all that work, she received only a "C" since she hadn't followed directions for an integrated lesson plan.

Syntax difficulties leave their mark on expressive language too. Your child may struggle to explain what he is trying to say because he can't handle complex grammatical constructions. This can result in disorganized or awkward speech patterns, misplaced phrases, unclear references, and general miscommunication of his ideas. When he says, "The dog is the old woman's that died," he doesn't see that his listener may think the woman is the one that died rather than the dog.

Children who have syntax problems are often underestimated by others. Their crude constructions will not be as effective or admired as the more refined speech of their peers. As a result, they may be judged as unintelligent. Their mixed up sentences may also give the impression that they don't really understand the substance of their topic. When he had to give an informative speech in his English class, seventeen-year-old Filipe tried to explain the way a car engine works. He was unable to explain the sequence and functions clearly, although he was a whiz at fixing cars and had been working on them at his dad's side since he was ten years old. His sentence constructions failed to convey sequences and cause-effect relationships clearly and his indiscriminate use of the pronoun "it" left his classmates and teachers unsure of what specific parts he was referring to. It was surely no failure of knowledge for Filipe, but a failure in his ability to structure his sentences in clear, unambiguous ways.

LANGUAGE-BASED LEARNING DISABILITIES AFFECTING SOCIAL SITUATIONS: PRAGMATICS

Devon stood on Alyssa's doorstep holding her forefinger stubbornly on the bell. She knew her two classmates were inside because Cherie's new purple bike was lying on the driveway. Why didn't they answer? Maybe the bell wasn't working. She pressed her ear against the warm wood and heard the faint chimes sounding inside. She decided to go around the side and bang on the back door. Maybe they were in the kitchen.

She rapped sharply on the screen and called out, "Alyssa, Cherie, are you there? It's me, Devon." Peering into the kitchen, she spied the two girls sitting at the kitchen table sharing a can of cola. Alyssa looked out at Devon's face, flattened as it pressed against the screen. Devon was getting to be a pain. They'd been best friends until this year. Both of their mothers were nurses at County Hospital and they often babysat for each other's children when they were working different shifts in the ER. On days off, they frequently took the girls on outings. Devon and Alyssa had practically been brought up as sisters.

But now Alyssa had a new best friend. Cherie had joined their sixth-grade class at Roosevelt Elementary when her family had moved in just two blocks away. Alyssa didn't mind hanging out with Devon at school, but after school she preferred to spend her time with Cherie. Cherie was easier to get along with. Devon was too demanding and stubborn. She never knew when to back off.

With a mixture of guilt and exasperation Alyssa approached the door and spoke to Devon through the screen. "What do you want?"

"Are you coming out?" Devon replied.

"I told you at school, Cherie and I are going bike riding this afternoon." She put a heavy emphasis on the words, "Cherie and I."

"Can I come?" Devon persisted.

"No, we have some stuff we have to do."

Devon had just opened her mouth to try another approach when the wooden inside door swung shut. Stung, she felt tears well up in her eyes. Blinking them back she stomped away. Flinging the words back over her shoulder, she shouted, "See if I care, losers!"

When her friend Alyssa had told Devon that she was going biking with Cherie after school, Devon may not have known whether this was an invitation for her to join them or a way of letting her know that Alyssa would not be playing with her that day. The impact of language-based spoken language disabilities doesn't end in the classroom. These disabilities take their toll on social situations as well.

The term "pragmatics" is often used to identify the use of language in real world social interactions. Developing skill in pragmatics is one of the most important aspects of language learning because failure to achieve it can result in a child becoming excluded, stigmatized, frustrated, and confused in her relationships with others and in negotiating the daily demands of human interaction. It may leave her unable to adjust to new social situations or to the changing landscape of familiar ones.

Receptive spoken language disabilities can result in your child's misinterpreting what another child is telling her. She may not understand subtly worded messages telling her to back off or to come forward. She may not be able to figure out the emotion conveyed in a friend's words, leaving the friend feeling "unheard" and uncared for. She may not be able to focus on a story someone is telling, leaving the speaker with the idea that she is uninterested.

On the expressive side of the coin, she may speak out of turn, make inappropriate or tactless remarks, and interrupt others. She may blurt out thoughts without censoring or hold back too long and fail to respond to what someone else has said. She may wander off the topic, interjecting unrelated subjects into a conversation. Some children with expressive spoken language disorders speak too loudly, are verbally aggressive, and come on too strong. Some speak in a monotone making it hard for listeners to maintain interest. Others become withdrawn, retreating from verbal interactions, becoming the silent ones in the group. Some do not know how to ask for something politely and may mistakenly be labeled as rude because of their curt requests. Many do not know how to express emotions like anger in socially acceptable ways and instead may swallow their rage or act it out inappropriately.

Being able to interpret and use language effectively in social situations is important to your child's adjustment. Deficits can have far-reaching effects, even into adulthood, and can have a negative impact on self-esteem and on success in personal relationships and careers. Helping your child to gain social language skills that may not come naturally to her can be one of the most important things you can do for her.

ASSESSING YOURSELF

Like Cora, in the story that opened this chapter, you've probably gotten used to your child's speaking and listening difficulties. You may even be compensating for your child without realizing that sometimes this can be counterproductive to his language development. It's tricky to get the balance between facilitating for your child in recognition of his current limitations and challenging him to go beyond his present levels of competence. So, in addition to observing and evaluating your child's behaviors, you also need to take a look at your own as well. Try to identify and then reduce any of your own behaviors that may inadvertently be contributing to your child's language problems.

If you have a child with receptive language deficits, you may have given up on expecting your child to process and remember what he hears. You may be excusing his behavior. Almost every night when Martin was ready to begin his homework, he would have to call his friend Jonathan to find out what they were supposed to do. By fifth grade, as she was clearing the supper dishes, his mother was in the habit saying, "Go call Jon and see if you have all your assignments for tonight." This reinforced Martin's reliance on others for a task he needed to learn to do for himself.

Martin's mom was also in the habit of repeating any important information several times for him. As he was watching cartoons on Saturday morning, it would be, "Martin, we're going over to Nana's this afternoon." As he headed outside to play at 10:00, it was, "Don't forget, we're going to Nana's after lunch." When he came in hunting for his baseball glove at 11:00, she'd remind him, "Don't make plans with your friends this afternoon, we're going to Nana's." After lunch, she'd say, "Go get ready to go to Nana's." Nine times out of ten, Martin would then express surprise at the plans, having effectively tuned out all of the earlier warnings as he pursued the activity of the moment. Sometimes a battle would follow since, of course, he had made plans to meet his buddies at the Boy's Club after lunch. Repetition becomes a way of life in some families and the child learns he doesn't have to listen the first time.

Some parents get into the habit of shouting at their kids who have receptive language problems. The parents are trying to get their children's attention or stress their message. This rarely works since the problem is not with the sensory act of hearing. Compare it to listening to someone speaking in a language that is foreign to you. If they speak louder, it doesn't help you to process what they are saying. Kids with auditory processing problems or receptive language deficits can tune out a loud voice as easily as a quiet one. It's not that they can't hear you!

Nonproductive compensations are often used to deal with children who have expressive language deficits too. Many parents inadvertently decrease the need for language in transactions with their child. The child points at an object, you hand it over. Or you anticipate your child's needs before he voices them. If you have a child who doesn't volunteer much in her speech, you may be tempted to "put words in her mouth." You may find that you ask and answer your own questions: "What did you do after school today, Honey? Go to the library?" This format allows your child to answer in one word, "Yes" or "No" instead of expressing a complete idea herself.

Putting words in your child's mouth can also take the form of supplying the correct term while your child is searching for it. For example, your son may say "The whatchamacallit on the door is broken." You respond, "The latch?" Perhaps with a little more time and a query instead of an answer, he could have supplied the term himself. You may also find yourself finishing sentences or making the point of a story your child has been "talking around." Your daughter is trying to tell the rest of the family about something that occurred when you and she went to the mall, but is getting bogged down in details. You finish her story.

If you see yourself here, there's no need to feel guilty. These are all perfectly natural behaviors. Some compensation on your part is necessary for practical reasons. After all, if you don't repeat your warning to your son at the beach, he may swim out too far and get into waters over his head.

Life moves fast, and it takes a lot of time and patience (sometimes time and patience you don't have) to hold yourself back from doing something that seems to facilitate the communication. In some ways, it actually does facilitate the issue of the moment. The problem is that you may be trading a short-term solution for long-term gains.

WHAT YOU CAN DO TO HELP YOUR CHILD OVERCOME SPOKEN LANGUAGE DEFICITS

If you want to help your child to develop to the best of his ability, the most important thing you can do is to create a language-rich environment involving all aspects of the language cycle. The child with a language learning disability whose brain does not take in, process, and produce language easily, will need more opportunities than other children before he can become proficient at language-related tasks.

DEVELOPING RECEPTIVE LANGUAGE ABILITIES

Let's start with the child who has trouble taking in what others are saying. The first thing you can do is reduce the impact of other distractions. Instead of telling your child something while he is flying by or when his attention is occupied doing something else, walk up to him and give him a cue that you are going to say something you want him to remember. Ask him to stop what he is doing while you talk to him. Many children can't easily integrate a variety of sensory inputs coming to them simultaneously. If they are engaged in a visual or motor task, you might think they could listen at the same time, but this isn't always so. Your voice may simply be perceived as background noise.

You won't need to yell to try to gain your child's attention if you look him in the eye and say, "Zach, I want you to listen to what I am saying," or "Slow down, I want to talk to you for a minute." If he's absorbed in a TV show or working on a puzzle, a soft touch can provide a signal that he needs to turn away and focus his attention on you. In the classroom, the child with receptive language problems should sit up front near the teacher so she can more easily make this kind of connection with him. There's no point in telling your child anything if you haven't gotten his attention first. Simply taking time to get his attention can eliminate the need for much of the constant repetition you may have been doing.

The next thing you need to do is control the rate and complexity of your communications with a child who has receptive language problems. A barrage of auditory input that overloads his "wires" will result in lost bits of data. The child may remember some of it, but not all. What he does remember may be scrambled. Slow down your pace and give him a chance to absorb one thing before piling another on top of it. Children with receptive language disabilities will often tune out if the listening task becomes too difficult.

Another idea is to ask your child to repeat what you have told him. This feedback is the only way you will know whether the message that left your lips truly found its target in your child's brain and was interpreted correctly. "So, let's go over it. What are you going to do when you come home from school this afternoon?" The fact that your child repeats orally what you have told him, in his own words, will also enhance the likelihood that it will be retained in his memory.

If there are many things to remember (or even if there are only a few), help your child to get in the habit of writing them down. The act of writing something down takes it from the intangible and very fleeting spoken word to a more lasting, concrete form in paper and ink. Most of us adults keep some lists and a calendar to organize our busy lives. Getting your child into this habit at a young age can help him to develop organizational skills as well as better listening skills. A bright calendar or assignment book with lots of room for each day is a good place for your child to write down reminders for himself. Another option is a simple spiral notebook for his "to do" lists. Single sheets of paper tend to get lost or forgotten. Having one place to use consistently works best. After completing each task, encourage your child to cross it off or put a small sticker beside it. This rewards him with a sense of completion.

Asking your child to write down directions or steps for doing a particular task can also be helpful. For example, don't just tell your daughter to clean her room on Saturday morning and presume she remembers all the parts of this task that you've discussed with her in the past. Help her to make a list including all the steps from putting her dirty clothes in the hamper to settling all her stuffed animals back in their perches. Once the list is done, you can have her post it on her closet door so the next week you won't have to repeat it again. Visual children can draw symbols or pictures on their list both to decorate it and to provide another avenue for the message to get through. Oral reminders don't work well for a child with receptive spoken language disabilities, but many people keep repeating the same ineffective method. They figure that quantity of spoken reminders can compensate for lack of proficiency in listening skills and that's just not so. It will only frustrate you to have to tell your child the same thing over and over again.

DEVELOPING EXPRESSIVE LANGUAGE ABILITIES

On the opposite side of the spoken language coin, getting a child with expressive language difficulties to express himself clearly and completely can present a different kind of challenge. One rule here is, ask, don't tell. Before you supply a word your child is searching for, ask him to clarify what he means. A word may be stored in his verbal memory but it takes him longer to access it than other children. If he points, gestures, or uses a generic word like "thing," ask him to specify what he means. Talk with him about this plan and be sure he knows what you are doing and why. He needs to be your partner in this effort. You also need to be able to "read" your child. If he is frustrated or anxious, that may not be the best time to challenge him in this way.

If your child does not know the specific term, that's a different problem and calls for different kinds of interventions. Building vocabulary takes time. Use the teachable moment to present him with new words to fit his need or a given context. Get him a hand-held electronic speller/thesaurus. See if you can interest him in crossword puzzles designed for his age group (or even younger). Playing word games as a family (Password, Scrabble, Scattergories, Pictionary, etc.) can help too. As much as possible, entice him to read. If reading is a problem, talk to his teacher or a librarian about selecting high-interest, low-reading-level books. He needs to enjoy the process if he's going to persist in it and put enough time into it to make a difference.

Use his schoolwork as a way to build vocabulary and at the same time improve his grades. Go through his current textbook chapters with him and select boldface, italicized, and other words of obvious importance to his grasp of the subject matter. Get your child to make flash cards with visual cues for the concepts. Post new words from any source on a magnetic white board and hang it on the refrigerator.

Reward and recognize your child's progress in expressive language skills. If he uses a difficult word appropriately, make notice of it. Praise him when he makes an interesting analogy ("Wow, that's a great way of putting it!"). Encourage a lot of talk in the family. Patiently draw your child's thoughts out of him. Sometimes this will feel like ice fishing in frigid weather, but if you are patient you should be able to engage your child in talking about some topic. If he doesn't want to talk about his own activities (the "Where did you go? Out. What did you do? Nothing." syndrome), find something else to talk about. Ask him to tell you about a movie he saw, a song he likes, a game played by the local sports team, his favorite car. Suggest that everyone at the supper table tell about their dream vacation, their most prized possession, or an animal they'd like to be and why. Remember the "monkey see, monkey do" rule too: parents have to model what they want from their children, so speak up!

Many less-expressive children need additional time to formulate their ideas before speaking. Your child's silence during a family conversation may be a time of mentally sorting out his thoughts and figuring out how to convey them. By the time he is ready to add in his piece, the conversation may have already moved on. Slow it down a little and specifically call on a quiet child to contribute. Sometimes the less verbal children don't know how or when to jump in and need a little probing to get them started.

If your child has a problem with social communication, you may have to teach her how to express her feelings verbally. Try role-playing or giving her a scenario and asking her what she would say in the given situation. When she comes home and tells you about a real-life problem she has had in communicating, take time to help her to process it. Be sure to be empathetic and not judgmental; otherwise, she will refuse to share these situations with you. Start by validating the way she feels: "Oh, honey, I'm sorry. You must have felt terrible when Suzie wouldn't let you play with her." Only after the child is feeling "heard" can you help her come up with alternative behaviors.

Be sure to help your child to practice ways to respond to criticism, to accept compliments, to ask politely for what she needs, to refuse graciously, to disagree without animosity, to stand up for herself without being aggressive, to defer to someone else in conversation, or to insert herself into an ongoing discussion. When she successfully negotiates these kinds of communications in actual situations, be sure to praise her: "I noticed how nicely you said, 'thank you' when Gramps complimented you today." These communication skills are essential in social interaction and are hard ones for some children to pick up without help. They need to be made explicit for them and they need to be practiced in a safe, comfortable situation.

DEVELOPING LANGUAGE SKILLS IN YOUNG CHILDREN

With young children, there are lots of games you can play to encourage development of rudimentary language abilities that will form the base for further language development in middle childhood and adolescence. You can build phonological awareness by asking the child (without watching your lips) to say "same" or "different" as you pronounce similar or identical pairs of words: cap/cab, bat/bet, sit/sit. Give your child a series of three words and ask him to tell you which one starts with a different sound than the other two. Have your child clap, tap, or stomp out syllables in words. Play rhyming games and read your child books and poems with lots of rhymes and strong rhythms. All of these activities build awareness of sounds and the ability to discriminate between different sounds.

To help your young child develop listening skills and explore the meanings of language, try giving her pairs of sentences and ask her if they mean the same thing: "Jane and Tom went to school/Tom and Jane went to school" or "Jane has some candy/Jane has no candy." Let your child make up some for you to do. Ask a series of silly questions, "Can a dog fly? Can a shoe sing?" being sure to toss in some that have "yes" answers as well so she'll have to pay attention to the auditory message. Give her a series of orders and let her try to execute them in order to develop listening, auditory memory, and sequencing skills: "Spin around, touch the counter, hop three times."

To develop expressive language skills, teach your child tongue twisters. Show him pictures and ask him to name the objects you point to. Give him a few elements (a horse, a king, and a carrot) and ask him to make up a sentence or short story using them. Or ask him to give you the elements and you make up the story. Have him complete comparisons, "Her eyes were as big as . . . " Show a picture and ask him to tell you what is happening in the picture. Challenge thinking skills further by saying, "And what do you think will happen next?" Make puppets with your child out of paper bags, socks, or other material around the house and have a puppet show. Your child is learning about dialogue and developing creativity at the same time. Encourage role playing games. A tea party is a chance to practice greeting guests and carrying on social conversation. Playing store lets your child develop communication skills needed to make requests or find out what others want. Real cookies or a funny hat can go a long way toward making these activities enjoyable as well as educational.

Life is full of learning opportunities and your home is the most important language classroom your child will ever enter. Make it a place full of gentle words, warm conversation, and careful listening. Make it a safe place where what your child says will be respected and what he doesn't say will be heard by the heart.

9

THE WRITTEN WORD: READING AND WRITING

Brian was a college freshman when he finally broke his silence about an incident that had occurred when he was thirteen. A bright, popular child who excelled in sports and had a quirky sense of humor, he had made it through elementary school earning mainly Bs and Cs, and the title of class clown. He had expected the same in his new junior high school. Behind his broad smile, however, Brian was harboring a painful secret: he could not read.

The incident occurred on a hot September day, a day when his classmates were buzzing restlessly and anxiously watching the clock, waiting to be released like a swarm of honeybees into the warm afternoon sun. Ten minutes remained of the school day. Brian was holding his breath as the teacher, known for her intimidating methods, randomly called on various classmates to read a paragraph aloud from the chapter. She seemed to be picking out the students who were whispering furtively or who were shuffling their feet or rustling papers. Though Brian couldn't read books, he was skilled at reading cues. He made himself smaller in his seat trying to evade her radar. He remained motionless even when a fly lighted on his hand. He clutched his pencil hard and prayed.

Suddenly, with one word from the teacher, Brian felt as if his world had imploded. She had called his name. His stomach lurched. Panic welled up from someplace deep inside. Maybe he was wrong, maybe she hadn't really said it. She must have read his records, hadn't she? All of his teachers at his elementary school had known and understood. They had helped him guard his secret. Not even his best friend knew. No one on his hockey team knew. The girl with the long brown hair who sat across from him didn't know.

His face burned. His mind sought frantically for something he could say, a way to refuse, a way to avoid the humiliation. A comic remark wouldn't work with this teacher. He shifted in his seat and deftly tipped his book over the edge of the desk. Only a few of the bravest boys laughed as he made a wisecrack and killed time retrieving the book. The teacher's face turned to stone as she watched him flipping pages, feigning excessive difficulty in finding the page, rolling his eyes and clowning to defuse the tension. It didn't work. The seconds dragged on with agonizing slowness. The silence was broken only by the bell signaling the end of the school day and the teacher's ominous pronouncement that the class would remain in session until Brian had read his paragraph. He sat there in stone-cold apprehension, trapped in a silence that was like ice. His vision blurred as tears rose and threatened to spill from his eyes. He blinked rapidly to contain them. Perhaps it was only a few more minutes, perhaps it was ten. It seemed like an hour. Suddenly Brian stood. He lifted his chair and hurled it toward the teacher. In a mixture of pain and rage, fear and humiliation, he did the only thing he could think of doing to end the standoff. He could see no other way out.

The chair broke the teacher's arm. Brian was condemned, excoriated, and finally expelled. That turned out to be a blessing. Soon after, he was placed in a private school for students with learning disabilities. Looking back, he says that saved his life. He's now a college graduate and doing well. And while his story may be more dramatic than some, it is not unique in its expression of the pain and even terror that can be felt by children with dyslexia and other language disabilities in the classroom.

Reading and writing are essential to so much of classroom-based learning. Their importance can't be overlooked without inflicting harm on the child who struggles with them. It takes compassion and the right strategies to help your child to cope with the challenges posed by written language. While most parents aren't reading or learning specialists, they can be specialists in understanding their own child. If you have a child like Brian, you can work together with the professionals to encourage and support his development of reading, writing, and coping skills.

CRACKING THE CODE: UNLOCKING THE MYSTERIES OF WRITTEN LANGUAGE

Written language is nothing more (nor less) than a code that allows us to record, send, and receive verbal communications in written form. The alphabet is the key to cracking this code. Within the framework of the language cycle, written language includes both an expressive form (writing) and a receptive form (reading). Frequently, disabilities involving written language (like dyslexia and dysgraphia) are part of a broader language learning disability that can affect speaking and/or listening as well.

Written symbols are only a fraction of the many ways in which we send and receive information, ideas, and emotions. In fact, they are latecomers to the banquet of communication that gives human life much of its meaning. For a long time in the history of humankind, written language did not exist. Later it existed only for the few most educated. Most people could get along fine, earn respect, and achieve success as skilled artisans, farmers, or hunters without it. But today, the ability to use language in its written form is a survival tool as important as the hunter's bow was to our early ancestors. Most occupations require it to some degree; many depend on it. An individual's intelligence and competence is often judged (sometimes erroneously) by his proficiency in it. Our grasp of it limits or extends our possibilities. It's an open door or a barred gate. Even our pleasures may be diminished or increased depending on our ability to enjoy the written word. Anyone who has spent a lazy afternoon curled up with a good book or savored a relaxing cup of coffee with the morning newspaper knows this. Many of our kids don't.

All of this places a heavy and undue burden on the child who, by some accident of brain structure, wiring, electrical activity, or chemistry finds incomprehensible what seems to come easily to others. And no place is the burden heavier than in the classroom. From kindergarten with its emphasis on identifying the letters of the alphabet and printing your own name, to graduate school where the written treatises become longer, more complicated, and oftentimes duller, the child with a learning disability in reading and/or writing will have a heavier load to carry.

Because reading and writing are multifaceted processes, problems in reading and writing can have many causes. They can stem from visual perceptual disabilities that make it hard for a child to "see" the difference between" "b" and "d," or from auditory perceptual difficulties that make it hard for him to "hear" the difference between "cob" and "cop" even though he can physically see and hear well. They can be related to disabilities in visual/auditory integration that prevent a child from sounding out an unfamiliar word or figuring out how to spell a word by the way it sounds. They can be connected to deficits in visual memory that leave him unable to recognize a word automatically or to remember the way a word looks when properly spelled. They can arise from visual-motor or tactile-kinesthetic disabilities that leave a child struggling to hold a pencil, form letters, write in a straight line, or space words and letters properly on the paper. They can come from language deficits that cause him to struggle to understand the meaning of a sentence or be unable to organize his own sentences into written paragraphs that make sense.

WHAT IS READING?

Ashley snuggled up to her mom on the couch. The big Dr. Seuss book lay open on her lap. She loved it when Mom read to her and waited eagerly each day as Mom rinsed out the sink and put away the supper dishes. This was the signal that their nightly ritual was about to begin. Tonight, Ashley had picked the book and had been waiting on the couch when Mom had joined her. "Oh good, you picked *The Cat in the Hat*," Mom said. "You can read that one to me!" Ashley's brow furrowed as she regarded her mom with an incredulous expression on her face. "mom," she explained with exaggerated patience, "you know I can't read." "Yes, you can Ashley," her mom responded. "You just don't know it yet." As the dusk darkened into night, the quirky and wonderful words of Dr. Seuss filled the air. Read in a lilting voice by Ashley's mom, they were punctuated by her daughter's giggles and, occasionally, by her accurate reading of a word to which her mom pointed.

Ashley was still at the stage where words were a mystery. She didn't yet know the secret that allows us to recognize that cat, hat, mat, and bat are not random squiggles on the page, but part of a system that makes sense, at least most of the time. Reading any word involves taking in a visual symbol through the sense of sight, recognizing and interpreting the symbol (perceiving it), connecting that symbol with a corresponding sound, and associating that sound/symbol with a particular meaning. It is seeing the letters D, O, and G arranged in a particular order and knowing whether they refer to an animal or a heavenly being. It is knowing that when we combine the word with other words in a particular order, it makes the difference between a common story of a man being attacked by an aggressive canine ("The dog bites the man!") and a more bizarre tale in which the normal order of things is reversed ("The man bites the dog!").

Reading with comprehension means being able to get the meaning the author is trying to convey. To be good at reading is to easily shift a mental image suggested by the same word in a different context: the face of the child, the face of the cliff, losing face, and facing death. It means being able to find the ideas that are stated in a passage as well as those that are only implied. It means drawing conclusions, questioning the author's statements, identifying biases, and opening your mind to ideas you may not always be ready for.

When something goes wrong in one of the many components of the reading process, it can have a domino effect, toppling the other components as well. The bright child who could understand the message of a story and see how it connects to other things he has learned (maybe even better than his peers) never gets the chance to do so if he doesn't know what the words say in the first place.

Reading problems also have a domino effect in other ways. Failure in reading often triggers failure in other subjects. It also triggers more far-reaching effects at the very core of a person's self-image. When we ask adults with learning disabilities to tell us about their first awareness of their learning differences, many talk with tears in their eyes about the reading circle. Twenty or more years later, they still recall the panic, the difficulty breathing, the red-faced sweating as they struggled to read aloud before a "jury of their peers." For many children, failure in the reading circle is often the beginning of feeling inadequate as a learner, feeling dumber than the other children, feeling humiliated in the classroom that should have been a safe place to learn, and ultimately feeling "less able" both in school and out.

Children aren't aware of the complicated neurological processes that reading involves. They simply know whether they can or can't do it. They are often mystified by it. It seems to be something that happens automatically for those who are good at it. Even teachers often have a hard time pinpointing exactly why an individual child is having a hard time reading. If you are a parent who has a reading disability yourself, you are already aware that reading is a complicated process. If you find reading easy, it will be good for you to think about the many things you may have taken for granted. Many students with dyslexia report that they have been told that if they would just try harder they would be able to read the mysterious text before them. They have been told that they were lazy or unmotivated because they didn't finish the book assigned in their English literature class. They've been accused of being stubborn or disobedient because they wouldn't read aloud in class. None of us would ever tell a blind child that he could read if he would only look harder at the book, pay more attention to the print. And yet, many people do this with dyslexic children.

If we want to help our children with reading problems, we have to do it in ways that allow them to experience success and that reduce the frustration they feel. We have to be sure that they have the current skill level to do what we ask of them. You cannot get from your home to the corner in a single step. You get there step by step (sometimes in very tiny steps), with each preceding step making the next step possible.

There are many things you can do as a parent to help your child take the steps needed to succeed in reading. You can help him get ready for reading, be open to working on it. You can reinforce and support the work that the teacher or reading specialist is doing. The child with reading problems needs much more support than even the best school system can provide in the limited number of hours available. That's where you come in and the importance of your role cannot be overestimated.

Instilling a love of reading is more important than helping your child acquire any particular reading skill or strategy. Reading has more competition today than it did when most of us adults were growing up. The pace of life has quickened, and children often have full schedules of afterschool and weekend activities. These activities have their place in the development of happy and intelligent children, but they can also limit the likelihood that your child will make room for reading in the midst of a busy life.

Very often, children who are having trouble in school are the least likely to pick up a book in their spare time. Reading is difficult for them. They don't find it pleasurable and (like all of us) would prefer to do the things they enjoy.

BEGINNING STAGES: START YOUNG

Marcus had a game he liked to play each day when his dad returned from work. The incongruous sight of the two of them made bystanders smile. His dad, tall, lean, and serious looking would invariably be carrying a briefcase in one hand. Marcus, still carrying plenty of baby fat on his stubby six-year-old legs would be clutching the other. Together, before his dad even had a chance to go into the house, they would march up and down the sidewalk in exaggerated rhythm. Stomping out each syllable, they would vie with each other to come up with rhyming sentences. "There's a skunk in my trunk!" his dad would say as they punctuated each word with a slap of a foot on the pavement. "My friend's dog is a hog!" Marcus would counter. It didn't matter if the sentences made sense or not. In fact, the one's that didn't were the most fun. "There's a mule in the pool" from Dad brought peals of laughter and "There's a snake in the cake!" from Marcus. This game had been going on for a couple weeks and Marcus didn't seem to be tiring of it. Sometimes his dad was longing to just slip quietly into the house and sink down into his comfy chair, especially on those nights when traffic had been a nightmare. But he was willing to play for five minutes each night. He realized that Marcus was experimenting with sounds and their relationships. He recognized that the feel of feet hitting pavement was a great way for Marcus to become more aware of the rhythms of language, the demarcation of syllables. He knew it was a way to play with language, trying out word combinations and constructing sentences.

The key at this stage is the same as for other developmental tasks your child is mastering, lots of enthusiasm, a willingness for untiring repetition, and letting your child move along at her own pace.

One of the most important things you can do for your young child is to have a regular story time every day. Reading aloud to your young children is invaluable in laying a foundation for reading. Read with lots of expression and emotion. Young children learn a lot about their world through nonverbal cues, so use gestures, facial expressions, and movements to go along with the stories where appropriate. Choose books with wonderful illustrations and ask your child to tell you about the pictures. Watch for your child's responses and try to find other books similar to those she particularly likes. Connect toys and videos with books. Audiotapes of books, especially with sound effects or songs that go along with the story, are also appealing to young children. Let your child act out the stories; movement is a natural way for a young child to learn and express herself.

We are surrounded by words. You can start building the concepts of reading and an interest in the printed word by helping your child to be aware of words in his environment. Point out the stop sign at the end of your street as you walk around the neighborhood with your toddler. A four-year-old will soon be shouting proudly, "S-T-O-P stop!" when she sees that sign in other places too. Give little ones a chance to succeed at the reading task before they've even learned to read. As you take a can of corn or peas from the cabinet, show it to your child, spell the word or ask the child to spell it from the label, and then tell you what it says. The pictures on the labels make it easy for the child to know what is in the can and thus to "read" the word correctly. This builds confidence in reading. Decorate your child's room with bright alphabet letters, choose blocks with letters, get a set of magnetic letters for the refrigerator door. Make large labels with bold letters to attach to household items (bed, couch, wall, etc.). It doesn't matter whether your child can actually read these words. You are simply building awareness at this stage. The key to these interventions is in taking advantage of the child's natural environment. Once you get started, you'll be amazed at the number of opportunities you'll find.

A trip to the toy store, educational supply store, or appropriate Internet site will provide an ample supply of games and toys that contribute to development of reading skills. Many of the best games, though, are the ones you make yourself. These are simple, economical, and have the advantage of being more personal. They also challenge your creativity as well as your child's. Matching games are good and easy to create. Cut pictures from magazines or use your own photos. These can be matched with letters or words printed on cardboard. The more you involve children in making the game, the more you stimulate their interest in learning. Even young children can leaf through magazines and select pictures to paste on the cards.

A general rule of thumb in creating any game is to progress from the simpler to the more complex. Matching pictures to single letters (h matched with hat) is easier than matching whole words or even phrases to pictures (a red hat). Simplicity can also be achieved by limiting the number of choices. Giving your child five letters and pictures to match is a much easier task than matching a set of twenty-six. Limiting the number of processes required also helps. For example, it is easier to match letters with pictures if you lay out the cards face up than if the cards are placed faced down and the child has to remember where he saw a particular letter to match with the appropriate picture. As the child becomes more proficient, you can add in more complicating factors to keep the game challenging. Games that are either too easy or too hard will fail to capture your child's attention.

Sorting games are also effective and teach organizational skills as well as reading. Children can arrange word cards in categories like clothing, animals, buildings, and so forth. Alternatively, you can have your child select a category card and give him an initial letter. The child supplies a word that fits in the category and starts with the letter you provide. Thinking of a toy that begins with "m" or an animal that starts with "p" stimulates your child's ability to make connections, develops vocabulary skills, and practices phonics. You can print the letters and words on paper as you play and afterward your child can make drawings of his words. Keep the pages in a three–ring notebook for review—lots and lots of review. Be careful not to overwhelm your child with too many words at once. This will only result in frustration and loss of confidence. The emphasis should be on success.

Possibilities are limited only to your imagination. You will gain confidence in your own ability to think up new games. Like any teacher does, you will soon build a repertoire of ideas to use. Swap your ideas with other parents and get ideas from them as well. If your child is in pre-school, or her early school years, consult with the teachers about activities and materials.

A multisensory approach is very important for children with learning disabilities. By engaging their other senses, you can utilize alternate neural pathways in their brains, help them build connections between these pathways and those involved in reading, and capitalize on their natural learning styles and preferences. The more routes that lead to a word stored in the brain, the more chance your child has of accessing it.

For little ones, this may mean textured felt or sandpaper letters that they can explore with their hands, or "writing" letters in sand to get the feel of the way they are formed. One little girl loved it when her mother spelled out simple words on her back. She'd squeeze her eyes tightly and concentrate on the path of her mom's forefinger as she printed "cat" or "fat," often correctly identifying words she missed in print. The sense of touch is one of the first senses we use to learn about our environment, why not take advantage of it for learning about reading, too?

Matching sight to sound, a key element in the learning process, is often particularly difficult for children with visual discrimination or sensory integration problems. One way to help your child with sound/symbol relationships is to use color-coding. For example, print the letters "ad" five or six times in bold black marker in a column down the center of a page. Then use different colored markers for each of the various initial sounds that can be used with this ending to form a list of rhyming words. You could make a red "h" to form had, a green "b" to form "bad," an orange "m" to form "mad," This kind of color-coding will help your child focus on the part of the alphabetic code that changes the sound and meaning of the word. When a child with visual discrimination problems or sensory integration problems sees the teacher change "ran" to "fan" on the blackboard, all in yellow chalk, she may not notice the small difference in the visual symbols. However, if these changes are made more noticeable by color changes, then she has a better chance of perceiving the difference and remembering it. You can also use the same strategy with word patterns in which the beginning of the word stays the same and the ending changes (e.g., man, mat, map, etc.). As your child progresses to multisyllabic words, you can use this strategy to emphasize the likenesses and differences of word parts in words like ration, duration, recreation, and creation.

A similar technique using color-coding involves printing the letters or word parts on multicolored squares of paper. Lay out a selection of these cards and ask your child to replace one of the squares in a starter word to form new words, either words you supply or words of her own choice. Thus the child can manipulate the word "man" to form "mat" or "pan," all the while building a better understanding of the keys to written language.

Experiment with color coding when you are trying to teach your child various word patterns for reading or spelling. The point is that your child gets to "see" the way words are put together and begins to understand the principles underlying the process. Always ask your child to explain what is happening so she can articulate the principles in her own words. Another thing to remember, especially with young children, is that exaggeration captures attention. Exaggeration can be used to emphasize the sounds that children with auditory discrimination problems may have difficulty perceiving, and they can make the activity more fun, too. When you are working with your child on phonics, stretch out that "s" sound on "snake" into a long sibilant hiss and extend the "z" on "buzz" until it sounds like a pesky mosquito is circling your child's head. Better yet, accompany these sounds with appropriate slithering or circling gestures.

Drama works in lots of other ways too, so draw on those skills you honed in your fifth-grade play. Get your child acting and moving too. Make a bowl of simple sentences on strips like those in fortune cookies. Have your child pull out a sentence and act it out. Some can be straightforward commands like "Hop ten times on one foot." Others can be more imaginative, like "Moo like a mad cow," or "Act like a sad cat." In this way, your child can have fun while practicing her word recognition and decoding skills, involve additional senses in her learning, and have some relief from the stress and tedium of focusing her brain on a difficult task.

Lots of children like cooking, and there are some good children's cookbooks on the market. You can write your own too by simplifying the language of recipes you already have. Cooking gives practice in reading and following directions, involves a multisensory hands-on learning approach, and has a built-in reward: mmm, smell those brownies! Watch for opportunities in your child's real world.

In the earlier years, the most important thing is to make sure the at-home learning activities are fun and not frustrating to the child. If the young child begins to show disinterest, fatigue, or stress, it's time to change the activity. If an activity is too hard, find a way to make it easier. It may be time for rest or free play. Lots of praise is important too. Evoking negative reactions to reading and writing will be ineffective in the short run and counterproductive in the long run. Learning activities, like all the other activities you do with your young child, should be opportunities for sharing love and developing in your child feelings of acceptance, joy, and competency.

THE STRUGGLING READER IN THE ELEMENTARY SCHOOL YEARS

"Dad, where's the dictionary?" Petey yelled from his bedroom. He'd gone right in after Cub Scouts and was doing his homework. Roger was proud of him. He'd been surprised at how much homework was expected of his son, only in fourth grade. He'd been a little embarrassed when Petey's teacher had called and told him his son hadn't been completing the papers she sent home with him. He felt guilty that he hadn't been doing his own job—making sure his son did everything expected of him. The feeling brought him back to his own school days and he found himself responding with that same mixture of deference and defensiveness he'd had then when his teachers had got on him about his missing assignments. "Yes, Miss Rodriguez, certainly Miss Rodriguez, but . . ."

He'd never really felt comfortable with his teachers and had barely scraped by enough to graduate from high school. His own parents had had little to do with his school work. Both worked long hours. His dad came home tired from a day of driving a big rig and his mom was gone at night, working at her waitressing job to bring in the few extra dollars that kept the family from drowning in debt. Now that he was a father, his own situation wasn't that different. His job as a production supervisor at the plant carried a lot of responsibility and left him drained at the end of the day. Nancy worked nights as a certified nursing assistant at the hospital. But Miss Rodriguez had given him a "wake-up call" and he was determined that Petey would get a better chance than he had had to do well in school.

Roger and Petey had made an agreement that Petey would work on his homework each evening in the hour before supper. Then if he still had more to do, he could finish after taking a break to eat dinner with the family. Roger would check the homework before TV time to make sure it was all done. Roger carried the dictionary into his son's room and affectionately rumpled his sandy hair. "What are you working on, Buddy?" he asked.

"Just some worksheets for reading." Petey was already flipping through the pages of his dictionary, anxious to get the work over with. His sneakered foot kicked rhythmically against the desk.

Looking over his shoulder, Roger read the directions printed in large, bold print at the top of the page: "Be a Word Detective: Use the Clues in the Sentences to Figure Out What These Words Mean."

Petey had just circled the answer to the first question and was now searching the dictionary for the answer to the second.

"Whoa! Hold on a minute, Petey. I don't think you're supposed to be using the dictionary for this."

"I have to use the dictionary, Dad. I don't know these words." Petey industriously went back to his work, thumbing through the dictionary and using his forefinger to track down the columns.

"Read the directions," Roger said. "You're supposed to figure out their meaning yourself. There are clues in the sentences. That's what you're doing this for. It's about how to figure out the meanings from the clues. Let's do a few together. Read me the sentence you're working on."

"The old woman handed her heavy grip to the conductor as she boarded the train," Petey read haltingly.

"OK, now figure out what a grip is and pick the right answer."

"I never heard of a grip," Petey answered with a hint of frustration in his voice. "Maybe it's her ticket," he continued, starting to circle the first answer among the multiple answer choices. "Remember when we took the Amtrak to New York, Dad?"

"Not a bad guess, Petey. But it says it was a 'heavy grip.' "

"Oh, that's right. Tickets aren't heavy. OK then it must be 'suitcase.' It can't be 'money' because that's not heavy either."

"Great! Now you're thinking like a word detective! Let's try another one, Sherlock, and see if you can find the clues again. This is kind of fun, isn't it?"

"Sure, Dad," Petey responded, drawing out the words and raising his blond eyebrows sarcastically. Roger wasn't fooled though. He had seen the hint of a smile on his son's face and knew Petey might actually being enjoying their detective game.

During the elementary school years, a wide variety of reading skills and strategies will be taught in school. In these years, one of your most important roles as the parent of a child with reading difficulty will be to keep him from getting discouraged and help him to make the transition to doing more work independently outside school. It will also be important to provide opportunities for your child to have more practice in the skills being presented in the classroom. Children with dyslexia or other language-based learning disabilities will need more opportunities than others to practice a reading skill to the point where it becomes automatic. Good communication with your child's teachers is critical during this period so you can monitor your child's progress and find out what skills you should work on with your child at home.

Children also need to have someone articulate what is involved in doing a particular reading task. Don't be sure this was done in the classroom or that your child absorbed it if it was done. Talk about processes with your child, asking him to explain how he is going about a reading task, and helping him to get a clear picture of what the task involves. Your child may not understand the concept behind such skills as finding the main idea or drawing a conclusion. Often the child is simply told to identify such elements and is not led through the process by which one does so. Whereas many children can do such tasks naturally, the learning disabled child may need step-by-step instruction on how to do them. So your child won't spend unproductive hours doing an assignment he doesn't understand, take the time to get him started and off on the right foot. Have frequent "learning conversations" with your child in which he is encouraged to think about his learning. Be sure to keep the conversation nonjudgmental. It hurts to be blamed for something you really can't do yet.

As children move up in grade, their grasp of content material in science, social studies, and other subjects depends very much on textbook reading. Children with reading disabilities often fall behind because they can't keep up with the demand for independent reading in these subjects. Textbooks on tape (available from Recordings for the Blind and Dyslexic) can alleviate this problem. In addition to keeping up with the content, reading the textbook along with the audiotape is a great way for your child to practice the eye movements involved in reading and to get exposure to the words he is expected to read at his grade level. The pairing of the auditory input (listening to the recorded voice) with the visual symbol of the word (seeing it on the page) may contribute to your child's ability to decode unfamiliar words when he sees them again. If essential books are not available on tape, you can record chapters yourself. Taping lists of terms your child has to study can also be helpful. Again, encourage him to look at the words and definitions in print as he listens to the tape. This way, he is learning the terms and also improving his word recognition. Be aware, though, that some children (especially those with auditory processing difficulty or visual tracking problems) may find the process of reading along with the tape very difficult. Some may want to simply listen, others will reject the tapes altogether. No one solution works for every child.

THE RELUCTANT READER

If you have a child who doesn't read by choice, there are some steps you can take to encourage reading for pleasure. Of course, this is a tall order, since for many of these kids, reading and pleasure are antonyms! Feelings and attitudes about reading (as well as about other things) are harder to change than skills.

The first step is to provide your child with role models. Your kids need to see that reading is a valued part of your life. One of the most important things you can do is build in some family reading time. It can be as short as ten or fifteen minutes a day in which the entire family sets aside all other activities and reads. Each person can choose any reading material. No phone calls or other interruptions are allowed. This few minutes per day of quiet togetherness may have benefits beyond an improvement in attitudes toward reading. At the end of the reading period, those who wish can share a little about what they've read. This may engender communication about topics the family may not have discussed otherwise or may help children and parents get to know each other a little more.

Though not lengthy, this strategy at least ensures that your child will have a chance of discovering something he enjoys reading. If you don't set the time aside, the children many never choose to use free time in this way. If required to read alone for a set period a day on his own, your child may feel like this is a punishment. Doing it together can reinforce the idea that you as parents consider reading important and enjoyable. Make the session as pleasurable as possible. You might want to put out a bowl of popcorn, fruit, or candy, and play soft music in the background.

You'll also need to help your child find reading material that interests her. Many kids who don't read for pleasure believe books are boring. Even voracious readers who will read almost anything in print have preferences that they discover through experience. Helping your child to discover the books that she enjoys may take some effort on your part.

Visit libraries and talk to the librarians. They have a wealth of information about books kids enjoy. Talk with your children about their interests and try to find books that are related. Take your children with you to bookstores to browse through the sections appropriate for their ages. Books that explore developmental issues children are facing are often favorites. The popularity of Judy Blume, M. E. Kerr, Norma Fox Mazer, Robert Cormier, and other similar authors testifies to that. As they change, children are searching to understand themselves and their experiences and books can be a wonderful way to do this.

The key for free reading is choice—the child's. Let your child choose comic books, sports stories, junior detective books, science fiction, or joke books—anything that will awaken her interest and help her to see reading as enjoyment rather than punishment.

Once your child has identified a book she likes, ask teachers and librarians about other books by the same author or books similar in style or content. Many adults report that they became hooked on reading by devouring series like "Nancy Drew," the "Hardy Boys," and "Encyclopedia Brown," so watch for series, too. The "Harry Potter" books are enticing today's children in the same way. Don't try to force your child to finish a free reading book she doesn't like. You may feel frustrated that the child doesn't complete a book, but remember that the key here is to help her experience the pleasure of reading. You need to let her explore to find out what she likes. For some children, magazines are a better alternative.

Another important consideration in choosing the right books is the reading level. A child who is struggling with word attack or comprehension problems may not be able to enjoy books written at his grade level. Many publishers provide high-interest, lower-reading-level series that give these kids easy-to-read books that aren't "babyish" to them. They are available through publishers' catalogs, so ask your child's teacher about them. Reading for pleasure shouldn't be a struggle. Don't worry about your child not being challenged; she gets enough of that at school. Free reading should be fun, and it's not fun if it's frustrating.

READING TO LEARN

Russell had always loved science. From the time he was six, Marcia had wisely tolerated the muddy sneakers he kicked off in the hallway when returning from one of his many explorations of the wetlands near their home. She had provided him with a magnifying glass and specimen bottles, nets and aquariums to support his interest. By the time he was eight, he knew the names of all the birds, butterflies, amphibians, and insects whose habitat surrounded their suburban home. He had touched many of them, been stung by a few, and would spend hours scanning the pictures in his Audubon field guide to identify a new bird that lighted in their woods. Marcia was sure he'd be a scientist some day.

That's why she was stunned when he brought home a D in science his first semester in seventh grade. A little investigation revealed that the grade depended upon weekly quizzes on the chapters assigned for homework reading. Marcia saw the thick textbook for the first time when she visited his classroom for the parent-teacher conference. Russ had never even brought the book home.

Much of what we've been talking about so far in this chapter is about learning to read; this section, however, is about reading to learn. As your child gets older, reading becomes more and more important as a vehicle to learning other subjects. While science and social studies in first and second grade are usually taught through hands-on activities, by fourth grade your child's teachers will begin to rely more on textual information to convey content. By high school, learning in the various content areas depends greatly on the ability to supplement in-class demonstration and discussion by careful reading and studying of textbooks. In college, the professors expect students to be able to read material and acquire much of the subject matter independently, using class time for clarifying and assessing comprehension, and for encouraging critical thinking and application of the material rather than for summarizing and spoon-feeding it to their students.

This puts children with reading problems at a great disadvantage in almost all subject areas from fourth grade on. Children who struggle with reading will find it not only distasteful, but discouraging and frustrating to do homework assignments involving large amounts of textbook reading. These children will often avoid the task, especially if it hasn't resulted in success. After all, who among us would spend hours every evening doing something that didn't pay off?

So, what can you do about this dilemma? You certainly don't want to encourage avoidance as a way of coping and yet you don't know how to intervene. You may not know any other way of getting your child to do the reading other than that time-tested (and often unsuccessful) method your own parents might have used: "Go to your room and don't come out until it's done!" This will most likely result in a variety of responses like daydreaming, doodling, tears, a little back-talk, and even lies—none of which gets the reading done.

Fortunately, there are some steps you can take to make the task more do-able for your child and more fruitful for him as well. The first is to assess whether your child can actually decode the words in the textbook. If he can't, you should talk with the reading specialist or resource room teachers at his school about getting the textbooks on tape.

The next step is to teach your child how to read the chapters. Don't presume that he knows how to do this efficiently and effectively. Children with learning disabilities, more than other children, need help with the "how to" aspects of textbook reading. A wide range of learning deficits, including problems with decoding, reading comprehension, vocabulary, organization, and memory, can require special strategies. Several methods have been developed for textbook reading including the Cornell method, PQRST, and SQ4R (Stahl, 1983). The suggestions below draw on all of these methods.

The first, and one of the most important steps in reading a textbook chapter is to preview it. Do this part with your child to get him started, set the stage, and build a framework for what is to come. Previewing involves reading the chapter headings and subheadings and making some kind of visual representation of them that shows their relationship to one another. This is just as important for the good reader who has spatial problems as it is for the child with dyslexia. Creating a visual helps the child to know what to expect, to see the part-whole relationships, and to build a mental structure to which he can attach the material presented in the chapter. The visual representation may be drawn as a web with the chapter title in the center and spokes radiating from the center. Each spoke is labeled with a major heading. Smaller spokes can be drawn from each major heading and labeled with the subheadings. The benefit of this method is that it helps your child to make sense of what could otherwise be a confusing jumble of details.

Another way to record the preview points is by dividing the paper vertically, creating two columns—one on the left about one-third the width of the paper and the one on the right about two-thirds the width. During the preview stage, your child should write the major headings and subheadings in the left-hand column. He should indent the subheadings a little to show that they are subsets of the major heading. Color-coding is also good. Your child can highlight all of the major headings in one color, subheadings in another, and sub-subheadings in a third. This method, like the webbing described above, will tell your child how many major topics there are and what he should know about each of them. It's a good idea to do this previewing with your child if possible. This will allow you to talk with him about what he will be learning in the chapter, be sure he sees the chapter structure correctly, and motivate him to read it.

Once the previewing is complete, your child is ready for the next step. Ask your child to read the chapter independently (with or without the audiotapes) and fill in details on the preview web or in the right-hand column of his paper. He can put in pictures and symbols as well as words. Depending on how much supervision your child needs, you can ask him to do the whole chapter or just one or two sections of it before you look it over. Doing the chapter in sections builds in some natural breaks for the child who is unable to maintain concentration for an extended period of time. It helps you to provide a balance of support and independence, structure and freedom.

Step three involves going over the notes to clarify, confirm, and review what was written. Ask your child to tell you about his notes and explain the chapter to you using the notes. Ask him to come up with some questions about the material, to react to it, or to connect it to other things he knows. At each step in this process, the material is being processed and stored in the brain. Make sure your child sees the value of this method by asking him some questions that will allow him to demonstrate what he has learned.

Don't worry if your child doesn't have perfect notes or perfect understanding of the chapter. This process can be difficult and some textbooks are harder to apply it to than others. Keep encouraging him to use this active reading method and assuring him that it will work. He will get better and faster at it and should see an improvement in his learning. But before he gets good at it, he will need encouragement and help to see that he is getting more out of the chapter.

The main drawback of this method is the time it takes. It's a lot faster to skim quickly through a chapter or even to read carefully from beginning to end without previewing or taking notes. The payoff is in the effectiveness. Your child will retain much more from this active reading method. He won't get to the end of the chapter and sigh, "I don't know a thing I just read! It's useless." The next day in class, he'll be able to participate actively in discussions. And when the time comes to prepare for a test, he'll have a solid foundation and good notes to use for his review.

WRITING: THE OTHER SIDE OF THE COIN

The paper was crushed into a corner at the bottom of Kerry's purple backpack. Rob found it when he was helping her to get her books, gym shorts, and lunch bag packed before the school bus came. Kerry had always been forgetful and now that she was in seventh grade, Rob and Julie realized they had to teach her to become more organized. Sometimes it felt like a losing battle, but they had finally realized that one of them needed to help her pack the bag each morning. It didn't seem to be something their dreamy-eyed daughter could do for herself yet, even though she was thirteen.

When Rob pulled out the crumpled ball of paper, he thought it was junk and started to toss it into the trash. Remembering that that had happened last week with an important school announcement, he smoothed it out on the tile counter instead. It was Kerry's story about a young girl living on a remote island off Cape Cod. She had gotten the idea of writing it after reading *Anne of Green Gables* and used a setting she was familiar with from frequent family vacations at the Cape. Rob remembered her excitement as she had described to the family at supper last week the events she would include in her story. They'd been impressed by the interesting story line and well-developed ideas for the characters. Most important, they'd been thrilled by Kerry's enthusiasm for the assignment. Here was a chance to show off that imagination, to capitalize on some of those creative fantasies she had as she stared out her window daydreaming.

Rob and Julie hadn't had a chance to see her finished version. Now, here it was, wrinkled and creased, covered with angry red markings that made Rob think of the welts that rise on a person's flesh when their skin has been raked by sharp claws. His heart ached for Kerry. He remembered his own lost dreams of being a writer, knew that he still harbored those dreams in his own heart though they were pretty much withered now. The word "disorganized!" was scrawled boldly at the top and the page was stained with numerous corrections of spelling and grammar. Rob looked up to see Kerry staring at him and at the paper in his hands. Her liquid gray eyes showed the hurt she felt. Her pain evoked a stab of recognition in his own heart as well as feelings of helplessness. He didn't know what to say to her to take away the hurt. "It was just a stupid story anyways," Kerry said defiantly as he turned toward her. "I hate writing!"

Reading and writing are just opposite sides of the coin that is written language. Many of the points made about reading in the first part of this chapter apply to writing as well. And many of the children who have trouble with reading will also have trouble with writing. After all, both are tasks involving written language. Reading involves decoding those symbols we call words, remembering what the words mean, and figuring out the meaning conveyed by the way those words are put together in sentences, paragraphs, and longer passages. Writing, on the other hand, involves encoding ideas using the alphabetic symbols and an organizational structure that will make sense to others. While children with receptive language problems may find reading more difficult, children with expressive language problems will find writing a bigger challenge. And, of course, since they are simply opposite sides of the same coin, there will be many interconnections. Children with other kinds of learning disabilities like spatial problems may also have trouble with writing because of its organizational demands.

One of the first steps in helping your child with writing is to figure out the nature of the problems she may be having. Writing problems can involve the inability to spell and physically write down the words as well as trouble remembering or recalling the words to express what you want to say. They also include difficulty with the rules of grammar and usage (syntax) that guide us in putting the words in order to build clear, correct sentences and paragraphs. In addition, they may involve problems in seeing the big picture and knowing how all the parts fit into the whole, especially in longer, more complicated pieces of writing.

Children with writing problems may agonize for hours just to come up with a few, scraggly sentences or may produce pages and pages that never get to the point or that hide the point in confusing, disorganized language. We can compare the child with a writing assignment to a chef asked to produce a tasty dish for us to consume. One child serves a big, empty plate with a few lonely peas on it. Another has an overflowing pile of ingredients that don't go together, all heaped in a jumble on the plate. A third tries to make a cake and uses all the right ingredients but doesn't follow the order prescribed in the recipe. It's time for some cooking lessons, but where to begin?

With writing, the place to begin is with talking. Talking is the oral form of expressive language while writing is its written form. Talking is the expressive form that comes first and that comes more naturally. With any writing your child may do, it's good to let her spend some time talking about it first. That way, she can generate ideas, clarify what she wants to say, and begin to organize her thoughts. You can ask questions that stimulate and guide her in this process.

WRITING: FIRST STEPS

The language experience approach is a wonderful strategy to use with a child (younger or older) who cannot yet encode her ideas efficiently. Ask the child to tell you a story while you act as her "secretary." Tape the story or write it down exactly the way the child tells it, using her own words. Later type or print the words neatly. Leave plenty of room for the child to illustrate the story or add extra pages for pictures. Bind the pages and have the child design a cover with the title and her own name as author. Save these books and ask the child to read them to you on later occasions. You will probably be surprised at how much of the book your child will be able to "read" to you. Working with her own language structures and with stories she herself created will aid her ability to read the print. The pride and accomplishment your child feels at creating these books is an added benefit. She can even give them to parents or grandparents as birthday or holiday gifts.

ENCOURAGING THE WRITTEN WORD

In writing, as for reading, your most important role is to encourage and motivate your child to want to write. Children learn to write by writing. There is no substitution, no computer program, no set of grammar exercises that will do more to develop your child's writing ability than actually using it. Help your child to see writing for what it is—a means of human communication—by encouraging letter writing to friends, relatives, pen pals. Involve your creative youngster in making her own stationery using crafts materials or computer programs. Long letters aren't necessary. Even a few lines on a card gives your child a chance to write a message that has a purpose.

Journal writing is also good for children who are interested in keeping them. Let them pick out an attractive notebook or one of the "blank books" available in stationery stores. Some children love the idea of a locked diary, while others will choose a spiral notebook with their favorite cartoon characters on the cover. If you can't get your child into writing paragraphs, suggest that she simply keep a log listing events and daily activities in her journal, maybe with a comment or two on the highlights of her week. Recommend using the journal to create lists: things about my brother that bug me, places I want to go, my best friends and their pets, five things I'd like to change about myself. The ideas are endless, and you'll have to know your own child to know which might appeal to her.

Children who are more visual will enjoy pairing words with images. Cut out interesting pictures from magazines and ask your child to write about what she thinks is happening in the picture. Give your child a Polaroid camera and set her loose to take pictures of anything she chooses.

Then ask her to paste the pictures in a notebook and put a caption under each.

DEVELOPING ORGANIZING SKILLS

Another way to build skills that are foundational to writing is to practice organizing and categorizing. Ask your child to list all the items in a room, then group them into categories. Challenge her to find a variety of ways to categorize the items (texture, color, function, etc.). Cut up newspaper cartoons into individual segments and ask your child to put them in order. Have your child draw her own cartoons telling the main events of a story she has read or an experience she has had. Create a word box (print words on small slips of paper) and have your child see how many different sentences she can create from a handful she pulls out. This is one the whole family can do together as a game with the winner being the one who uses the most words in a given amount of time. Sequencing skills can also be built by asking your child to write a list of all the steps in a process and then following them to see if she put them in the right order and included all of them. Processes can range from the simple (making a peanut butter and jelly sandwich) to the complex (how a baseball game is played). Children who like science will enjoy performing simple science experiments right in your kitchen. (Yes, it may make a mess!) Libraries carry many books with suggestions for such activities. Ask your child to make a simplified list of the steps after reading about the experiment in the book, then let her try it. Suggest that your child create a new board or yard game and write down the rules of play. The family can play the game after supper.

All of these activities aim at developing an understanding of the need for clarity and organization in written expression. Perhaps most importantly, they also help your child to see the value and use of written words and the fun she can have in manipulating them.

IMPROVING THE WRITTEN WORD

As your child moves up in grade, more emphasis will be placed on correctness of expression and on the rules for grammar and usage. This effort has been the bane of even some of the most creative and successful writers. If your child is bringing home grammar exercises that require her to identify parts of speech (nouns, verbs, adjectives) or sentence parts (subjects, predicates, etc.), try using multicolored markers to help her. Give her models to follow like lists of nouns in red, verbs in blue, and so forth. Then ask her to highlight the words in the exercise with the appropriate color. Use squares of multicolored paper with nouns printed on one color, verbs on another, and adjectives on a third. Let your child make a variety of sentences by arranging and rearranging the words. See if you can find a good computer game that will provide plenty of practice.

For some children with language learning disabilities, the way their brains are wired makes it very difficult for them to acquire grammatical concepts and structures (syntax). It takes lots of meaningful repetition. Anything you can do to make this process less tedious and frustrating will be helpful. And don't expect that what your child understands one day she will be able to apply the next. Neural pathways aren't built in a day. It's like making a path through a grassy lot. The first few times you walk that way, you won't be able to see the path. It's only after many times retracing that path that it is clearly evident.

WRITING AS A MULTISTEP PROCESS

Carla had been hunched over her desk for an hour when Maddy decided to check on her progress. Since her daughter had started high school, Maddy had seen the length and complexity of her assignments increase. Unfortunately, along with that, she'd also seen a decline in Carla's English grades. It was puzzling because Carla had done well in English up until then. Although she had been diagnosed with some spatial organization problems that required her to have additional time on some tasks, her written work had always been excellent. Now it seemed that her learning disability had caught up with her and was interfering with her success in writing English compositions.

"How's the essay coming, Honey?" Maddy asked, looking down at a lone page littered with cross-outs and arrows indicating the changes Carla was making. Maddy knew the essay Carla was writing had to be at least three pages long. She was worried that her daughter would never finish it if she kept on going the way she was. She'd seen it before. Carla would labor over the beginning, spend a huge amount of time refining, editing, and improving the first part. Then she'd run out of steam or tolerance, rush through the rest, and turn in disorganized papers that teachers often labeled with comments like "Uneven!" or "Great start. What Happened?" It was beginning to be a pattern.

"This is the fourth time I've started it," Carla groaned, casting a hopeless glance at the wastebasket containing the crumpled remains of several earlier starts. "I've got a lot to put in and I can't figure out how to do it."

"What does the teacher want you to do?"

"I need to compare and contrast the main characters from two different stories we read. I know a lot about the books, but I don't know how to make it all fit together."

"Well, tell me what you're doing now. Maybe I can help," Maddy replied, recognizing that her daughter was feeling overwhelmed by the process of deciding what to include and how to organize it. Maddy divided up a clean sheet of paper into three columns and two rows. "Let's make a chart to sort out the stuff first," she said handing the paper to Carla. "Write 'Characters' at the top of the first column, 'Likenesses' at the top of the second, and 'Differences' at the top of the third." She watched as Carla labeled the columns, holding her breath hoping that her daughter wouldn't resist and refuse to try the strategy the learning specialist had suggested. "Great!" she said as Carla finished. "Now, what will you write in the two boxes under 'Characters' in the first column?"

Carla neatly printed the names of young girls who were the main characters in *The House on Mango Street* and *A Tree Grows in Brooklyn*. "They were both young girls," Carla said, and without further prompting printed "young girl" and their ages in the "Likenesses" column beside each of their names. Next, her thoughts jumped to a difference. "But they lived in different times." She wrote the information for each in the "Differences" column. "And in different places. One lived in New York and the other in Chicago," she continued, writing as she spoke. "But the neighborhoods were the same in some ways." She started filling in some details in the "Likenesses" column. "And they both had to cope with some of the same things . . ."

She was off and running. Finally she had a structure for her abundant thoughts. After she filled in her chart, it would provide the guide she needed to write her paper in a clear, logical way. Now that she had a roadmap, she didn't need to stay at the starting point.

An important thing to remember as your child gets older is that writing a composition is a multistep process. Carla's mistake was in trying to do several of those steps at once. She was trying to write before she had worked out an organizational structure and sequence for her essay. And she was editing the first part before completing her first draft. Carla's method of handling her assignment was one that was sure to confuse her and was likely to leave her with an unfinished or poorly constructed piece of work.

You can help your child to avoid this kind of frustration and failure. Start by encouraging her to separate the steps of the process. Take time before she starts writing to clarify what the assignment is asking her to do. Then spend some time on brainstorming to generate topics that might be included. Your child can make a list or write her ideas on a web such as that described earlier in this chapter for reading textbook chapters. Some topics lend themselves to a chart like the one Maddy did with Carla. At this stage, encourage your child to let her thoughts flow freely and not to censor or judge them. If a child has difficulty generating enough ideas, help her to learn how to branch out from the ideas she has.

The next stage involves focusing in on what your child wants to include in the composition, choosing or discarding some of the ideas she generated. Then, guide her in deciding the order in which she wants to express her ideas. She may want to make a flowchart or an outline to show the sequence she will use. After this, she should write the first draft without trying to edit her work. She should just let the ideas flow, using her organizational guide to keep on track.

Editing should come last. At this stage, she should check first for clarity, completeness, the flow of the ideas. She may want to move, add, or delete something. She may find a better word or phrase to express a thought. Lastly should come the nitty gritty corrections to spelling, grammar, and usage. Too often it is this last step that becomes the major focus of writing, and that discourages children who could be excellent writers in spite of some problems with grammar or spelling.

Using a word processor is strongly recommended because it makes the process of writing and editing much more efficient. Children will find writing and rewriting by hand tedious and frustrating. They will even avoid making changes that would make their work better or more accurate because they don't want to rewrite it. This is especially true for children with dysgraphia or other fine motor problems. Once your child is comfortable with a word processor, she can write her compositions directly on it from her organizers.

Don't expect perfection. Pay attention to where your child is and then help her to move to the next step. Even small improvements in writing take time. If you try to do too much, your child will simply become discouraged and give up. Every time you read your child's composition, find the positive in it ("Great ideas! Interesting ending!") before helping her to fix errors. Even adults are sensitive about criticism of their writing, why should we expect children to be different?

THE TEACHABLE MOMENTS IN READING AND WRITING

For schoolchildren with reading and writing problems, it's important to take advantage of the teachable moments in their everyday lives. This is true for the older kids as well as the younger ones. Capitalize on your children's interests and get them involved in reading recipes, creating arts and crafts projects, doing research about a new pet, reading travel materials to plan a family vacation, using computer games, skimming popular magazines, studying the driver education manual, and doing a host of other activities in which reading and writing are components.

If children dislike reading and writing, you have to relate these activities to more pleasurable pastimes. Doing this also allows you to capitalize on your child's learning style as well. What works for one child doesn't work for the next. You have to be a good detective and a sharp observer of your own child. No reading specialist, tutor, or classroom teacher will know your child the way you do.

The things we know will work are in your hands: role modeling and creating a home culture that values reading and writing; associating reading and writing with good feelings like warmth, pleasure, comfort; helping your child gain a sense of achievement and accomplishment from these written language activities; finding books and writing projects that engage the child's mind and emotions; providing support and structure for difficult reading or writing assignments. The fact is that there are many simple acts and choices you can make every day that can and will contribute to your child's growth in reading and writing. Be patient (with your child and with yourself), and you will find the ways.

10

The Language of Math

It is often when children have reached adulthood that they can reflect upon their experiences, especially those experiences that presented a challenge to them, and articulate their feelings about specific aspects of their educational histories. In this case, we are talking about mathematics, an area that possesses an exclusive language of its own consisting of numbers, symbols, and concepts. For the purposes of this chapter we will refer to arithmetic as the process of computing numbers; addition, subtraction, multiplication, and division. Mathematics is the umbrella under which mathematical concepts, problem-solving, and higher mathematics such as algebra, geometry, trigonometry, and calculus exist.

The language of mathematics is an unfriendly minefield for some individuals. When symbols and numbers are introduced to children, language as they know it takes on a different meaning. It's no longer like a child's first or primary spoken language. It's another language, an additional set of rules and directions. For one child, math presents a welcome challenge and justification for how the world around him is ordered. For another child, a child with a math disability, math is not connected to the naming of numbers, to quantities of candy or toys, or to daily life. It's a separate entity, a new enemy, and a new stomachache in the morning.

First let me tell you a timeless story about Jeddie and Miss Halliday, her fourth grade teacher. Today Jeddie is a middle-aged adult who can still vividly recall the events she experienced with long division in the classroom. She can envision the classroom of the 1950s with its tall wood-framed windows, the dark stained wooden desks with ink wells, and the contemporary idea that Miss Halliday was attempting to employ by seating her students side by side in large groups, and not in traditional rows. Jeddie missed a few weeks of school in the fourth grade as a result of a childhood illness. When she did return to school, her fourth-grade peers were in the throes of long division. With wide eyes, Jeddie watched some of her friends move through this new phase of learning with ease, and she watched some of her friends with wrinkled frowns as they struggled. They would whisper to her in class, "This is really hard! How're you gonna catch up?" She didn't know.

"What is this?" she wondered with sweaty palms and a fluttering heart. New symbols, numbers lined up horizontally, columns lined up vertically? It looked like something new, and it looked like the old addition and subtraction she was familiar with, only all mixed up. And the language, there were terms she didn't understand. Jeddie was mystified by the process being thrust upon her by Miss Halliday, who gave Jeddie a few extra minutes to catch up when possible and a couple of after school sessions in an effort to align her with her peers' progress.

Jeddie just "didn't get it." She couldn't grasp the concept of division and its ensuing mechanisms until two years later with the help of an understanding teacher and a developmental leap in her life that allowed her to see and sense what the idea of division meant. Consequently, in the fourth grade Jeddie went to school most mornings with a sick feeling in the pit of her stomach, dreading the moment when Miss Halliday would say, "Now let's take out our workbooks, and look at our long division." The concept of "our long division" was anger provoking to Jeddie. Long division belonged to other students, not to her.

ARE WE BORN WITH THE LANGUAGE OF MATH?

Decade after decade theorists have deliberated over young children's inborn ability to understand the idea of *more than* or *less than*. In fact, human infants do seem to have a natural sense of quantity. "As both Mom and Dad hover around the infant, the infant not only perceives their physical features, such as the shape of the face, but also seems to be aware that there are two, not one or three, people milling about. *Twoness* is abstract because it is not an attribute of either parent, but rather represents an important feature of the set of parents, that is, how many" (Geary, 1994, p. 3).

We can all remember that as young children we knew when a play-mate or sibling had more gum or more little trucks than we possessed, and that we needed to add items to our inventory in order to have the *same* or *greater quantity* than the other person. We knew by looking and sensing, just as mother birds know when someone is missing from the nest. We also knew that when an item was taken away from us, for whatever reason, that we then possessed *less than*.

Even when we didn't know the names or words for numbers, we counted. We looked at and touched all our dolls, our blocks, or animal cookies. We counted, using our own language of mathematical reason-ing. We evolved to the inner language of mathematics, a dormant abil-ity of varying levels that awaits our cognitive and neurological awakening by employing our visual perceptions and our haptic or ki-netic beings. This seems to happen within different frames of time for everyone, and the revelations or aha! moments for each child vary ac-cording to cognitive style and individual human development. Very simply, this means that all children do not learn or understand mathe-matical concepts or principles at the same time. For some children, the learning of such complex constructs occur much later when their neu-rological wiring is ready to handle the job. For some children, the lan-guage of mathematics becomes a disability, just like any other learning disability.

Human brains are not equipped with reading or math programs. However, the human brain in its beautiful and mysterious complexity possesses many of the channels or pathways for developing individual-ized learning and understanding of such tasks or concepts. The process of learning and understanding numbers and mathematical concepts is often interfered with by external factors such as traumatic brain injury, physical illness, psychiatric disorders, learning disabilities, or some-times by ineffective teaching methods. These factors can certainly slow down development, and in some cases contribute to such a fear of math that it appears to become a "math phobia." If a child repeatedly experi-ences failure, or consistent confusion at the very least, she will eventu-ally avoid math. She will avoid math well into adulthood.

A lag or impediment in math development can be detected in early years, or is sometimes identified as a student moves from computational skills to a more abstract, problem-solving mathematical task. Whatever the challenge or the time frame in which the difficulty reveals itself, the feelings of inadequacy connected to what is looked at as a dysfunction remain. To put it simply, no one likes to feel dumb in math.

THE EXPERIENCE OF OTHERS

Many sculptors report that they can envision a three-dimensional object that lies embedded within a piece of wood or marble. Their envisionment, their seeing and sensing, is an unknown reality at that moment and may lie dormant for long periods of time. For some artists, the freeing of such an image never occurs. It remains a captured mental image, never to be brought to life for others to see, or for the artist to understand as a concrete reality. Some children and even adults view math as that kind of mystical process. While a sense of math may exist internally in one's thoughts, it's difficult to articulate the understanding in an exact way. After all, math is an exact science, demanding specific kinds of language to demonstrate the process and eventual correct answer. Albert Einstein walked around with the theory of relativity in his head for many years before he found the means to carve and chisel the idea and its accompanying details and language so that the world might see and understand his thoughts and processes. It's bridging the sensing of mathematical concepts to revealing and articulating an understanding of them that becomes difficult, and for children with a disability in this area, a gut-wrenching task.

Often what may be embedded in a child's thoughts or understanding is as difficult to free as the sculpture that the artist may envision trapped inside a piece of marble or wood. Unless practical experience coupled with expressive language occurs, the artist-child may not be able to free her understanding or connection to the mathematical concept that has been posed. Learning to add and subtract might be learned in the home environment as well as in the classroom. It can be talked about, discussed, and turned into a metacognitive experience for both the child and the parent or caregiver. Metacognition means gaining a deeper insight into how we learn, think, and function. This is achieved by becoming more aware of how we approach a problem or a new concept, something we have all experienced. Some of us have become aware of ourselves and how we learn. Others need a guide, a mentor to assist in the process of self-discovery.

Although we often observe how our children gain understanding, we are not always aware of whether they are aware of their learning process. Did your teacher ever ask you how you arrived at your answer in math? Were you ever puzzled yourself about how that magic actually occurred? Maybe you were able to articulate your process with relative ease. Or, maybe you scratched your head, wondering how you could explain the steps you took. If you felt you intuitively leaped to the answer, how did you chisel out and reveal your steps?

Jules, a very quiet young child, used to like to line up his little plastic cowboys in front of the TV and count them. Every day he counted them, rearranged them, and then recategorized them according to color and size. One day his friend called and invited him over to play, asking him to bring his cowboys, but just the brown ones. While his mother watched, Jules counted the brown cowboys, packed them in a plastic bag, and announced his plans to his mother. She ushered him across the street to play and returned home. She thought she might pack up the remaining cowboys in the shoe box Jules used for their storage in order to clean up the living room.

When Jules returned home, a look of panic crossed his face when he noticed the remainder of his cowboys were missing. "Where are they?" he demanded of his mother.

She explained that she had cleaned up the living room, and that his collection of cowboys were in his bedroom. She seized the moment to ask her son, "How many cowboys do you have?"

He said, "I have forty-three cowboys."

"How do you know this?" she asked.

He rolled his eyes in exasperation with her. "I counted them."

"How many brown ones did you bring across the street today?"

He looked thoughtful. "I think eleven."

"Let's look at them, and count them, OK?" He looked suspicious, but ran to his room to retrieve the collection. Immediately he began the ritual of lining up his cowboys against the TV. All the brown ones were together, the red ones, the blue ones, the white ones.

Jules's mother sat down on the floor with a large pad of newsprint paper and some crayons. Together they made four circles; one brown, one red, one blue, and one white. Jules counted the cowboys in each color category, and with his mother's assistance wrote the number in the appropriate circle. He was very proud of his accomplishment. He then crowded the brown cowboys into the circle, then the red ones, until he finished the task he created for himself. He began to develop new ways to count, to document his thinking, and to dialogue with someone about his understanding of quantity.

Over the years I have observed children, adolescents, and adults go to excessive and creative lengths to avoid "doing math." Why is this? It's from the stories of adults with LD/ADD/Dyslexia that I have learned what kinds of feelings and eventual attitudes lurk within the hidden recesses of children's minds. Many children with learning disabilities find it difficult to articulate to us why "math is hard," and often it's not until years later when an astute diagnostician or practitioner puts the pieces of the cognitive and neurological puzzle together that we can enlighten that individual, and ultimately the professionals who oversee the education of our children.

Sometimes adults tell us that they experienced gaps in their learning as a result of illness or truancy. Others explain that as children, computing numbers and moving to other mathematical processes was like a foreign language in which they could never gain full literacy. Covering up what they perceived to be an inadequacy took a great deal of energy and planning. Teachers with large classrooms often didn't have the knowledge to diagnose a math disability, nor the time to devote to working individually with children who might have been capable of moving along at their own pace. This is a very sad scenario, considering the consequences in older adolescence and adult life.

Some adolescents and young adults never learned as children sufficient computational skills to make change with their own money, or from the money they are handling at their jobs. They become adults who develop fears of working behind a cash register, despite the technological ease that has been placed at their fingertips. We stand in lines in drug stores and witness the painful humiliation of a teenager as he struggles with an angry customer who has been short-changed. We are saddened by the young adult who cannot understand the cost of her new suit as a result of a 25 percent off sale. What happened? Do they all have a math disability? Were they absent during multiplication and division week like Jeddie? Did no one notice what was occurring all the way through elementary, middle, and high school? Where was everybody looking when this atrocity was occurring?

How can we be sure that the children today are being taught the most basic math skills? We can't be sure. That's the scary thing. But parents *can* take control of what looks to be a most precarious future for children who might have a tendency to struggle with learning how to add and subtract, learning how to solve a word problem, and figuring out the cost of their favorite toy in relation to the dollars and cents they hold in their hands.

IS IT A MATH DISABILITY?

It's important that we first look at what a math disability *is* so that as you progress through your thinking you will feel more confident about what it isn't. In other words, you want to understand your child's struggles and abilities before you approach a teacher or clinician to argue your case, or to even ask for assistance in determining the best educational choices for your child in the classroom and at home.

The *Diagnostic and Statistical Manual* IV (DSM-IV) is a book that school psychologists, psychiatrists, and other kinds of learning specialists and diagnosticians use in order to sanctify a profile that requires special kinds of services in the educational system and/or the mental health system. You will often find that whomever administers diagnostic testing to your child will cite a specific passage or definition in the written report, and sometimes at a core evaluation. You can purchase DSM-IV in paperback at most larger bookstores in order to read the section on Learning Disorders if you feel that you want to gain a deeper understanding of the language or jargon that may be used in evaluations and at meetings where your presence is requested.

Under the heading of Learning Disorders you will find the following information:

315.1 Mathematics Disorder

Criteria for Mathematics Disorder

- As measured by a standardized test that is given individually, the patient's mathematical ability is substantially less than would be expected from the patient's age, intelligence, and education.
- This deficiency materially impedes academic achievement or daily living.
- If there is also a sensory defect, the mathematics deficiency is worse than would be expected from it.

For some children, the only identified learning disorder they might receive is a math disability. However, in addition to that diagnosis other children are diagnosed with a reading disability as well, compounding their difficulty with math, especially when computational skills move to the world of problem-solving. Adding language that must be read and understood in relation to the computing of numbers makes the language of math yet more complex, requiring another layer of expectations. According to DSM-IV a reading disorder is much the same as what you see listed as a mathematics disorder (listed as "315.00 Reading Disorder" in the manual).

In David Geary's book, *Children's Mathematical Development*, he refers to reading disability as RD, and to math disability as MD, an easy way to follow and discuss these issues as they relate to our children's existing or potential diagnoses. He refers to three subtypes of mathematical disability:

Subtype 1: Semantic Memory
This subtype often coexists with RD; children may experience difficulty with fact retrieval/memory.

Subtype 2: Procedural
This subtype may or may not coexist with RD; immature approaches to problem solving that may improve with development.

Subtype 3: Visuospatial
This subtype does not appear to coexist with RD, but is marked by visuospatial difficulties (aligning numbers, columns, decimals). (Geary, 1994)

Some children's spatial skills are better than others, whether their difficulties rest solely in math or coexist with RD. Depending upon the severity of their spatial skills deficit, difficulties in math may remain undetected, leading to a profile that does not reflect the true abilities or difficulties of the child. The ability to read is considered the primary concern in literacy and in the global perspective of American education. However, the ability to understand and demonstrate competency in math is not regarded often enough with equal concern, nor is it investigated in conjunction with reading. With a purely visuospatial deficit, RD may not be evidenced. However, a child may experience a visuospatial deficit and not be up to par with her reading skills. A double whammy!

When MD coexists with RD, and children are being introduced to word problems, any competency they have exhibited or may sense within themselves can be thwarted or masked by their language-based difficulties. Word problems become a maze of language. One misread or misunderstood preposition within a word problem changes the pathway to understanding and the eventual road to demonstrated competence.

The multifaceted issues of RD and MD, as they exist in isolation or in conjunction with one another, become problems not only worthy of our political scrutinization in terms of national and international competitiveness in math literacy, but also become areas that deserve careful vigilance for the sake of individuality in human learning and development. If we care about our children, then we need to communicate to them and to their educational institutions that we acknowledge their unique abilities as individuals, and that we will find ways to mentor their progress, their abilities, and eventual competence. We will help them to find the right sculpting tools to free the image and understanding that is trapped inside their thinking. And, we will do this work together on the children's timeline, not ours.

What many professionals consider to be a math disability looks to some parents and professionals as being a black hole in the education of that child. This may be true, and for a variety of reasons. Again, it is important to state that each child's development occurs at a different rate. The timeline for learning new skills or bringing to understanding the sense of a concept is like looking at the individuality of a fingerprint. We have fingerprints just as we have our own unique set of neurological wiring, like an electrical system. Even though we might all possess a set of wiring or equipment, the intricacy of its network is specific to each child's genetic coding, or to each child's life experience or culture. These networks are set into motion only when the conditions are right for that specific system. Each time we learn something new as children, or as parents, we experience a sense of disruption within our beings (Fuqua, 1993). Our systems are rattled, and we seek to find ways to fit this new information into our internal landscapes or filing systems. Eventually, after some shifting and sorting and an occasional wrestling match, whatever is new finds a place to fit. A mathematical leap will occur when the internal clock and environment says that the developmental phase of that child's life is ready for newness, ready for acceptance, ready for a new fit. This will occur when the teacher is a mentor and when the caregivers in that child's life are providing the encouragement of sculpting tools and proper lighting to chisel the meaning and language of math.

RECOMMENDATIONS

Hopefully, you feel better able to watch your child at play to determine how she sees and senses what's *greater than* and what's *less than*. This might be accomplished through informal conversation at the kitchen table or by sitting on the floor with her and asking her to tell you how many dolls she has. When you watch your child's math development hit bumps and curves, maybe you'll know what questions to ask her teacher. If you have to sit through a core evaluation feeling very threatened and defensive about your self and your child, maybe you'll better understand the language of the professionals who sit in judgment of the profile before them. Maybe you can ask questions that will give you more specific information about what you can do at home to foster a greater understanding of our mathematical world to your child.

GAMES AND ACTIVITIES

The bookstores are full of wonderful publications that offer suggestions for math games and activities at home. The Internet is an infinite source for connecting with parents who share the same fears that you feel. Start your own parent support group with a focus on math. But keep in mind that the richest resource for you and your child is what you embark upon together to explore the world and language of math.

Kerri used to count her dolls by touching each of them on the head and singing, "One potato, two potato, three potato, four . . . " Eventually, the concept of her counting to the rhythm of a familiar song took on a different meaning as she conceptualized quantity. She began counting her dolls' dishes and her stuffed toys, and began to learn new songs that incorporated computational skills. Often we engage in this kind of learning with our children and are very unconscious of the process that unfolds before our eyes.

Brian developed an attachment for an old worn out deck of cards his parents used when they played gin rummy. When he was very young he would sit for long periods of time touching each of the symbols on each card and making a noise. Eventually his mother began to question him about how many diamonds he counted, and they would sit at the table and count together. He carried this activity to counting animal cookies, lining them up on the table to match the way the diamonds lined up on the playing card. As you can guess, he began to experience *less than* when he began eating his cookies and comparing cookies to diamonds.

There are endless games that can be played in the car; counting red cars, blue cars, traffic lights. How many trips did we make to the grocery store this week? In the grocery store, the task of loading the basket can be turned into the language of math. Let your child count the oranges you need. How many bananas are in this bunch? You can pick out one prize, one pack of gum, two boxes of cookies—the games are endless.

Dervla loved it when her parents planned parties. She and her mother would write out a list of people to invite. Her mother would ask, "How many chairs do we need for all these people?" Then the counting and lists would begin. How many hot dogs? How many bags of chips? Candy? It was always Dervla's job to count the guests as they arrived, and then count the napkins, the place mats, and so on. An activity of this nature leads to further activities such as dividing the extra or left over items.

Four-year-old Joseph loved music, and when he received his first set of drums his father bought him a metronome. He learned to tap his foot in time to the little instrument that helped him with his rhythm, and eventually began to tap his foot and click his drum sticks together in unison. "One, two, three, four!" he would click and tap, and then begin his drum solo in time to the metronome. His counting transferred to more sophisticated rhythms. He was learning the language of math as it encompassed the world of music.

PREPOSITIONS

As children with a math disability or difficulty get older and math problems become the layer of expectation that crosses them over into a world of mental confusion, chaos, and avoidance, pay some attention to prepositions. We use them in our daily language all the time, but are usually not aware of the power of those small words. Prepositions denote the abstractness of time, direction, or position. They can be small yet mighty words that have the power to change our interpretations of written and spoken language as it affects our general and specific understanding of an idea or a direction.

"Please pass the cookies *by* me" is much different from "Please pass the cookies *to* me." For the child who misuses the preposition, your misinterpretation of his intent makes you wrong. However, when the child has misinterpreted the preposition in written language, his inappropriate interpretation walks him down the pathway to misunderstanding, and eventually to an incorrect answer.

For young children a game that asks them to do something in the house or in the yard that includes the word *under* can be revealing about their understanding of the spatial aspects in language. Children may hide under the table or place one toy under another. If they are misinterpreting the word, you can do the activity with them, thereby mediating their learning of the preposition that becomes the abstract of time, direction, or position. Adding other prepositions in daily household activities can be helpful in building upon their existing understanding of spatial language. Just remember that it's OK to make mistakes with it. This becomes a mediated learning experience that is ongoing. Making mistakes is one way we construct knowledge.

When children are older and prepositions are embedded within word problems it can be helpful to work with your child to identify the prepositions and then determine how that preposition impacts the meaning of the statement or question. Never hesitate to encourage your child to draw out her understanding of a key word on graph paper; of, from, in, except, and so on. Each tiny preposition has the power to change meaning in a sentence, in word problems, in directions, and in how the language of math is interpreted.

TECHNIQUES: I LOVE GRAPH PAPER!

When children begin to learn how to add columns, subtract, multiply, and divide, it's helpful to give them graph paper to assist in their new visuospatial tasks. The object is to teach them how to align columns, not to see if they fail at the task. Many math teachers today do not offer graph paper when children are introduced to columns. You can suggest that your child begin by using graph paper, and then gradually see if they can align columns by themselves, or if their visuospatial ability level requires that they continue to use an aid of this nature. Graph paper is not cheating. It's a technique that can only help in being able to do math within specified guidelines. Look at it as being akin to the colored bookmark or index card that helps you keep track of what line you're on when reading your favorite magazine or a required textbook.

Graph paper is equally as helpful when children have difficulty in placing a decimal point in the appropriate space. This may be a temporary measure for some children, and again, for others it may be a technique that will need to be employed for a longer period of time. When students begin to understand how the misplacement of a decimal point changes their answer to a wrong answer, they look for ways to manage their visuospatial difficulties. Graph paper is just one way that is relatively inconspicuous, and it is available in any office supply store.

The concept of fractions is extremely difficult for some children and adolescents. By using manipulatives designed for classroom use, or materials from the home, it becomes clearer to some students what one-half means, a quarter, and so on. When these concepts are brought to written exercises, graph paper can be used to draw out the relationships.

CONCLUSION

This chapter has given you an overview of the language of math, and indeed math is a language of its own. It communicates an exactness to us through numbers and symbols, and sometimes requires that we arrive at correct answers through a great deal of mental language as we engage in computation. As children, we first learned quantity through our experience and relationships with concrete objects, nature, and other human beings in our lives. Then the task became much more sophisticated as the written and spoken word accompanied or prefaced the computation of numbers. Word problems! Can you remember them? Do you watch your child as he tackles these various levels of development and expectations?

A metacognitive experience, or becoming aware of how we learn, can be achieved by looking at how we ourselves learned and how we parent our children. We can also facilitate this process in our children by asking that they become observers of how they arrived at an answer. We can help them to construct their knowledge and create a constructivist learning environment at home. We can encourage children to talk to us about how they counted their toys, and how they knew Lori had more candy pieces than Brandon did. We can help them add to their existing language of math by coaxing them to draw pictures of their activities. The world of visualization is another layer of language that can unlock doors to understanding for some children, and add the richness of diverse thinking for others.

If your child has been diagnosed with a math disability, begin to pay closer attention to the jargon used in the evaluations and individual education plan. Buy the *Diagnostic and Statistical Manual* (DSM-IV) in the bookstore, and keep abreast of the latest books and/or videotapes on learning disabilities. Be a savy consumer of education for your child. Experiment with math at home. Play games. Have some fun with it, and try to take some of the sting out of what might have become a task that is dreaded by both you and your child.

If your child has not been diagnosed with a math disability, but does experience difficulty in other areas of her learning, bring this to the attention of the teacher. If a language-based disability or difficulty exists, it may eventually interfere with being able to interpret word problems. Although as parents, it's so difficult to be ready for everything that is tossed our way, we can try to stand guard against some of the issues that may be camouflaged. On the other hand, it's important as well to not look for problems where none exist at that time. Sometimes it feels nearly impossible to be vigilant enough in order to intervene when necessary, and other times it feels as if our vigilance is overwhelming to our children and to ourselves.

It would be so simple to sit back and let the school systems take care of everything. If your child is not doing well in math, the teacher will know what to do and will make sure that good judgment is employed in the best interest of your child. Are you comfortable with that? Classrooms are still too large in most public schools, and a math disability can go undiagnosed in many cases for years. Maybe you're not equipped to teach your child all that math he has to know in order to survive school and the world that awaits him, but you can begin by just noticing, watching, and talking to your child about numbers, arithmetic, language, problem-solving, games.

If you remember nothing else, please remember that mistakes are OK—yours and your child's.

11

Tools of the Trade: Using Technology to Enhance Learning

Kristian's handsome face flushed with a pride he could not contain. His mouth twisted in a quirky grin as he struggled to contain the exuberant joy he was feeling. "The handcuffs have been removed!" he proclaimed as the smile spread across his face. He brought his wrists together forcefully, then snapped them apart with a flourish, flinging his arms outward. "I am free!"

Janna regarded him with affection and a joy that almost matched his own. This was a different young man than the one who had arrived at the college four months earlier. He had come with lots of "baggage" and the expectation that his instructor would tutor him in the content matter of his college courses, do his homework with him, and perform as his scribe, writing down what he dictated when he had papers and other writing assignments. Though accomplished and self-assured in other areas of his life, Kristian had no faith in his own ability to handle the written language tasks essential for college survival.

Janna remembered in her mind's eye the tall, elegant stranger who had appeared in her doorway that first day. She was struck right away by his self-contained composure, his refined politeness and cosmopolitan air. At only twenty-one, he was already a successful entrepreneur in his native Sweden. His competence was also evident in his successful negotiations of the ins and outs involved in applying and getting accepted to a college in a foreign land, figuring out how to get the best exchange rates on his money, settling into a cozy apartment in the Back Bay, mastering the public transportation system and the tangled layouts of Boston's winding streets, and making the hundreds of adjustments necessary when one leaves the familiar far behind. Most people would find this a significant challenge, but Kristian handled it with equanimity. He seemed surprised that Janna regarded his success in these matters as an accomplishment. She remembered the way he regarded her unbelievingly when she confessed that her own spatial difficulties would have made all this exceedingly difficult for her.

In spite of his competence in real-world, common-sense ventures, however, Kristian's self-assurance didn't extend to the academic sphere. Though he had tried mightily to conceal it, Janna had recognized the fear he hid behind his mask of politeness that first day. His posture was rigidly erect. His intelligent gray eyes tracked her every move warily, the way a cat, feigning indifference, keeps careful watch on an unfamiliar intruder. He felt threatened, and it would be a challenge to get him to trust her enough to remove the armor.

As Janna had expected, during his first few months, Kristian protected himself against vulnerability. A highly intelligent young man, Kristian's performance throughout school had been severely restricted by dyslexia and dysgraphia. Held in bondage by his inability to transcribe his thoughts in written language, Kristian had developed a variety of coping mechanisms, many of which were ineffective. His strategies had allowed him to survive, but not to thrive academically.

Chief among his survival tools was avoidance of writing. He used his excellent negotiation skills to procure accommodations that allowed him to demonstrate his knowledge orally. He enlisted parents, friends, and tutors as scribes. When Janna tried to get him to work on doing his own writing, he flatly refused. When she pushed, he resisted even more stubbornly. She tried to assure him that his ideas were superior and that he was ready to take the next step of putting his thoughts down on paper independently. It didn't work. So strong was the bondage in which he was held, so firm his belief that he could not break free, Kristian steadfastly refused to work on acquiring new writing skills and strategies. Janna was concerned about the reliance he had on her for help with written assignments. She didn't want to foster dependency. She knew only too well that a child who was always carried would never learn to walk.

One day when Janna had been pushing him a little harder than usual, Kristian had exploded in frustration. For the first time he openly revealed what he was feeling. The pain on his face was evident as he described years of schooling in which he had been separated from his peers and made to attend "special classes" for children with disabilities. He had missed out on opportunities to study foreign languages and other subjects of interest to his alert and questioning mind. He was forced instead to spend his time on unproductive remedial reading and writing exercises.

In high school he was channeled, angry and disheartened, into a vocational curriculum though he had made it clear that he wanted to attend college. Finally he had heard about a college in the United States that would provide support for him and that believed in his potential. Two years after high school, he left his homeland against the advice of well-meaning teachers and parents and set forth in search of the dream he wouldn't let die. Now Janna's efforts to get him to work on improving his writing were bringing back all of the unproductive and humiliating moments from his past. His shame at his inadequacies prevented him from even attempting to put words on paper. Janna guessed that he thought he would, once again, be judged less capable, less worthy.

It took months to build trust with Kristian, but gradually he came to understand that he was in a safe place, a place where he could put words on paper (no matter how creatively they were spelled!) and wouldn't be judged as stupid or relegated to a back room. He began to take a few tentative steps forward. He was using prewriting strategies for generating ideas and organizing them. He was using textbooks on tape and scanning other reading matter into a computer equipped with software that read the material back to him. But the major move occurred when he finally agreed to try a software program that would convert his spoken words into text on the computer screen. It was this that freed him from bondage. Within days of his initial training, he was independently completing assignments that had always required help from others. He was dictating his answers for essay exams into a microphone connected to the computer instead of recording them on audiotape. He was printing them out himself instead of having someone else type them from the audiotape. He could add, delete, and reorganize his ideas. He was soon proudly announcing to Janna that he wouldn't need her help any more to write weekly journals for his management class. He was sending long e-mails to friends and relatives back home. Once the handcuffs had been removed, there was no stopping him!

THE TOOL BOX

Picture a well-stocked garage or basement workroom filled with all sorts of machinery and gadgets. To those of us who are mechanically challenged, some of them look like weird medieval torture instruments. We have no clue as to the purpose of many of them; we're afraid to operate others. But to the artisan, carpenter, or mechanic, they are the instruments of expression, creation, and restoration. Tools for learning are like that, too. Learning what they can do and how to use them properly opens the door to many possibilities.

There are a number of tools that are available today to help individuals with disabilities of all sorts. Some of them are low-tech tools that have been around for a while. Others are more modern tools based on the advances in computer technology that have revolutionized so much of life today.

LOW-TECH SOLUTIONS

Low-tech tools have long been used to help students with various disabilities. Tape recorders can be used to tape classes, record material for study, and provide assistance in reading. They can also be used to listen to recordings of books and magazines. Books on audiotape are available in libraries and bookstores. Textbooks and magazines on tape are provided by Recordings for the Blind and Dyslexic and the Library of Congress National Library for the Blind and Physically Handicapped. A teacher or learning specialist can help you apply for these materials. Special four-track tape players are often needed to play tapes from these sources. These tapes make it possible for a dyslexic child to keep up with reading in the various subject areas. Following the printed text while listening may even help him to improve his word recognition skills.

Calculators are a low-tech solution helpful for children with dyscalculia or with memory problems that make it difficult to recall math facts like multiplication tables even though they have the reasoning to do the problems. They are also very useful for checking answers after doing the problems manually. If an answer is wrong, your child can go back to find his error and learn from it. Some "talking calculators" will read back the numbers that are entered, a helpful check for children who tend to transpose numbers or make other errors in copying problems. Large key, colorful calculators will be easier to use and more attractive for young children. High school students will need more functions and college students enrolled in statistics or science courses will probably need a scientific calculator.

HIGH-TECH SOLUTIONS

We can group these computer-based solutions into five categories according to the various roles they can play in your child's learning: assistive or adaptive technology, instructional software, organizing tools, writing tools, and information sources.

ASSISTIVE OR ADAPTIVE TECHNOLOGY

The voice recognition software that made Kristian feel as if his hand-cuffs had been removed is an example of one type of assistive technology. The term assistive technology refers to hardware and software that help individuals with disabilities to perform activities they might not be able to handle without assistance. These tools can help your child to work around his disability. Instead of enlisting the aid of a human helper, assistive technology provides the learner with a tool he can use himself, resulting in greater independence and sense of self-efficacy.

There are new developments in this area every day, resulting in improvements to products, greater ease of use, and lower costs. Among the types of assistive technology used for students with learning disabilities are voice-to-text systems, text-to-voice systems, scanning pens, software that enlarges the size of the characters on the computer screen, and personal data managers.

Voice is converted to text through speech recognition systems. These programs (like *Dragon Naturally Speaking*), installed on your home computer, allow your child to speak his sentences into an attached microphone and see his words appear miraculously on the screen. For the child who can express himself orally, but has trouble encoding his ideas in written language, this is truly a wonderful product. It does, however, require practice and programming the computer to recognize each individual's particular vocal quirks and local pronunciations. The more your child uses it, the better the program will be able to accurately convert what he is saying.

Text-to-voice systems have the opposite function: converting the written word into speech. Text-to-voice systems include speech synthesizer/screen readers (like *Cast eReader* or *Real Speak*), which are programs that will read out loud whatever the child downloads or types with his keyboard. This allows him to listen to his own compositions. Hopefully, in hearing what he wrote, he can find errors he may have missed in visually checking his printed words. Besides reading material typed in through the keyboard, many of these programs can read text from disks, CD-ROMs, and the Internet. This makes them very valuable to the dyslexic child who is doing research for a project but can't read some of the material he finds on his topic.

Text-to-voice systems also include products meant to be used with a scanner (like those made by Kurzweil/Lernout and Haupsie). In these systems, text from noncomputerized sources like books or newspaper articles is placed on a scanner attached to the computer. Once scanned in, the optical character recognition (OCR) software can read the print and convert it to speech.

A major benefit of text-to-voice software is that the student can see the words on the screen as he hears it in his earphones. Most programs highlight each word on the screen as it is spoken. This provides practice in reading as well as a way of accessing needed material. The main drawback of text-to-voice systems is the computerized voice that sounds like a robotic friend rather than a real person. It's not perfect, but it is a workable solution for many children, especially those in higher grades with heavy reading demands and materials that are beyond their word recognition levels.

Hand-held scanners or reading pens work on similar principles and provide the advantage of portability, being not much larger than a thick marker. One type, WizCom's Quicktionary, allows a student to scan a single word in a book, hear the word read aloud, and see its definition in a small built-in display screen.

Another hand-held scanner, the QuickLink Pen by WizCom Technologies, doesn't have the direct capability of converting text to voice, but does have an array of other helpful functions. It allows you to scan text from a print source into its memory, save it in a file, and then transfer it to your computer. Once the text is transferred to the computer, you can use your screen reader to convert it to voice. You can also read the files directly from the pen through a small display window. The QuickLink Pen could be used to scan important facts and definitions from a textbook chapter. Once transferred to the computer, your child could print out the file, producing a neat, readable set of notes to study—a boon for the child with visual-motor problems or dysgraphia that makes note-taking difficult.

At this stage in their development, however, hand scanners are somewhat difficult to control and are not perfectly accurate. They would be most useful for high school and college students to aid their acquisition of course content.

INSTRUCTIONAL SOFTWARE: THE COMPUTER AS TUTOR

Christopher sat glumly at the kitchen table. He picked dejectedly at the sleeve of his Chicago Bulls sweatshirt. Tomorrow was the big test on all the multiplication tables from one to twelve. He'd been trying to learn them for the past three months, but still hadn't mastered the higher ones. Some tricks he had easily mastered allowed him to figure out multiples of five, nine, and ten. But even in these, he wasn't as fast as he needed to be. He couldn't get the answers written down before the teacher moved quickly on to dictate the next question. He kept copying the lists, reciting the math facts over and over, sometimes out loud and sometimes in his head. He was getting discouraged because he couldn't recall some of the ones he had known just last week.

"Need some help, Champ?" his Dad asked as he made tuna sandwiches for their lunches the next day. His dad wanted to help, but he had a lot to do being Mr. Mom since Chris's mother had died last year. Most nights he brought papers home from the office that kept him up late after getting dinner, doing laundry, and shuttling Christopher and his brother Mark to hockey practice or scouts. Christopher wished his dad had time to help him practice his multiplication tables every night like his friend Michael's dad did, but he knew he didn't. "I'm OK, Dad," Christopher answered and took out a clean piece of paper to copy the sevens table one more time.

Many parents have wished they could have a live-in tutor to provide additional educational support for their children. Children with learning disabilities do need more time from caring adults and sometimes their parents just don't have enough time to meet their needs. The computer can be a tool to assist with this. It will never (we can't emphasize this enough) replace the human presence. However, it can do some tutoring tasks for you and your child, leaving you free to do the things no machine can.

Instructional software run on your computer can remove some of the burden on both parents and children and can make many learning processes more efficient and faster. This is important in our time-short lifestyle and helpful for the child who does take longer to do his work. Computer software can provide "drill and practice," especially in some of the rote memory tasks that some learning disabled children struggle with. Many children with learning disabilities need more exposure to a new word or a new math procedure than the typical learner needs. Neither the teacher nor the parent may be able to provide the number of exposures that would firmly record the new skills or facts in the child's memory. Too often the child with a learning disability who needs additional instruction and reinforcement in basic skills doesn't receive it. The class moves on to the next level before the child has achieved mastery. This sets up a chain reaction in which successive levels of learning are also compromised because the child is building on a weak foundation. The outcome is sadly only too certain—a bright student reading or performing in math far below grade level and getting further and further behind as he moves up in grade.

Software programs providing instruction in a wide range of reading, math, and English skills at all levels are readily available. Children can practice word recognition and phonics skills as well as higher level comprehension, thinking, and problem-solving skills. Older children who need further development of basic phonics can use these programs in the privacy of their own homes and can get the multiple exposures they need in order for the skills to become automatic.

The computer has infinite patience and doesn't mind going over the multiplication tables or the spelling rules hundreds of times. It can provide practice in math facts like the multiplication tables and in performing mathematical calculations quickly and correctly. It can reinforce spelling words and give your child the opportunity to apply essential reading and grammar skills like phonics and sentence completion. And it can do it in a way that your child may actually enjoy!

The best learning software provides interaction, allowing your child to be actively involved in games and activities related to building skills. It avoids mindless repetition in favor of exercises that demonstrate underlying concepts, patterns, and principles. It teaches material through lively, visual and auditory modes of delivery and not simply through lines of text on screen. Some of this software concentrates on teaching new skills while other programs provide opportunities for drill and practice. Drill and practice software has sometimes been given a bad name, but it does have its place, especially when material your child needs to master is presented in a creative, interesting way.

Other instructional software gets your child thinking by engaging her in activities involving problem-solving, classification, logical sequencing, and identification of cause-effect relationships. Simulation games allow her to apply creativity and critical thinking to novel situations. Still other software programs are basically electronic storybooks that attract children with bright visuals and sound effects. They're not so different from the comic books many of us devoured in our youth, but these stories are accompanied by movement and sound as well as pictures! Many of these storybooks highlight the words as they are read aloud on the computer. This opportunity to match sound and symbol can improve word recognition. Even more importantly, these electronic books may decrease frustration and increase your child's interest in literature.

Because of their excellent graphics capabilities, computers aren't limited to development of mathematical or language skills. They provide ample opportunities for children to build visual-spatial skills, too. Using maps; making charts and graphs; following mazes or visual clues; performing visual-motor tasks; changing the orientation, shape, or size of figures on the screen; identifying details in pictures or matching visual images are all helpful ways for your child to develop her abilities in this area. Some of these programs encourage creativity by allowing your child to create visual designs, photo slide shows, animations, greeting cards, banners, and multimedia presentations.

Software programs in the content areas can also support your child's learning. Science programs allow kids to dissect virtual organisms, see close-ups of microscopic cells, trace the path of the bloodstream through the human body. Social studies games expand your child's knowledge of geography, history, and social concepts. Foreign language programs provide essential auditory input that no textbook can. The multisensory approach used in the best instructional software accommodates various learning styles, allowing children to use the channels that work best for them while at the same time developing those that are weaker.

ORGANIZING TOOLS

Another challenge your child can use the computer for is getting organized. Organization doesn't come easy for many kids with learning disabilities. These are the kids with the messy bedrooms (watch out for those cookies under the bed!), notebooks full of torn and wrinkled papers, and ideas swirling through their brains in everchanging patterns. When it comes time to produce an important phone number, they've often misplaced or lost it. When they need to organize ideas for a paper or report, they are helplessly overwhelmed. Fortunately, there are lots of ways you can help your disorganized child to create some order in her life. Some of the strategies make use of high-tech solutions.

Personal data managers can be used by older children to support both their organization and their memory. These electronic phone, address, and date books have miniature keyboards to enter information and small screens to access it. Some even allow voice input of data. Data from some of these devices can be downloaded onto the computer so you can print out the contents. Some are equipped with alarms that can signal the child who loses track of time that she'd better leave for her dentist appointment. The teenager who resists using a regular calendar may be intrigued by the novelty and find a personal data manager a more agreeable way to keep track of her schedule.

High tech has solutions that can help your child to organize her own thoughts or the ideas contained in a textbook chapter, too. Outlining programs set up the format and automatically adjust the numbering and lettering when additions or deletions are made, keeping everything in sequence. These programs can help your child see the structure and relationships in the material. There are also programs that allow more free-flowing, visual representations of relationships. These mapping programs (like *Inspiration*) are designed so your child can put a main topic in the center and draw lines to branch out from it, placing subtopics in circles or squares around the center. The resulting graphic will help them to see both the forest and the trees. When used as a prewriting exercise, both outlining and mapping programs can provide a place to begin and help prepare your child for the next step.

Word Processing Software: A Writer's survival Kit

The dining room table was a mess! Books and articles were strewn haphazardly across the surface of the big oak table. Crumpled pages littered the floor. Brownie crumbs left grease stains on a sheaf of pages covered with handwriting Aisha's teachers had referred to as "chicken scratch" or "hieroglyphics." Cross-outs, arrows, yellow stickies, and notes written in the margins were evidence of the major reorganization effort under way. In the middle of it all, Aisha slumped in her chair. "Aaargh!" she growled. "I can't stand this! I'll never get my report finished. I'd like to throw this thing out the window!"

Her complaints brought her mother into the room. "Aisha, you go through this every time. And every time you get it done in the end. And usually you end up with a good grade too. So just stick with it."

Aisha pushed her fingers through her thick chestnut curls and massaged her aching head. "Why does it have to be so hard?" she wailed. "There must be an easier way."

There is. The word processing software on your family's personal computer is a survival kit for the child with learning disabilities. Once your child has reached the age and grade where he is writing reports and research papers, this tool becomes practically indispensable. The task of collecting, organizing, and integrating various pieces of information into a written product is like climbing Mt. Everest for children with a variety of learning disabilities ranging from dyslexia and dysgraphia to visual/spatial and organizational problems. The word processor gives these children the equipment they need to make the climb successfully.

There are lots of reasons why writing on the word processor may be superior to handwriting for your child. First, once the child knows the keyboard and has developed a minimal level of typing skill, the fine motor skills involved in striking an individual key are not as involved as those involved in printing or handwriting a letter. Children with visual/motor deficits or with dyslexia who may struggle to get the direction correct each time they write a "d" or a "b" will find that the word processor removes some of the burden involved in physically encoding letters and words on paper.

Children who have trouble organizing their thoughts and expressing ideas in logical sequences will be able to move their paragraphs and sentences around, add and delete ideas, and insert needed transitions between sections. Those children whose handwriting or poor spatial organization results in messy and confusing papers will be able to hand in reports that not only look better, but are more understandable to the teacher. This simple fact contributes to your child's pride in his work and has been shown to improve grades.

In addition to the basic writing functions, word processors have additional features that can improve the quality and accuracy of your child's written work. Spell checkers allow your child to discover and correct spelling errors and also build awareness in your child of the need to edit his work for such mistakes. An added bonus is that spell checking provides your child with immediate feedback and multiple exposures to the correct spelling of words. Over time, this can contribute to improvement of reading and spelling skill.

Spell checkers, of course, are not a cure-all for children who have major spelling and reading deficits. These children will need your help to spell check their work because they may not be able to select the correct spelling from among the suggested alternatives when the computer identifies a mistake. One college student, a male, wrote an entire paper about his bout with "vaginal meningitis." He had been unable to spell or select the proper spelling for the word "viral" and accepted the first suggestion made by the spell checker. Fortunately, his tutor caught the error before the paper was handed in to his English professor. He was able to enjoy the joke in the safe confines of the academic support program. However, he might have felt humiliated in the classroom where the teacher often read student essays aloud and where students were required to swap papers and give each other feedback. So after your child has done as much as he can independently, it's a good idea for you to take a last minute look at the product, remembering always to comment on what's right about his work before pointing out what's wrong.

Grammar checkers are even trickier. For example, many of them routinely question anything written in passive voice ("Mark was bitten by the dog.") and suggest using active voice ("The dog bit Mark."). Your child may not be able to distinguish between what is actually an error and what is simply a style choice. The grammar checker is more helpful to someone who knows grammar fairly well and uses it to find an error he may have overlooked. At this point, the human approach is still better for most kids for checking grammar and style.

The thesaurus can be very helpful, but again has its drawbacks. For example, if you look up the word "drawback" you will find "side effect" among suggested alternatives. A child with limited vocabulary might choose the latter when it is inappropriate in the context. Again, let your child experiment and then go over his written work with him. This will provide opportunity for discussion of word meanings and their connotations. Regular discussions like this can do wonders for raising your child's level of verbal awareness and expanding his vocabulary.

The very children who most need to clean up, edit, or revise their written work are usually the ones who find this task the most burdensome. They loathe copying or rewriting their work, even if they recognize that it needs revision. You may have had your child tell you not to mark the errors on his handwritten paper because he is not going to copy it over again. He'd rather pass it in knowing there are errors than subject himself to the stress or tedium of laboriously handwriting the work again. The computer removes that problem. Corrections are easy.

In addition to the basics of allowing your child to type in, edit, and print his work, word processors also have several formatting features that can be helpful for school work. For example, they make it easy to create tables that your child can use to organize data in a research report. They allow your child to insert clip art or put boxes and shading around particular material in a report. They let your child insert footnotes or endnotes, automatically reserving correct spacing at the bottom of the page and allowing for new footnotes to be added as needed—a blessing for kids with spatial problems and for those who might forget to include a reference.

Word processors or writing programs designed for younger children provide many of the same features found in standard word processing programs, but are easier to use and have formatting features geared to elementary and middle school writing assignments. For example, some have book report templates and project templates. These templates help your child to organize his work and remind him to include such essential information as his name, the date, and the title of his report. Formats like this build mental templates too so as the child becomes more and more familiar with them, he forms in his own mind a concept of the standard formats for various types of writing assignments. Writing programs for children usually include fun and easy-to-use graphics your child can insert into his reports as well. This provides motivation and enjoyment for a task that may seem like drudgery for some children.

There is a wide range of specialized writing software available for getting your child interested and involved in writing for pleasure. These are tools to trigger imagination and creativity. They include storybook makers that allow your child to write and illustrate original books. These programs let your child experiment with dialog, plot, and characters, familiarizing him with the basic elements of literature as well as developing his expressive language and thinking abilities. Some of these programs provide "triggers," ideas to help children get started on a story. Others allow your child to add clip art, musical background, and even moving illustrations. You can also help your child to print and bind his own work. Writing his own books gives a child a sense of accomplishment and a greater appreciation for the written word. These original books make great gifts for Grandma and Grandpa too!

You should also be aware of some excellent portable solutions for writing that can be used as supplements to the word processing programs on your home computer. Consider getting your child to use a hand-held electronic speller/dictionary/thesaurus combination. Some of these devices even read the word aloud so your child can be sure that the word he has found is the word he thinks it is. He can carry his electronic dictionary with him from home to school to library and back again. If specified in his educational plan, he can use it in class for those spontaneous writing assignments that dyslexic or dysgraphic children dread.

Another wonderful portable device is the AlphaSmart from Intelligent Peripheral Devices. This keyboard with a small viewing screen is no bigger than a three-ring binder and weighs only about two pounds. Your child can use it for notetaking in class, writing essays at his desk, doing assignments in the library or study hall, or creating poems on the beach. The AlphaSmart stores the text and later your child can download it to your home computer or directly to your printer. It is inexpensive to buy, truly simple to use, completely nonthreatening. It's a great place to start for the child who might have trouble learning the ins and outs of a more complicated word processor, but is also popular with advanced computer users who employ it as a portable peripheral.

INFORMATION SOURCES

Maya, true to form, waited until 8:00 P.M. to announce that she had a report on Martin Luther King, Jr., due the next day. While it still frustrated her mother, Eva knew they'd be able to handle it. It wasn't like it used to be—piling into the car for a frantic trip to the town library, an anxious search of the shelves, furious page flipping and photocopying, and all the while their enemy, the clock, moving ahead faster than it should. Now that they had a computer, the job would be a lot easier. In a flash they saw Reverend King's face fill the screen, heard his resonant voice deliver his haunting and inspiring words: "I have a dream. . . " It still sent chills up and down Eva's back. She hoped it would inspire Maya, too. The encyclopedia on CD-ROM was far, far removed from the worn *Britannica* she and her sister had used as kids.

Computers have put a world of information at our fingertips. Some of it is contained on disks and CD-ROMs. Even more is available through the Internet. This worldwide network allows access to databases containing print documents, images, music, and other resources right in our own homes. Whole books can be read in virtual libraries. Search engines sort through the online reference sites and find what we need in the blink of an eye (or the touch of a mouse). Tutors provide help with math homework. Chat rooms allow us to join conversations online with experts in all fields: politicians, astronauts, and ordinary people who live in our town. Each site we discover provides us with links to others.

Of course, this is when it's all working well. As with any tool, you do have to develop some proficiency in accessing this powerful resource. More is not always better. For a child who has trouble distinguishing significant from nonsignificant details or relevant from irrelevant information, it can be a nightmare. For the one with attention deficit disorder, it can provide endless distraction that keeps him from accomplishing his goal. Children need instruction and practice to develop skills and strategies for using the Internet. If you haven't become familiar with it yet, you can learn together. You may want to pick up a guidebook, take a course, or visit your local library to get some help. Check out the resources listed in the Appendix of this book, too.

CHOOSING TECHNOLOGICAL SOLUTIONS

There are many things to consider in choosing the technological solutions that will work for your child. It's a good idea to get some advice from an expert in educational technology before you invest a lot of money in something that may not be right for your family. Always consider where, when, and how any particular technological tool will be used. For some families, a laptop computer fits their needs best while for others a full-sized computer with scanner, printer, and CD-ROM drive is needed.

Compatibility is another consideration. You don't want to buy an expensive printer only to discover it won't work with the rest of your hardware. Software too has to be compatible with your hardware. Check out the kinds of programs you want to run and be sure the computer you purchase has the power, speed, and memory requirements you'll need. When buying equipment for your child, consider what type is used at school. It may be confusing for your child to switch back and forth between different systems and there are advantages to his being able to carry a disk between home and school.

You also want to find out how complicated any piece of technical equipment is to use. A data manager with too many bells and whistles may end up gathering dust. A simpler one with only the functions your child needs would have been more useful. In this regard, don't forget to consider the no-tech options as well. While an electronic speller is great for one child, a plain paper dictionary is better for another.

When selecting educational software, check out reviews in newspapers, educational publications like Scholastic's *Parent and Child*, and parent magazines, as well as in computer magazines and guides like *Family PC*. Ask teachers and librarians for suggestions. Talk to friends who have computers. Whenever possible, try the program out first. Involve your child in the selection, too. The more involved he is at every stage, the more likely he will be to use the material. Look for software that fits your child's learning style. Most children will enjoy programs that make learning a game, have attractive videos, and provide lively sound effects. Choose software that requires interaction rather than passive viewing. Children will tire of programs that are basically text on screen. That's no different from a traditional textbook and most kids feel they have enough of that in school. Look for programs that gradually build in difficulty. As your child masters one level, he can move to the next.

If your child is using the Internet, be sure to provide careful monitoring of his choices. If you wouldn't let your son wander around the local train station chatting with strangers, you wouldn't want to let him do this on the Web either. Some Internet providers have special connections for kids that limit them to child-safe sites. You can install software programs on your computer that will do this, too. Still, there is no substitute for your guidance. Experts recommend locating the computer in a family area rather than in your child's room. This reduces isolation and makes it easier for you to know where your child may be in cyberspace. Remember the old public service announcement on television: "It's ten o'clock. Do you know where your child is?"

LIVING AND LEARNING IN THE "BRAVE NEW WORLD"

Technological solutions have the potential to change the world of students with learning disabilities. Of course, the true transformation occurs within these individuals, as it did with Kristian whose story opened this chapter. It is the transformation from learned helplessness and feelings of inadequacy to a sense of self-efficacy and pride.

While technological solutions are wonderful, you can't expect them to work miracles. They are not electronic babysitters that can take care of your children's needs by themselves. The virtual world is not a replacement for the real world and real human contact. The best way to use technology is within a human context.

Neither is assistive technology a "cop out." Many children with learning disabilities do need the help of screen readers, voice-to-text systems, and other accommodations. These provide your child with the tools he needs to do the job. It would be foolish to try to pound in a nail with your bare hand when a hammer was available.

Technological solutions should, of course, be integrated into the broader context of your child's educational plan. These solutions should be part of a large web of interventions and support systems. They should be tailored to your child's specific needs and to her uniqueness as a person and as a learner. What works for one child does not work for another. You want to choose the right tool for the job. A hammer is great for pounding a nail, but it makes a poor screwdriver. Be sure your child is ready for the demands of any program she uses and consider both her abilities and disabilities. Programs that require a lot of on-screen text reading without audio accompaniment aren't the best way to reach a dyslexic child, and those that require careful listening may not be the best avenue for a child with receptive language deficits. As we have said so often throughout this book, it's important to know your own child. This is just as true when it comes to technology as it is in other areas. Walk this journey with her.

12

Navigating the System

Dr. Evah Nellsom sat with her head in her hands at her desk. Behind her was a picture window that overlooked the thick woods of coastal Maine. Occasional glimpses of cobalt blue peeked through the dense pines. Another window behind Evah was propped open with a copy of *A Closer Look*, its cover worn and wrinkled. The curtains gently billowed from the wind that brought the aromas of pine and salt air that comforted Evah during her most anxious moments.

She had just completed a tour of North America's west coast, and was exhausted. Before her was an open manila folder that contained the most recent case from her private practice. It was propped open next to a large pile of folders. She ran her fingers through her short hair, hoping to gain some sense of clarity from just staring at what lay before her. The work! The deadlines! She couldn't concentrate because she was so tired, and she instinctively knew that to tackle any files today would be counterproductive and more exhausting. She quickly jotted down the phone numbers and e-mail addresses of several parents to let them know that she was back in her office, and that she would be in touch with them within the next several days.

"Hmmm, navigating the system," she thought. "It's so difficult to learn. Parents of kids with learning disabilities have to *know* so much more, have to learn the ropes, the rules, and how to ride the waves of change that occur almost daily in education." She shook her head and thought how unfair it all was. Then she remembered the old red row-boat that rested on her front lawn that was now laden with colorful annuals, but reminiscent of years past when she navigated her way around the tiny harbor by herself. It was so like life itself she pondered, only navigating life for some families was like weathering a storm each day.

Evah began pacing her office in her bare feet, thinking about the file that lay open on her desk. It was her first priority. She picked it up and began carrying it under her arm, hoping that somehow the physical contact of the written material would transfer a groundbreaking idea that would help the Horton family. As she paced slowly back and forth in front of her old oak desk, she deeply inhaled the aromas coming through her window on this beautiful spring day. She paused to listen to a mockingbird, and smiled. Life really does go on, she thought to herself. Evah vowed to do the best she could for the Horton family, who were so obviously in distress.

A month ago, prior to leaving Maine for the west coast, Jeannette Horton called Evah from Boston. "Dr. Nellsom? I got your phone number from a brochure I found in the pediatrician's office. I would like to make an appointment to talk about my son, Casey."

Evah asked Jeannette Horton about the nature of the visit, and Jeannette related her past experiences with her son at home and in the classroom. Casey attended an exclusive private school in New England that claimed to be able to assist students with learning challenges, but seemed to be unable to help Casey. Jeannette Horton didn't know whether to keep him in this private school or move him to their local public school. She just didn't know where to begin. The private school told her that her son could receive educational diagnostic testing through the town in which she lived, and the public school in her town told her that she needed to seek private testing. It was an old story for Evah. And it was just as frustrating to hear it this time as it was to hear it for the first time years ago. Casey's story reminded her so much of Brian's story (chapter 9, this volume) some years ago. Now he was a college graduate!

The wind blew a strong scent of earth and sea through the room. It sounded like a heavy sigh and billowed the curtains as if to whisper a message. Evah knew that if she did nothing else today she would develop a preliminary plan of action for the Horton family. This would be her project for the next few days, until she felt she could tackle the growing pile of folders that sat menacingly on the corner of her desk. As she left the room she looked back at the pile. It seemed to look back at her. She walked with a purpose out of the office and into her kitchen, the Horton family's file still under her arm. The curtains flapped as if they applauded her decision.

Evah sat down with her mug of tea at the kitchen table and dialed Jeannette Horton's number. Three rings. "Hello?"

"Hi Mrs. Horton. This is Evah Nellsom. I just returned from the west coast and thought we should set up a meeting for this week. Is that possible for you? Can you drive to Maine? You're north of Boston, right?" There was a silence that Evah guessed stemmed from the element of surprise.

"Yes, yes, of course I can. Tell me when. It will take me about three hours I think."

"How about tomorrow? About noon?"

Jeannette was shocked. She never expected that Dr. Nellsom would call today and invite her to meet with her tomorrow. But it didn't matter. She would do whatever it took to make the meeting. Dr. Nellsom had an international reputation as a professional who genuinely cared about the educational success and well-being of her clients.

Jeannette quickly made arrangements and informed her family that she would be gone for the day tomorrow and would probably return later in the evening. She explained to her husband and two other children that this was all about Casey, and finding the best possible setting for him. No one questioned her decision to go to Maine. No one questioned the history of frustration and devotion the family had experienced in their efforts to make life easier for Casey, and for other family members.

Evah Nellsom sat at her desk late that evening, drafting an outline for Jeannette Horton. It looked something like this.

    I. Casey's educational history
   II. Casey's socioemotional history
 III. Casey's medical history
 IV. Casey's family: who are they?
   V. Options for educational diagnostic testing
        A. Pursuing the public school for accountability
            1. Parental rights and student rights
            2. What kind of testing is necessary?
        B. Pursuing private testing
            1. Who should do the testing?

2. How much should you pay?

3. What kind of testing is necessary?

VI. Options for schools: which one to choose based on Casey's needs

A. Teachers you know

B. Teachers you don't know

C. How to approach the schools following the testing

VII. The biggest question: *What does Casey want?*

VIII. How will we develop our recommendations together, as a team?

Evah felt better. The plan was on paper. It looked similar to this in most cases, with some variations according to the nature and severity of the problems being presented. She wished she could create a format, a formula, a one-size-fits-all recipe for every client. It just wasn't possible. By the time she was through with the session tomorrow with Jeannette Horton, there would be the beginnings of a picture of a boy, a learner, a human being who needed a plan, a map, and a reason to keep plugging away at his educational career. Then she would need to meet Casey. Alone. This needed to happen without his mother or the rest of the family around. Evah pulled out her organizer. She would be in Boston the end of the week. If she could manage to visit their home . . .

TUESDAY

At 5:00 A.M. the following morning Jeannette Horton was on the Maine Turnpike. She knew it was hours too early to be on the road for the noon appointment, but she was desperately afraid of getting lost, of losing the directions, of getting her right and left mixed up. She did that a lot, especially under stress. She'd find Dr. Nellsom's office, and then go find a place to have breakfast and read the newspaper.

Evah woke up early and reviewed her outline, crossing things out, adding last minute thoughts. Then she put on her sweatpants and T-shirt and went for a walk in the woods. It always helped to clear her head. She deeply inhaled the crisp air and moved briskly through the smooth pathways between the pines. She walked about a half mile and stood on the edge of the cliff staring at the water. It reminded her that on the larger scale of things in life, our frustrations seemed so tiny, so insignificant. What was important was the quality of our relationships and the sense of peace with ourselves we managed to salvage.

Jeannette found a coffee shop at 8:30 A.M. She only took one wrong turn, and it didn't take her too long to find her way back to the highway again. As she sat down, she noticed that her knees were shaking. Her hand trembled as she lifted the menu. A nice waitress a little older than Jeannette approached the table.

"Can I get you some coffee?"

"Oh! Decaf please. I'm so nervous this morning. I just drove in from Boston."

The waitress smiled and brought her coffee right over. Jeannette splashed coffee all over her suit because her hand was so unsteady.

"Whoa girl! What are you so nervous about?"

"Well, I have to find Dr. Evah Nellsom's office when I leave here. I should have done it first, but then I thought I'd just get lost again. I have an appointment at noon."

The waitress smiled again. "Oh, we know Evah real well here. She's in for coffee a few mornings a week—when she's around that is. She travels a lot, you know."

"Oh, really? You know her? What's she like?"

The waitress was thoughtful for a minute. "Well, she's just an ordinary woman I guess, but that's because we know her. She's from here. But her work. That's different. If it wasn't for her my Brian would never have gone to college. She really helped us get the kind of help we needed for him when he was in high school."

"That's really nice to hear, uh . . . what's your name? Mine is Jeannette."

The waitress held out her hand. "Nice to meet you Jeannette. My name is Lorna. You're going to be in good hands with Dr. Nellsom. Now what can I get you for breakfast?" She glanced at her watch. "It better be a big, long, breakfast because you've got a lot of time to kill."

At 12:01 P.M. sharp there was a polite tap at the front door. Evah didn't even hear a car pull up she was so engrossed in reading a new article on the new Wechsler Abbreviated Scale of Intelligence. She opened the door and smiled at her old friend. Aromas from the rowboat at rest on her front lawn drifted up to the front porch.

"Hi Lorna. What brings you out here?"

Lorna reached behind her and pulled Jeannette out in front. "Evah, this is Jeannette Horton, and I'm just making sure that she finds her way to your office OK." Lorna winked.

Evah opened the screen door wide. "Jeannette I'm so pleased you made it here alright. Thanks so much Lorna for making sure she arrived safely." Lorna waved good-bye as she climbed into her car and headed back into the center of town.

Jeannette felt speechless, and a little silly that her waitress had to deliver her for her appointment. Evah showed her down the hallway, past her living room and dining room, and to her office at the back of the house. A scruffy gray cat peeked around the corner of the kitchen to investigate.

"You have a lovely home Dr. Nellsom. Do you mind having clients come to your house?"

"No, of course not. I found after all these years that I had to create a work environment that was comfortable and therefore productive for me and for my clients as well." She seated herself in a chair next to Jeannette, careful not to separate herself behind her desk and away from her visitor.

Evah began by offering Jeannette a copy of the outline she created last night. She always tried to keep preliminary outlines to one page in order to keep the beginning of the process as simple and nonthreatening as possible.

"Please keep in mind Mrs. Horton that this is just a place to begin. Our discussion and follow-up meetings will take us to many, many places, and this outline will be reorganized over and over again until we have developed a plan for Casey that will work for him, and for all of you."

Jeannette nodded, scanning the outline, not knowing where Dr. Nellsom would begin. Evah thanked herself for keeping the outline brief.

"Let's start with the first item. Good place to start, huh?" Evah was trying hard to relieve some of Jeannette's obvious anxiety. Jeannette just nodded, frantically trying to decode the language. She was so full of fear she couldn't read the words. Nothing was making sense.

Evah began slowly. "OK now. Roman numeral one. Casey's educational history." She paused to study Jeannette's face. Jeannette nodded.

"Yes, I can fill you in if that's what you want."

Evah reached over to the tiny table between the two chairs and held up a tape recorder the size of a candy bar.

"Do you mind if we tape some of this Jeannette? I'll take notes, but I also would like to tape some of our discussion. This way we don't have to break the flow of our conversation, and I have a backup system for information if my notes are illegible—which they often are." She smiled at Jeannette. Jeannette nodded.

"OK with me. I just want to help Casey." She paused in thought for a moment. "I guess I should begin with preschool. Casey couldn't sit still. Everyone said he was hyperactive—you know how some people say that instead of saying your child is ADHD. I tried not to pay too much attention to what people said, but then his preschool teacher said that she didn't know if he was ready for kindergarten. That shocked me."

"Did Casey pass the kindergarten screening?" Evah immediately thought of several former clients whose stories began much the same.

"Well, yes, he did. And I did send him to kindergarten at the public school in our neighborhood. Maybe I did it just to prove the preschool teacher wrong. You know, you feel like people are being unfair when they judge your child like that. And, how would she know anyway?" She paused for a moment. "I guess I just didn't want to believe her."

Evah prodded a little. "Tell me what kindergarten was like for Casey."

"He was just as flighty there, too. I was always getting notes from the teacher telling me that Casey wouldn't cooperate, that he wouldn't stay in his seat. As the year progressed he began to get aggressive with the other kids. You know, get into tiffs. He would throw things, break things. Soon the principal called my husband and I into her office to tell us that she felt Casey needed diagnostic testing done for learning disabilities. Again . . . I was shocked."

"Did you follow through with testing Jeannette?"

"Yes, we did. He was tested through the school, and they said that he didn't have a learning disability. Or at least they didn't think so. They said he needed to be retested in another few years." She handed Evah a large white envelope.

"They said that he knew his alphabet, was beginning to read, and could do most of the things expected of him. They said he was just very, very difficult. Every time I asked what exactly was wrong then, they would become very evasive."

Jeannette pointed to the overstuffed envelope Evah held in her lap. "There are copies of the first testing, and then the testing he had when he was eight years old. The second testing also said he didn't have a disability, but that he was a behavior problem."

"Thank you Jeannette. I'll go over these later when I look through my notes and listen to the tapes. This will really help me to build a picture of who Casey is. Now . . . can you tell me what the rest of elementary school was like for Casey?"

"Well, it seemed to go from bad to worse. He was retained in the third grade—he couldn't get any of his work done. By that time he had a reputation for a badly behaved child in the classroom. He was a clown.

We always suspected it was in an effort to divert everyone's attention away from what he couldn't do."

Evah nodded. "Often that's true. Behaviors like that are sometimes masks that disguise what's really going on. That's perceptive of you and your husband, Jeannette."

Jeannette felt affirmed. It made her feel more confident. She continued. "In the fifth grade—and I don't know how we all made it that far—Casey was caught trying to steal a computer from his classroom. He set the hamsters free and burned a little girl's hair with a lighter. The list goes on and on." She began to cry. Evah handed her a tissue and waited patiently. She learned how important it was to let parents have quiet time as they collected their thoughts and emotions. She knew she couldn't fill up the space with chatter because she didn't want to take Jeannette away from her story. They needed to stay on track. Evah's cat, Naomi, peeked around the corner of the office and flicked her tail.

"Thank you Dr. Nellsom," Jeannette sniffed.

"Whenever you're ready Jeannette."

"Well, the principal finally suggested to my husband and me that Casey be put into a special class for kids who had behavior problems. This time I wasn't shocked, I was horrified. I felt that I had done everything that was asked of me, and that the school just couldn't figure out what was wrong with Casey. I also felt that they were somehow blaming me, like I was a bad mother or something. If they only knew the hell we went through at home!"

Evah knew that this is where her outline would be derailed, but necessarily so. Navigating always became tricky at this point. All of the aspects of Casey were intertwined and helped to make Casey who he was. This was just another case of integrating all the information in order to build a comprehensive picture.

"Well . . . at home Casey was more relaxed, and I found that we seemed to be able to handle him better than the school did. When he became frustrated we would either try to talk to him, which was often futile, or ask him to go to his room and work it out. As he got older, my husband put a chin-up bar and a punching bag in the garage. Casey would go out there and spend a half hour or so, and most of the time return to the house a much calmer person. We started doing that when he was about six years old."

"That's an excellent strategy, Jeannette. How was he at home with other family members?" Again, Evah realized they were wandering away from the outline, but it was necessary to gain as much information in order to integrate the aspects of self that made Casey who he was.

"He loves his older brother and sister. And they love him, although Casey has stretched their patience to the limit as well. He rarely needs help with his homework, but when he does, either his brother or sister will help. It seems though, that as he gets older he can't read the higher level books, and this is upsetting to him. His frustration level hits a peak quicker these days over his schoolwork. He can talk about the work they do in class, but he can't seem to get through the reading."

"You're giving me some good information, Jeannette. How does your husband interact with Casey?"

Jeannette looked uncomfortable. "Well, OK I guess. I told you that he put the punching bag and chin-up bar in the garage for him. Actually, my husband doesn't have much patience with Casey's antics and tantrums. When he has trouble in school he demands that Casey get his act together and request help from the teachers. Then Casey tries to explain what is happening with his learning, and his father just doesn't want to hear it. He wants to help, but wants it to go away. I guess we all do." She started to cry again. By this time Naomi had settled herself at Evah's feet, and was watching Jeannette carefully. Naomi resented intruders taking up so much time.

"Casey gets frustrated and then he gets his words all mixed up. This used to happen when he was a little boy, and now of course it's more noticeable. His father tells him to grow up and stop being such a baby!" She paused. "You know my husband loves Casey. I think he just doesn't know what to do, and wants him to be—you know—normal I guess."

"How old is Casey now?"

"He's fourteen. In the seventh grade. Should be the eighth but he was kept back, remember I told you that?" Evah nodded as she made a few notes. Naomi swatted at Jeannette's handbag that sat on the floor. She sank her teeth into the leather strap.

"What are his grades like, Jeannette?"

"Well, when he's in a class where he's not causing too much trouble, they're As and Bs. When he hates the class, they're usually Ds or Fs."

"When does he get Fs?"

"Usually in English and Spanish. He does write beautiful poetry though. And nice stories. He won an award last year for his short story. We were all very proud, especially his father. Although he ruined it when he asked Casey why he couldn't do that in every class!" Evah nodded again. Jeannette rolled her eyes in disgust.

"Dr. Nellsom, is my husband's attitude part of the problem?"

Evah fielded questions similar to this in most of her cases. Parents needed to place blame, and often mothers—or the chief caregivers—are the ones feeling blamed the most. If in turn they can find other people and circumstances to blame, the burden feels so much lighter, so much easier to manage.

"Jeannette, we all respond and react to our children's challenges in different ways. You have been watching Casey struggle all of his life. As his mother, you have tried to patch things up for him, go to meetings, meet with teachers, and probably feel very apologetic most of the time because of Casey's behaviors." Jeannette nodded understanding.

"Your husband is as frustrated as you are and wants his son to behave in a way that will bring him success. He will say and do different things than you do because he feels Casey's struggles in a very different way than you do. It's really alright to have these differences, Jeannette. It's normal. You're a family, and you're trying to do the best you can."

"Now tell me, Jeannette, how is Casey when you have company or other family over to visit?"

"He's OK. He's a very friendly young man actually. He likes to help people and wait on them when they come to visit. He likes to please I guess. He does get out of hand when there are other kids around his age . . . you know, it's when he gets kind of hyper. Will he ever stop that?"

Evah smiled and tried not to answer the question right away.

"How is he with younger children?"

"Great. As a matter of fact he babysits now for two families in the neighborhood. They love him. He's very responsible. He cooks, cleans, plays ball with them, plays games, and reads them stories. Little kids love Casey."

"Does he mind reading to them? I mean, does he initiate this, or do the kids ask him?"

Jeannette responded quickly. "Actually, I think Casey does most of it on his own. He's always picking up books for them at the mall, at yard sales. He has quite a collection . . . hey! I see where you're going with this, Dr. Nellsom."

They smiled at each other.

Evah said, "I didn't think for a minute that you wouldn't see where I was going with this. You are an excellent observer of your child's behaviors and feelings, Jeannette." Again, Jeannette felt somewhat empowered.

"He likes to read these books, doesn't he Dr. Nellsom? He feels in charge, doesn't he? Why wasn't I seeing that before?"

"Sometimes we just get so immersed in trying to make things better, we don't see the obvious. It was there for you to see, but you had to sit down and begin talking about it before it would surface in your conscious mind."

"Now, Jeannette, I want you to just glance briefly at the outline I gave you. We have already touched upon the first four items, some in more detail than others. And we will continue to add to this as time goes on. But you are giving me a good picture of who Casey is. That's very important in our work together."

Jeannette exhaled audibly. "This is hard work, isn't it?" Evah nodded.

"But it feels very good to talk about it Dr. Nellsom. Very good. I feel as if I'm finally doing something that might make a difference for Casey. You know, like we're fighting back."

"Yes, I understand completely. Now why don't we have some tea and lunch and resume our conversation about Casey. Let's go into the kitchen." The two women walked slowly down the hallway, with Naomi in the rear trying to figure out how long yet another intruder would stay in her house.

Jeannette and Evah sat at the kitchen table with their sandwiches and mugs of black tea. With Jeannette's permission Evah again snapped on her tape recorder. Naomi meowed from the other side of the old screen door. Jumping on top of the kitchen table to scare Jeannette had earned her an immediate dismissal from the kitchen.

"Tell me a little about Casey's medical history, Jeannette. Start with his birth, and then try to outline for me any significant illnesses or injuries he may have sustained in childhood."

"I guess the birth was normal. He was just over five pounds. I nursed him for six months. He was very, very alert. Too alert sometimes. He never slept. He watched people carefully. Like a cat."

"When did he begin to talk, Jeannette?"

"He babbled on time I guess, but he was pretty late with actual words, and didn't string a sentence together that made any sense until he was almost four. He had a really difficult time pronouncing his words, and in preschool and kindergarten the kids made fun of him. That's when I noticed the behaviors change to being more aggressive. More hitting and lashing out." She thought about what she had said. "Do you think he was angry and frustrated, Dr. Nellsom?"

"It does sound that way, doesn't it, Jeannette?" Jeannette nodded sadly.

"And, his brother and sister teased him sometimes. I don't think they meant to hurt his feelings, but they did I'm sure." There was a pause in conversation.

"At the dinner table Casey started speaking less, and started acting out more at around that time. He would clown around, spill things, annoy his father. Then the trouble would begin."

Evah knew she had to prod Jeannette back on track. "What about any illnesses, injuries?"

"Oh, yes . . . Casey had a head injury that resulted in a concussion when he was seven. He fell off the garage roof. Don't even ask! He was always in trees, on roofs, in situations where he constantly flirted with danger. It's amazing my hair isn't completely white by now!" Both women laughed.

"How long did he have the concussion?"

"Oh, I don't know. A few days. But he didn't lose consciousness."

"Did you notice any change in him? In his behaviors? His school work?"

"No, although his concentration seemed a bit off. But I think it returned to normal—or at least what is normal for Casey."

"Any other injuries or illnesses?"

"He had the usual childhood illnesses. But then he did have a second concussion two years after the first—when he was nine. He was playing hockey, got into a fight after the game and took a nasty blow to the head from a stick. Actually he did lose consciousness briefly, but it didn't seem to affect him too much." Evah nodded.

"Dr. Nellsom do you think the concussions made Casey's behaviors worse?"

"It's pretty hard to say. Casey was experiencing problems with concentration prior to both injuries according to your recollection. They may or may not have exacerbated his already existing difficulty with his ability to attend, to concentrate."

"It's part of the puzzle, isn't it, Dr. Nellsom?"

"That's right."

Jeannette and Evah continued their conversation, moving back and forth from Casey's medical history to his family life, his socioemotional development, and the behaviors and attitudes he exhibited presently. Finally, at 5:00 P.M. Evah put her pen down and clicked off the recorder for the last time. She sat back in her chair and ran her fingers through her hair, a gesture Jeannette had become accustomed to over the past several hours.

"You probably need to be getting back home Jeannette, and I need to rest. Tonight I'll review my notes and look over the testing. We'll meet again in a few days, OK?"

"Just name the time. I'll be here."

"Actually, I was hoping to visit with Casey at your home. Would that be convenient? Possibly on Friday? I'll be doing some business in Boston in the morning."

Jeannette's mind was tired, but she made a quick mental scan of the house and decided she could get everything in order within three days.

"And please Jeannette . . . don't clean your house. I just want to meet with Casey. And would your husband be at home on Friday?"

"Ah, not normally, but he can manage it if you think it's important. Maybe for lunch. He could come home for lunch, and we could all eat together. Is that alright?"

"That would be wonderful if it's not too much trouble for any of you."

The women said good-bye at the front door. Naomi sat guard on the front porch, relieved that she had Evah to herself again.

WEDNESDAY

It was raining today, and Evah welcomed the opportunity to curl up in a chair with Casey Horton's testing. She pulled out her outline and felt good that they had covered so much territory yesterday. Jeannette had good recall and was willing to mentally step back into time, offering Evah information about Casey's history that was useful in creating a profile. Naomi sensed that Evah was embarking upon another project that would keep her occupied. She leaped onto the back of the leather chair where Evah sat and swatted at her mistress's hair.

Evah looked at the first testing, administered too early in life she thought. But then each school, each system, felt very differently about when to introduce testing into the circle of problems that manifested itself as unmanageable behavior in the classroom. Everybody needed an answer, she thought. And of course, the testing would magically conjure up an answer, and a solution! She snickered softly. Why couldn't people just talk through the history, the behaviors, the attitudes of all the people involved in the life of the child? Why did people think that testing always gave the answer? Did they think that a huge neon sign would flash "DYSLEXIA" or "MATH DISABILITY?" Mischievously she thought that would be interesting, especially if the marquee also included a recipe kind of solution, a little like watching Martha Stewart explaining how to take care of pesky weeds.

Casey's first testing didn't reveal anything out of the ordinary. There was a ten-point discrepancy between the verbal and performance modes of intelligence on the Wechsler Scale. Evah had seen worse, much worse. There wasn't a great deal of intratest scatter. What was notable was the teacher's concern with Casey's language development, coupled with his classroom behaviors. As Evah read through the several accounts of classroom episodes the teacher offered, it seemed as if Casey created a conflict in the classroom whenever he was expected to join in on an activity that included language. He seemed content to print his letters and words and draw and paint along with his peers, utilizing his own mode of expression. However, at storytime he would create a situation where he was either removed from the group, or the activity was temporarily put aside as a result of the disruption he had created. As Evah read on she discovered that following storytime the children were asked questions about the story and were expected to articulate their understanding of the characters and the sequence of events. That pesky language again! Just like one of Martha Stewart's weeds!

"Aha!" Evah said aloud. Naomi jumped off the chair, her back up.

"I knew I'd find this!" As Evah read the second report she noticed there was still no significant discrepancy in his Wechsler, although the verbal mode dipped more precariously. The backup achievement tests showed that Casey was battling language and seemed unable at this time to understand what he read. He knew the words, and could read them, but wasn't understanding what the language really meant. Additionally, his ability to follow verbal directions was taking a nose dive. His receptive language was giving him even greater difficulty now that the academic demands were increasing—the expectations were constant, never ending, relentless—this is the way it would seem to someone like Casey. Evah was gleaning most of her information about Casey from teacher reports.

It appeared in the second report as if Casey had shut down in terms of his expressive language. He didn't want to talk, to read, to articulate his thoughts in any way with language. He was unconsciously acting out his feelings and thoughts, although unfortunately it was usually through conflict. However, at this time Casey began to write short poems, and this was expression! His own expression! They were brief, and the language was simple, but the message was clear and full of feeling and humor. He could rhyme. He had a sense of rhythm. Evah knew that Casey had a great deal of potential that was locked inside him and that he needed some help in opening up his gifts to the world.

There was a case for an expressive and receptive language disorder, and Casey did need further diagnostic work to confirm the label of ADHD that the school was only too willing to put in place. Lately, this seemed like the all encompassing label that explained any behavior that appeared outside of established norms. It would be difficult to tell if Casey's concentration problems were due to his receptive and expressive language disabilities, or if the alleged ADHD was present due to a chemical imbalance. The chicken or egg again. When would science make her job easier!

Evah arranged the papers neatly and slipped them inside the large white envelope again. "Well, Martha Stewart! Guess we've got the weeds under control for the time being." Naomi flicked her tail at Evah's feet, daring her to notice.

"OK Naomi. Time to play. Let's go out in the garden and weed."

Naomi ran through the hallway and sat patiently at the kitchen door. Evah scooped up her pail and gardening tools and shooed Naomi through the door and into the backyard. Evah stood and faced the woods, and saw the glimmer of cobalt blue again through the pines.

FRIDAY

"Oh my gosh you people! You are not helping me. Dr. Nellsom is coming here today. Today! Do you hear me?"

Four people stood woodenly in front of Jeannette Horton. They were afraid to talk back. They were afraid to make a move. They hadn't seen Jeannette like this since she rehearsed for the lead role as Miss Jane Maple in the Community Theater Club.

"Kevin, please sweep the driveway. It's a mess!" Her husband looked puzzled.

"Sweep the driveway? What's wrong with it? It's a driveway for goodness sakes. It has dirt on it." He looked down at his clothes. "And look Jeannette, I have my suit on. I just came home for lunch to meet Dr. Nellsom. You didn't tell me I had to clean the driveway or whatever it is you want cleaned outside."

"Sweep the grass and clippings and stuff. Make it neater looking." He shrugged helplessly and headed toward the back door.

"Cathy and Corey! Your rooms!" She rolled her eyes. "They're a disgrace. Clean them, and then pick up your stuff in the den. It's a disaster!" They skulked away as quietly as possible. They were grateful for the afternoon off from school, but dreaded the tension the visit from Dr. Nellsom threatened.

"And Casey! Your stuff is all over the garage. And your room! My gosh, this woman will think I am a completely hopeless slob of a housekeeper!"

"No, Mom, she won't. She'll think I'm a slob. I am. I'm a teenager. It's OK. She won't care. Really." His mother dug her heels in and put on her most fierce mask.

"But never mind. I'll pick up, I'll pick up." Casey always had to have the last word with his mother. "But she won't care, I'm telling you!" He slammed the back door and headed to the garage. He began picking up his hockey equipment and board games and placing them on shelves he and his father built together last winter. He loved that his father gave him half of the two-car garage. It was his own, for his own stuff. Cathy and Corey never came in to bother him. They had their own spaces in the attic and in the basement. Everybody had their own space. Casey liked that.

Casey started banging away on the punching bag with a steady rhythm, one, bang, bang, bang, two, bang—then he saw a car pull into the driveway. Oh, oh, he thought. Dad wasn't through sweeping. Mom would kill him. Casey peeked through the garage window. A woman got out of the car. She wasn't very tall, and Casey could see that she was older than his mother, but he couldn't say how old. Real old he thought because she had some gray hair. She was dressed in slacks and a jersey. She looked around appreciatively at their yard. Casey knew she liked their house. He could tell.

He whistled. "Boy, Mom will be wild. Dr. Nellsom is early!"

Evah shook hands with Kevin Horton. He looked relieved. He thought Dr. Nellsom looked very ordinary, very nonthreatening. Right now his wife was much more threatening than this woman who stood her five-foot frame in front of him.

Kevin led Evah up the driveway to the back door. He opened the door and yelled, "Jeannette! We have company!" Jeannette whirled around and gasped.

"Dr. Nellsom! You're early! My gosh, the kitchen is a mess!"

"Well . . . first of all, I'm sorry if I'm early. My business was finished on time for a change, and the traffic was reasonable, and here I am! And your kitchen is not a mess. It's so pretty! I knew you would have such wonderful taste, Jeannette! It's so like you." Jeannette looked immediately relieved, and smiled modestly. Kevin let out a sigh.

Evah knew that Jeannette would obsess about her house and was afraid that it might get out of control, but she had to gain at least a peek inside the family dynamics. This was the part that usually helped her to fit the pieces together into a cohesive whole. She suspected that Jeannette had sufficiently terrorized her family into shaping up for her visit.

Forty-five minutes later the six of them were seated at the dining room table sipping chowder. Jeannette was a perfect cook, and as Dr. Nellsom looked around she noticed that everything else looked perfect. Nothing out of place. No lint on the rug. No stains on the white linen tablecloth. Cathy's braid was falling out. It probably irritated Jeannette, Evah suspected.

Evah looked across the table at Casey. He looked back and smiled, showing sparkling braces. Cathy and Corey smiled also. Evah wondered why they were home, but figured that Jeannette probably arranged for them to be there. The lunch passed with some discomfort, small talk about Boston, questions about vacationing in Maine, and then on to school, the dreaded subject. Cathy and Corey politely excused themselves. Evah knew they wanted to be anywhere else but at the table.

Casey pushed his chair back and folded his arms across his chest. "So I guess this is all about me now, huh?" His mother gave him another fierce stare.

Kevin cleared his throat. "Um, Casey, I think Dr. Nellsom just wants to ask some questions. That's all. Right Dr. Nellsom?"

"Yes, and Casey this is not like an interview. I really want to know what you want, what you're feeling about how school is going." There was silence.

"Casey, maybe you could take me to the garage and show me the chin-up bar and punching bag your mother told me you have. She said you're really good at it. I'd love to see it."

One corner of his mouth turned up in a half-smile. "OK. This way."

She followed him to the back door. Kevin and Jeannette watched.

Evah was led to a seat on an exercise bench in the garage. Casey demonstrated his punching bag skill, and when coaxed, did a few chin ups. He looked pretty proud of himself.

"You're pretty good Casey. You have a nice rhythm. Do you like to dance?"

Casey blushed. "No . . . ah, I don't really dance. But I know how I guess."

"Do you play an instrument?"

"I played the drums for a while. See?" He pointed to the back of the garage. "They're stored back there. I gave them up for a while."

"Think you'll go back to them or take up another instrument?"

"Hmmm. I thought maybe I'd play guitar, but the music is much harder to read for me. I'm better at drums I guess. I guess I don't know yet. Maybe I'll just experiment with a few things." He stood with his arms crossed, protecting himself, trying to be very grown up.

"I think that's a good idea, Casey. Don't make a decision right away. Try some instruments out first." Evah was careful with her questioning. She didn't want to scare him off.

"Casey, you have pretty good coordination from what I can see. Do you like to play other sports? Your mother said you used to play hockey."

He blushed again and stared off into space. He spoke without making eye contact. "Yup, I used to play, but I kept getting into trouble. I kept having fights and stuff. I don't know why. Honest I don't."

"I believe you."

"But I really hate it when people crash into me, like in hockey, and in football. I'm not big enough for high school football—it's a relief I guess. Dad can't ask me why I don't try out because he knows I'm not a big guy."

"Why do you hate it when people crash into you?"

"When they bump me, I lose my thinking. I can't concentrate. Then I mess up and people get mad at me. Then I just want to hit someone cause I'm really trying to play the game, but I get all thrown off when I'm hit or bumped."

"I understand what you're saying Casey. How about when someone bumps into you in the hallway at school or at home?"

He was thoughtful for a minute, and then gave her his half-smile again. "Hey, you think one thing is connected to the other, don't you?" He was making direct eye contact with Evah again.

"Maybe. Who knows? It's worth exploring, don't you think?"

"I guess. Well . . . I got into two fights last year because some guys bumped into me in the hallway and in gym. They were horsin' around . . . just being clowns I guess. It made me so mad that I shoved them back even harder, and then it wasn't funny anymore. It was a fight. They didn't know why I got so mad, and afterward I didn't know either."

"What about at home?"

"Well, we don't horse around like that as much here. It's calmer I guess. But I don't like to play football with my father and brother when they tackle. They hurt. I hate it. But I like to play catch. I'm really good at it. They think I'm not a good sport sometimes because I hate the tackling."

"Did you ever tell them how it feels for you when you're tackled?"

He shrugged. She interpreted that as being embarrassed to tell his father and brother that tackling was physically painful for him in a way that he couldn't articulate.

"Casey, I'm going to ask you what you would really like to be doing in the fall. Where would you like to be going to school?"

He shrugged again.

"Try to think about this, because you are the person who knows what kind of setting will work for you."

"I really don't want to go back to my private school. They don't believe me when I tell them that I have trouble with some of my reading. They think that if I can read—you know, just *do* the thing—that I know what it means. They think I'm faking. I'm not. Do you believe me?"

"I most certainly do believe you."

"I think I might like to go to the school here in town. I still have my neighborhood friends who go there. Maybe I can get help there, and they'll believe me."

"OK, that's a good place to start. You've given me a lot of good information, Casey. Now . . . let's see a few more chin ups. I'm so envious that you can do them."

He offered her the chin-up bar, but she declined. They had casual conversation for a while longer and looked over all Casey's board games. He said they were gifts, and he just stored them in here because he hated playing them.

"I never win. I hate it." They laughed together and shared some similar kinds of experiences with games.

Evah knew instinctively that Casey was misunderstood by his family members about his tactile defensiveness. This was a common mistake made by families and by teachers alike. It was literally painful for some children and adults to hug each other, to play contact sports, to be surprised by a tap on the back from behind. She remembered the story of Rob, certainly a boy who suffered a great deal more than Casey as a result of his vestibular system, but nonetheless an example of one of Casey's complaints about playing tackle football.

Casey's reading difficulty was well documented in his formal testings, but misunderstood by his teachers and probably to some degree by his parents. The testings indicated that Casey experienced difficulty with reading comprehension, and as the material he read in school became more sophisticated, his struggle to understand what he read increased. He was at risk for becoming repelled by the thought of reading, and at risk for lacking the pleasure this task might bring him later in life. The chief challenge here was to explain to Casey's teachers and family that although Casey appeared to be performing in a manner that far surpassed his reading assessments, he was still not understanding the material. He could read the words, but they remained words; meaningless words that were connected by conjunctions, included nouns and verbs, and ended with periods or question marks. For Casey, they lacked meaning, substance, and feeling.

Evah realized that she would have to tread carefully when counseling the Hortons about family therapy. Casey's temper was borne out of frustration, but other avenues must be explored as well. Did Kevin have a temper? Jeannette? Was she too much of a perfectionist, and despite all her good intentions, did she exacerbate the situation with her demands? Were Casey's siblings tough acts to follow? Did Casey feel that he was disappointing Dad by not wanting to play contact sports with him? The questions went on and on, and Evah knew that her friend in Boston, Dr. Leo Charles, could help this family.

Casey and Evah walked back to the house together. She looked up and caught Jeannette and Kevin peeking between the kitchen curtains.

"They can't help it, " Casey began, "they are so worried that I'm going to keep having fights, and flunking and stuff. They don't believe that's not the way I want it to be." Evah patted Casey gently on the shoulder.

Jeannette, Kevin, Casey, and Evah sat at the kitchen table. Evah checked her watch and knew she had to head back in order to avoid the worst part of the rush hour on the Maine Turnpike.

"OK folks. Casey and I had a nice talk." She looked steadily at both parents. "Casey would like to attend his neighborhood school. He explained that he has friends there, and that he maybe will get the help he needs from the school system."

Kevin interrupted. "What if the school can't give him the help he needs?"

Evah had heard the questions so many times before, and although she wanted to think her answers could be rehearsed she knew that each case presented such individual circumstances.

"Well you'll be saving a great deal of money from tuition, so some money might be spent in private tutoring for a while. It might not be forever. But if you're feeling at any time as if the school is not doing enough, hiring a private learning specialist or educational therapist is certainly an option. I know several in your area that I can recommend." Kevin looked as though he were trying hard to process all the information. He nodded agreeement.

Jeannette looked from one face to the other. Casey looked hopeful.

"Look folks. We can start by calling the public school and asking for an appointment. I'll go with you. We'll bring the former testing and Casey's transcripts. I have a feeling that you will be pleasantly surprised if we approach the situation in a way that will encourage the school system to form an alliance with you. It's teamwork. It's their job. We make friends in this business, not enemies."

Evah looked carefully at all the faces at the kitchen table. Casey gave a half-smile. Jeannette exhaled audibly. Kevin nodded, loosening his tie. Evah knew they had a tough road ahead of them. She hadn't even approached the subject of therapy yet, and she needed to sit with them again to prepare them for the meeting with the school. She felt her eyes burning with exhaustion.

The hardest part was convincing families that they were the best support networks for each other. Some of the answers were there already. They just couldn't see them yet. It was like trying to navigate a rowboat through the fog and bringing it safely to shore. Things never looked very clear until you were almost on top of them. Then they took on a new clarity, and it felt good. It felt safe.

FOUR WEEKS LATER

Evah dug her fingers deep into the soil that was banked against the old red rowboat in her frontyard. She added water, pulled a few nasty weeds, and immediately thought of Martha Stewart again. Why did that woman make everything look so easy—so fixable?

A baby blue sports car pulled smoothly into Evah's gravel driveway. She looked up and smiled as she recognized Jeannette Horton step gingerly out of her car.

"Dr. Nellsom! I'm so sorry I'm late! The Maine Turnpike was so slow today—vacationers I guess." Jeannette stooped down to admire the annuals. She ran her hand over the outside of the old red rowboat.

"Dr. Nellsom, how many people learned to navigate on this old boat?"

"Just me. My father bought it for me when I was a teenager. It holds many fond memories—a few scary ones too—and it reminds me that nothing is ever easy. But . . . it's always worth the effort."

The two women walked inside and sat down with a cup of tea. Naomi quickly trotted under the table to assess this new visitor. She sniffed her shoes, rubbed her face on her stockings, and swatted at her handbag. Naomi knew it was someone who had been here before, and knew she would stay a while. With this in mind, she perched herself on the wide windowsill in the kitchen and stared at Jeannette, demonstrating her ownership of the house and her mistress.

"Tell me, Jeannette, how your most recent visit to the school went."

"Well, after our first visit with you as the advocate, we received a call from the director of special education the next day. He invited us in again to talk about an education plan, based on our private testing, and some further achievement testing they would like to do. So far, Casey has been OK with all this. Kevin is feeling better about it. Actually, Casey has become a little more hopeful, and has reconnected with a few neighborhood kids that will be in his class." She crossed her fingers on both hands and held them out for Evah to see.

"And what about the neurologist?"

"It went very, very well with her. As a matter of fact, she's going to do a little testing with me." Jeannette looked sheepish. "And . . . I really feel alright with this. Maybe it's long overdue."

Evah smiled and nodded encouragement for Jeannette to continue.

"Your next question will be to ask if we've seen the therapist. And yes, we've had two sessions as a family. Now we will see separate therapists for a while, and come back again as a family. Actually, it felt pretty good although I know that we'll have some rough times with this. All kinds of issues will come up for us: present issues, past issues, problems from our collective families. The list goes on, doesn't it?"

Evah smiled again. "You're doing so well, Jeannette. You've really stepped up to take charge of coordinating all the services that have to be in place in order to navigate the system that seems so overwhelming most of the time. This is where your own preference for structure and attention to details will benefit all of you as a family."

"Yes, I know that sometimes my style helps . . . and, sometimes it doesn't. This is like an exploration of sorts, isn't it?"

The women continued their conversation, and mentioned the teachers that Casey would be dealing with over the upcoming academic year. Kevin said that he would take control of that matter and volunteered to speak with them, offering his services whenever necessary at school events. He offered also to be available if there were questions about Casey's classroom behaviors—hopefully there wouldn't be a need at all—and clearly stated his interest in maintaining a consistent communication with the school and the teachers who worked with Casey. He was epitomizing Evah's rule about making friends and not enemies.

As Evah waved good-bye to Jeannette from the front porch, she conjured up a mental image of the sea of faces that had come before Casey in her work. Brian, Lorna's grown son, came to mind immediately. His family was so proud of his accomplishments as an adult, but navigating the system was so difficult for them to master. The families at Kiley Cove came to mind, the inner-city families, the families who came with layers of issues that were culturally driven, economically driven, or driven by the pure need to succeed in an academic world of rapidly changing rules and expectations that functioned as land mines to those who had not as yet learned to navigate the system. Each one was special. Each one required their own unique blueprints in order to set out on this voyage that would ultimately lead to a sense of power and control over their lives.

Evah returned to her gardening. Naomi sat watch at the bow of the old red rowboat, flicking her scruffy gray tail. Now and then she yawned, always with an eye on her mistress, wondering when she would drop her gardening tools, pick up the car keys, and be off with a folder tucked under her arm.

Evah was born on a Saturday.

13

THE HOLISTIC APPROACH: CRUNCHY GRANOLA, INTELLECTUALISM, AND WISDOM FOR THE FAMILY

Each family learns or chooses to deal with LD/ADD/Dyslexia in a different way. One size doesn't fit all. The approach, or more aptly put, what works for each family's survival depends entirely upon the individual family culture, the availability of facilities and services, and the nature of the learning difference or challenge that faces each child. In most cases, what the child with learning disabilities faces each day both in and out of the classroom becomes what the family faces each day in their life together.

A typical model of the traditional family today has stretched far beyond the boundaries we were familiar with prior to the 1970s. Most people today are well aware that the divorce rate has zoomed, burdening single parents with the added responsibilities that are often difficult to navigate alone. We have stretched our traditional vision of the family unit yet again by recognizing that many parents who live together with their children both have jobs outside the home. As a result of single parenting, and cases in which both parents work, most children today begin their formal education much earlier than they once did. Preschool, nursery school, and day care have added new levels of child care and learning opportunities for children while providing parents with assistance as they often juggle one or two jobs, a family, and other responsibilities.

Some children spend a great deal of their time with other family members such as grandparents. Remember the story of Gemma? She's not at all unlike many children who live with and love being part of what is acknowledged as family life in North American culture. The idea of extended family has taken on new meaning and has become an inclusive acceptance of the people who love and care for each other in the life of each child.

This chapter will offer you a peek into the lives of several families and how they coped and adapted as families dealing with the complex issues raised by learning disabilities. Each of these scenarios takes place in the 1990s in North America.

THE HEALER

Roberto sat on his back steps watching old Mr. Carpo carry his groceries to his front door. He closed his spelling book and sat on it—out of sight, out of mind he thought. Roberto, waiting for a valid reason to leave the back steps, sprinted across the narrow street, meeting his neighbor just as he was inserting the key in his front door. Roberto glanced back at his back door to see if his mother had discovered his absence.

"Grazie, Roberto. Grazie. You always come to help a poor old man!" Willingly, Mr. Carpo let Roberto take the plastic bags from his hands and carry them into the house ahead of him. Mr. Carpo limped along behind Roberto, holding his aching hip as he walked into the kitchen.

"Roberto, does your mama know you're here?" He picked up the receiver of his old black dial phone and handed it to Roberto. "Here, you call her. I don't want her mad at me because you took off."

Reluctantly, Roberto dialed his home. "Hello Mama."

"Where are you Roberto!" It was more of an exclamation than a question.

"I'm across the street helping Mr. Carpo with his groceries. I'll be home in a minute." Roberto was glad for the break he gave himself. He didn't know how much longer he could stand staring at those spelling words. They didn't make any sense at all, and no matter how much help he got at school, he still couldn't remember how to spell them nor how to sound out the letters. He still couldn't remember what a vowel was. He thought it was a stupid word. That's what he told his sister who seemed to be having an easier time adjusting to another language in a new country. She looked at him as if he were crazy.

Last year when Roberto was in the third grade his mother was called into a meeting at school to discuss his academic progress. Roberto's mother, Louisa, who was vigilant about attending her English classes, was proud of her progress and newly acquired command of the English language and hoped to set an example for her two children. Carla, Roberto's sister, seemed to sail through her ESL classes in the fifth grade last year, and this year required little or no help in the full cycle of literacy in either language.

With a heavy heart and a firm approach Louisa was determined that Roberto would get through his fourth grade experience. She struggled with her decision not to have Roberto repeat the third grade; she knew he could do it! However, as she watched him now she doubted her wisdom as a mother and feared that the teachers were right. Roberto had an attention deficit disorder that impeded his already shaky academic progress. He couldn't focus, he couldn't concentrate, unless he watched his favorite TV shows. This infuriated Louisa who then enforced strict rules about TV.

After school each day Roberto was ordered to sit at home for an hour with his spelling or his reading. In the winter Louisa made him sit at the kitchen table where she did her own homework. Carla preferred to work in her room, undisturbed by other family members. This worked for a while until Louisa realized Roberto was more interested in her work than his own. She then moved her studying to the living room and left Roberto in the kitchen, armed with snacks and drinks, sharpened pencils, and restful music in the background. Louisa heard during her classes at the community college that soft music could help some people's concentration. Roberto was able to concentrate for short periods of time, and Louisa learned through observation and many arguments, that Roberto needed to get up and move around every ten minutes. Once she resigned herself to the fact that forcing him to sit wasn't going to get any homework done or any spelling words memorized, she complied with what looked to be the new guidelines for success. Removing herself from the kitchen helped her to cope with what she saw as Roberto's different style.

During warmer weather Louisa let Roberto sit on the back steps with his work. This proved to be more ineffective than the kitchen because everybody liked Roberto and stopped to say hello. Only too happy to interrupt the imposed study hour, Roberto would rise to the occasion and be his charming self, patting the next door puppies, helping Mr.

Carpo with his groceries, or babysitting little Jose next door while his mother ran to the post office. Louisa felt she couldn't win, and found that on Friday nights she was exhausted and cranky from the energy expended on Roberto's homework, running back and forth for meetings with teachers, and then trying to divide her time up equally between Carla and her husband as well.

Roberto's family was very religious and spent a good deal of the weekend at church. Saturday mornings Louisa volunteered her time in the parish to families she recognized as being less fortunate than her own, packing food boxes for them and delivering them often with the help of her two children. Louisa discovered that Roberto's obvious gift for helping people also put his excess energy to good use. Eventually, she started giving Roberto the lists of food to be packed per family and left him in charge of delivering boxes to the families in their immediate neighborhood. It gave Louisa a break in order to spend time with Carla and the other women at church, laughing, drinking coffee and planning the social hour after Mass for the next day. She found this small opportunity on a Saturday gave her back some of the socialization she felt she had lost somewhere along the way, and it gave Roberto his moment to shine, to socialize, to help others. He experienced a sense of competence and independence.

Soon Roberto was called upon by the priest to assist him in parish visits. He was amazed at the gift Roberto possessed for talking with people and the genuine pleasure he demonstrated when he was able to assist another person in need. Roberto's family and community culture were instrumental in uncovering his talents as a human being. When Roberto and his mother talked about the difficulties he had in school, numerous people stepped forward and said they would help him study and memorize his spelling words. Some parishioners offered to pray with Roberto, asking that his own burdens be lifted and made more manageable for him.

Roberto was a very lucky child and grew to be a very successful and loving young man. His success and feelings of well-being unfolded with the guidance of his family, a tight-knit community full of people who cared about one another, and a deep faith that kept Roberto moving ahead in his life, one day at a time.

BE A STAR

Twelve-year-old Lise skipped over to her mother's side. She was a rising star in her rural French community in Canada.

"Maman I've been chosen for the part! The leading role! The star!" She spoke rapid French and was motioned to slow down by her mother. Lise was always in a hurry to do everything. When she first learned to speak it was only tentatively, as if she were trying on new shoes to see what fit properly. When she felt a command of her first language, she became a powerful little locomotive, racing ahead, adding new words to her vocabulary, asking questions, and engaging everyone in conversation.

Her mother, Paulette, beamed. A few years ago Lise was demonstrating clear signs of childhood depression as a result of her learning disability. After endless visits to the city hospital, testing, testing, and more testing revealed that although Lise's classic dyslexia was impeding her progress academically, the larger problem resided in the regional school she attended. They just weren't equipped to deal with learning disabilities at this point in time, and no matter how angry and vocal her parents became, the fact that Lise could not be effectively educated in her district's school system became glaringly apparent.

Paulette's husband owned a small business in their community, and while they made a respectable living, private schools that catered to Lise's specific needs were out of the question financially. Besides, they didn't want their daughter to attend a boarding school. She belonged at home with them, with her six brothers and sisters, and a community that encouraged the preservation and daily integration of her French heritage.

After much research and a great deal of support from their community, Lise's parents made the decision to educate their daughter at home, privately in her own community. Four of Paulette's children decided they would prefer to be schooled in this manner as well. By the time Paulette had conferred with the local and provincial authorities, three other families in the small French community decided to pool their resources with Paulette's. The following summer seven adults and seventeen children ranging from the ages of four to sixteen reorganized the abandoned community center attached to an old church. It became simply, "L'ecole."

By September, a visiting special educator was developing individual education plans for eight of the seventeen children and making suggestions for materials and new books. She volunteered her time training the parents/teachers in methods that would help to remediate some of the identified reading problems that needed immediate attention.

L'ecole joined forces with the two existing churches in the community, devoting one school day of each week to the call of service to the community. These special times were spent reading to the elderly, helping in the local day care center, and assisting in the gift shoppe in the small hospital located in the adjoining community. The list of services grew as the year passed, and before long Paulette and her group of parent/teachers had recognized what a rich experience they had created for their children and for themselves. Some children were actually engaged in apprenticeships while they contributed their time to the community. They were learning in ways that were not possible for them before and were experiencing competency that provided them with a sense of worth.

By the third year of L'ecole's existence, many of the community's parents felt empowered by their contributions to the education of their children. The children were learning, and in fact they were thriving. The humiliation of feeling different, of feeling singled out, pointed out, and left out was gone for those students who were diagnosed with learning disabilities. L'ecole left no room for the humiliation of children, only for the humbleness that came from an education that embraced home, community, and unconditional acceptance.

Lise truly became a star.

THE ARTIST

Marshall whistled as he rounded the corner to his apartment house. His mother leaned out of the second-story window watching him carefully, one eyebrow raised.

"Thought you were gonna be home to watch your brother." She knew where he was, and luckily she could rely on the charity of her next door neighbor for babysitting.

Marshall looked genuinely shocked, and smacked his forehead. "Honest Ma, I forgot!" He took the front steps two at a time. "But you should see the painting I finished today. It's HUGE!"

Carrie let out a belly laugh. She knew what a talented artist her son was and remained thankful that there were programs in this end of the city that offered support and guidance to a budding artist. Marshall burst through the door to their apartment. Before Carrie could speak Marshall was sketching on the pad of paper Carrie learned to keep handy for her son. He diligently sharpened his pencil and sat down at the kitchen table, motioning for her to sit down next to him.

She watched as Marshall quickly sketched a scene of neighborhood people who were waiting for the bus. He talked as he sketched, and she nodded understanding of her son's interpretation of people, of life in the city, of the human condition. He was a marvel to her. She knew that her son's work had been chosen for a mural in their city hall, and she was so proud of him she could burst.

After about fifteen minutes of rapid sketching and explanation to his small audience, Marshall asked, "So whaddya think Ma?"

Carrie shook her head. "I hate to bring this up, but do you have any homework?"

Marshall made a sour face and thought for a minute. "Nope." He then yanked open the refrigerator and bent down to peer among the offerings.

Carrie took a deep breath and exhaled slowly. This part was always painful, but nevertheless had to be faced. "Marshall, I am so happy you are so talented . . . and everybody knows how talented you are . . . your dad would be so proud if he were here." Carrie's eyes filled up, still missing her husband who had passed away three years ago when Marshall was just nine. It was frightening to be left by herself in charge of two boys. The city. The risks. The temptations. Marshall's talent would be his salvation, and her's as a parent.

"Marshall, we have to find a way for you to do your work at school. Mrs. Garvey called again and said you weren't doing your work. How come Marshall?"

Marshall sat down again with a loud plop! on the padded kitchen chair.

"Cause I hate it Ma. I can't do it. I hate goin' to the resource room . . . you know, that special room they have for the dummies. That's what they call it ya know. And know what they call the special bus? The vegetable truck!" He chewed on a cracker and thought for a minute.

He turned to his mother with a disgusted face. "Georgie upstairs takes the special bus, and he goes to the special class. They make fun of Georgie all the time, and they know I go to that room too! I hate it Ma, and I don't wanna go there anymore. Can't I just take art?" He looked imploringly at his mother who was all too familiar with the validity of Marshall's complaints. She too hated the fact that her son was shoved into a special education room that seemed to be the dumping ground for any academic or social problem that couldn't be taken care of in the regular classroom. She felt her blood pressure rise. And, what was all this talk about inclusion? Marshall said he hated it more when the man from the special class would come and sit down with Marshall in his own class—"Right in front of everyone Ma!" he would wail. "Then all the kids know I can't do my work . . . right in front of everyone Ma!"

"Let me think about this Marshall. Let me think, OK?"

"OK Ma. Just don't make me go there anymore." With that he stuffed several crackers into his shirt pocket, returned the pad of paper to its proper place by the phone, and sped down the hallway, humming a TV jingle. Carrie knew that he felt trapped at school, and that the methods they used to ameliorate his learning difficulties were suffocating his creativity and his will to succeed academically. His art was his passion. She needed to find a way to bridge his passion for art with his intellectual and academic growth.

The next day Carrie stopped by the community center where Marshall took his art lessons on Mondays, Wednesdays, and Saturday mornings. Ken, Marshall's art teacher, recognized Carrie and came to greet her. Carrie immediately launched into a description of what life had been like these past few years, trying to make Marshall go to school and participate. Kevin looked thoughtful, but nodded understanding. He had listened to Marshall complain about not wanting to do his homework and about his level of discomfort in his classroom.

"Why don't we try an approach where Marshall doesn't feel that his art is being threatened because he's not finishing his work at school. Let me try a few things with him, and I'll drop by and visit with his teacher. In the meantime, I have some equipment I'd like you to consider including in your home—art equipment—this will give Marshall a sense of seriousness about his art work."

Carrie nodded. "Anything Ken. Anything you want to try."

Later that afternoon as Marshall again took the front steps two at a time, his mother leaned out of the window and asked if he would please stop outside the door to their apartment and wait until she let him in. He looked puzzled, but nodded agreement.

Outside the door Marshall waited patiently, placing his ear against the worn, smooth wood of the door. He couldn't hear much and began to feel uneasy. Did she remove the TV? Move the furniture around? She was always doing that. As soon as he heard his mother turn the knob, he stood up straight.

"Cover your eyes," his mother whispered before she opened the door all the way. Marshall smiled. This was getting exciting. But wait . . . it wasn't his birthday. Carrie gently steered her son to the left into the living room area and told him to uncover his eyes.

Marshall looked straight ahead to see the window where his mother usually kept the desk where she did all the bills. Frantically, he scanned the room. In place of the desk was an easel and a stool and an old cabinet he had seen in the basement of the apartment building. He walked around the easel and touched it. It was one of the old easels from the community center. He peeked inside the cabinet his mother had filled with supplies she had gathered from his room and donations Ken had made to Marshall's new "studio corner."

"Ma! This is great! I'll be like a real artist!"

"You *are* a real artist Marshall. Now you have to start behaving like one."

Marshall raised an eyebrow suspiciously. What could she mean?

Carrie said, "All artists have to know more than how to put the paint on paper, canvas, or a wall Marshall. They need to really know about their subjects. They need to know about anatomy, about people, about things, about culture. There's a whole lot more to this you know."

"Yeah? So what does that mean, huh?"

"It means that you're gonna have to buckle down to your work in school, Marshall, if you really want to be a success with your art. Ken says he'll check your homework with you for fifteen minutes before your sessions at the community center. He really believes in your talent Marshall. And so do I. Now, will you give it a try?"

"No more resource room?"

"We'll try it without the resource room for a little while and see what happens. I talked to your teacher and so did Ken. She said that her part of the deal includes you helping her out in the art room every afternoon instead of a study hour. She said you can stay after school and get help any day after school that you want, but . . . we all agreed that you have to do your work. You can't pretend you lost it, or that you don't have any. You have to bring your work home, Marshall. Got it?"

"Got it Ma."

"You're sure no more resource room?"

"I'm sure. We'll try. I promise."

By this time Marshall had pulled out the acrylic paint and was filling a large jar with water at the sink. He was mumbling about how he would ask Miss Garvey to change the furniture around in the art room tomorrow.

"Life with an artist!" Carrie said as she rolled her eyes.

BREATHE, ONE, TWO, THREE. . .

"Breathe in . . . one, two, three. Hold it, hold it. Breathe out now . . . one, two, three." Becky felt her abdomen with her hand and imagined her stomach, lungs and throat fill with cleansing air. As she exhaled she imagined all the toxins from her body being expelled. Becky learned how to meditate and practice yoga when she was only six years old.

Now that she was getting ready for high school she felt quite proficient in yoga, and she felt in control of her life following a very long battle with learning, and with depression.

When Becky was in kindergarten the teachers told her parents that she should repeat the year and then be reevaluated. It seemed at that time that Becky was having difficulty with directionality, with listening, and with focusing on any given task for more than a few minutes. Becky's mother, Martha, cried for days, blaming herself for the obvious difficulties her daughter was experiencing in school. Becky was their only child, their pride and joy! How could this be happening?

At home Becky was a bouncing ray of sunshine, flitting from one activity to another, always smiling, always ready to please. Martha couldn't understand what went wrong. She thought that possibly she didn't prepare Becky enough for school. She thought that maybe their vegetarian diet was doing it. She spent days on end running through the list of things she needed to blame Becky's trouble on, all of which stemmed from something she and her husband were or were not doing. It never occurred to Martha that it wasn't her fault. It doesn't occur to most parents.

Martha watched her ray of sunshine turn into a storm cloud. First it began by Becky's attempts to avoid anything that required focus, anything that included books, reading, coloring, taking directions—the list grew. Becky's need to avoid most things that caused her to be disappointed in her self and embarrassed by her peers and teachers eventually grew to a retreat into self. She became quiet, nonresponsive to the things she usually loved, and began to demonstrate a smoldering anger that frightened Martha and her husband.

One day when Martha was assisting her with getting ready for school, Becky had her first panic attack, or at least the first one that Martha was aware of. Becky cried. Martha cried. They stayed home together that day and watched mindless television and ate popcorn. By the end of the day, a little of the old Becky had returned. She smiled a little and seemed to take some pleasure in helping with dinner. Of course the next day was Saturday. Becky knew in her six-year-old-mind that she had a respite coming.

Martha had been meditating since she was in college, and in fact was a yoga instructor. She loved her work, loved helping people learn how to heal themselves, to respect themselves, and to forgive themselves for pushing their bodies, minds, and spirits to unforgiving levels of expectation. As she watched Becky with her second, third, and fourth panic attacks within a week, she knew something had to change. The medication the pediatrician prescribed wasn't enough, and she didn't want her child to become dependent on drugs in order to move through the demands of each day.

After two weeks of staying home from school, flatly refusing to get dressed, eat breakfast, let alone look at a book, Becky consented to accompany her mother as she instructed her yoga class held in the basement of their home. Usually this was off limits to Becky, not that she was interested anyway. Staying upstairs during the yoga class gave her an opportunity to watch uncensored TV, and eat whatever snacks she wanted.

Recently Becky had become very moody, and Martha was never sure what to say or how to say it in order to keep the peace. The past few weeks had the household walking on egg shells.

"I really could use your help today, Becky. My back is really bothering me, and maybe if you model one or two poses for me it would help." Becky stood with her feet apart, arms folded across her chest, a frown working its way into an angry scowl. She sighed disgustedly. Oh well, it would give her a chance to see what was really going on down there anyway. And, it was so boring staying home, not that she wanted to go to school.

She shrugged. "OK."

Martha put on her best "thank you very much for saving my life" look. Together they waited in the kitchen for the women to arrive. Becky rolled her eyes as the visitors patted her on the head, asking politely why she wasn't in school today.

"She's a bit under the weather this morning, but has agreed to help out. My back is a little sore today, so Becky will demonstrate some of my more challenging poses—she's so young and flexible." Martha laughed nervously, hoping that her plan would work. No one seemed to mind.

Martha began with some breathing exercises and asked that Becky sit next to her and move through the exercises with the rest of the group. Becky reluctantly admitted to herself that she felt rather important, sitting next to her mother in front of the group. She breathed in, out . . . in, out . . . and learned to rest a hand on her belly, feeling it fill up with air, visualizing crystal clear air bathing her insides, and with her exhalations visualizing the poisons from her body being expelled. Eventually she closed her eyes and trusted that she could follow her mother's directions just as the other participants did.

Proudly Becky demonstrated her flexibility and allowed her mother to assist her with poses that required some concentration. Her cobra pose was perfect with the help of her mother, and she went on to demonstrate the ease with which she held the mountain pose, working her way into a tree pose for balance. She was proud. And it felt good! By the end of the session Becky found herself wanting to do more breathing exercises; she knew on some level that it made her feel better, calmer. She stayed downstairs while her mother escorted the women out through the kitchen. Becky clicked on the Enya tape and began breathing exercises on her own. In and out slowly through her nose . . . one, two, three. Out slowly . . . one, two, three.

About twenty minutes later after the women had left Martha peeked downstairs and watched as Becky moved with ease through several poses they had tried that morning. First she experimented with the seal pose, and then the crab. Her flexibility was amazing! Martha said a silent prayer that Becky would find some solace in yoga. When Becky came upstairs Martha said nothing and continued about her business as if this morning had never taken place. Two days later Becky still refused to go to school. Martha had another yoga class scheduled for that morning and again asked Becky to assist her.

Becky eyed her mother. "I thought your back was better."

"It is. I don't want to risk straining it just yet. Would you mind helping me again?" Casually Becky nodded. Secretly, she was pleased with herself that she did so well. Last night she practiced the breathing and worked on several of the poses again. She loved the animal poses, and borrowed the yoga book, *Fly Like a Butterfly*, by Shakta Kaur Khalsa from her mother's bookcase downstairs. Martha found it under her pillow, but said nothing.

Martha watched with pride as Becky guided the group through several poses. She sat right next to her mother and moved in unison with her through each exercise. Again, Martha left Becky downstairs while the women filed out, chattering about how impressed they were with Becky's "yoga talent." Of course Becky overheard them, and smiled to herself, proud of her accomplishments over the past few days, but pleased as well with the difference the exercises made in how she felt. The last two nights she practiced the breathing exercises her mother taught her and she fell asleep more easily. She practiced in the morning and felt a little more like eating. This morning she ate a piece of toast.

The days became weeks, and still Becky would not go to school. However, she practiced yoga every day and assisted her mother on a number of occasions. Becky boasted her flexibility, and the women loved to watch her attempt some of the more difficult poses. Slowly, her appetite returned, and Martha breathed a sigh of relief one morning as she heard Becky request pancakes for breakfast.

Becky's third-grade teacher came to the house to visit and brought some of Becky's work. Becky agreed to meet with a tutor daily and said she would think about returning to school. She had not had a panic attack in two weeks. The doctor was pleased, the psychiatrist encouraged Martha to continue yoga with Becky, and the school principal said they would work with Becky and her family.

Eventually Becky did return to school. It did take another month, but within that period of time she caught up with her work, developed a good relationship with her tutor, and most importantly, became proficient in yoga. With her mother and her psychiatrist she discussed how different the exercises made her feel, and how she began to understand what kinds of events in her life triggered panic.

Becky's yoga worked for her. Her parents took an active role in the initiation of the activity and skill, and worked toward making yoga something the whole family enjoyed and benefited from. This was a family practice, and one that was able to assist in healing the wounds caused by the impact of learning disabilities on the life of a child.

Breathe . . . one, two, three. Feel better?

AN ARTFUL DODGER

Daniel took his young daughter's hand, and began searching the aisles of the video store for his son, Todd. He heard someone humming the tune to a popular TV commercial and knew he'd find Todd around the corner. Sure enough, there he was balancing three videos under his chubby arm as he inspected a fourth one about alien visitations.

"Choose *one* Todd. Remember we agreed?" Todd ignored him.

"Remember? One for you, and one for Lizzie?" Still Todd acted as if he were alone in the aisle.

Daniel's voice got louder. "One Todd. Pick one!" Todd thought he'd better not push it any further. He kept the alien visitations and put the others back.

Todd followed his father out of the store and helped to buckle his sister into her car seat. He unwrapped a lollipop for her so that he could monopolize his father's time while keeping her occupied.

"Todd, you know your mom hates it when we give Lizzie candy."

"I know Dad, but we never get to talk if we don't give her candy." Daniel chose not to start an argument. Their time together was so precious he hated to have it laden with conflict and tears. Daniel had been a single parent for two years now, and some days felt as if he maneuvered his parenting fairly well. And then, there were other times.

They were on their way back to Daniel's apartment for a Saturday night of videos, pizza, and ice cream sundaes. Tomorrow it would be a visit to Grammy's for breakfast, a walk around the mall, and home to Todd and Lizzie's mother. Same thing every weekend. It was a routine, and it took Daniel, Todd, and Lizzie two years to perfect it. They all hated it when something occurred that derailed their routine, their ritual.

As Daniel got Lizzie into her pajamas, and busied Todd with setting the table he thought back to that afternoon. Daniel and his former wife agreed that on Saturday mornings Todd would finish his homework before they all became involved in a family activity. She felt that if Todd postponed his homework until Sunday evening, it would never get done.

Todd had been having a very difficult time in school and had been diagnosed with a learning disability last year. The divorce didn't help, and both Daniel and his former wife were honest about how their life choices had impacted their children. Now all they could do was to demonstrate their unconditional love to their children, especially in the face of a stormy educational experience for Todd this year.

Last night when Daniel picked the kids up at their mother's house, Todd threw his suitcase into the backseat and climbed happily into the front with his father. Daniel had learned to be observant of what Todd brought with him, but more importantly what he didn't bring.

"Hey buddy! So where's the books?" Todd pretended he didn't hear his father, a perfected act by now.

"Todd. Where are your books? Look at me." Reluctantly, Todd looked at his father. He shrugged.

"What's that? A shrug? Does that mean you don't know where your books are?" He opened the driver's side door. "Guess I'll check with your mother. Stay here and watch Lizzie." Todd stiffened, but knew now he had to stand his ground and act as if he didn't care. He shrugged again and watched his father retreat into the house. Two minutes later Daniel appeared at the doorway with Todd's book bag in hand. He opened the trunk of the car and flung the book bag inside.

Daniel started the car up again. "Your mother found your book bag in the laundry room. Strange place for a book bag, huh?"

Todd shrugged again, looking convincingly puzzled. Lizzie giggled, as if she understood.

That evening passed uneventfully because Daniel wanted to enjoy his kids, watch a little TV, and talk to his children about what was happening in their Monday-through-Friday lives. Lizzie couldn't contribute much to the conversation, but showed off the new doll her mother bought for her as she climbed onto Daniel's lap. Todd kept his father's attention through constant conversation, answering questions before they could be asked. Sometimes Daniel was in awe of his son's ability to anticipate what he might ask, especially as it related to school.

Daniel interrupted a riveting story about gym class. "So Todd, Mom told me you were beginning to really read now in school, and that you guys have storybooks to take home. That must be nice, huh?" He hoped he wasn't treading on forbidden ground.

"Yup. One's in my book bag. It's about some boys at camp. But I already read it. Don't need to do it again." He wheeled around and gave his father an affectionate punch in the arm. Lizzie squealed with excitement. Then Todd made some faces and attempted a deliberately botched cartwheel to keep Lizzie laughing. Daniel sighed. His son was a master of manipulation. He thought he'd attempt the subject again tomorrow after breakfast.

The morning was quiet. Both Lizzie and Todd watched cartoons in their pajamas while Daniel coaxed breakfast into them. He tried to devise a plot in his mind to get Todd to talk about his reading, because he knew that's where the knot was located, that's where it had been for him when he was in school. Those were painful times for Daniel, and his heart went out to his son whom he knew was experiencing the same kind of humiliation and fear in relation to school.

They ate lunch at a fast-food restaurant and planned their usual Saturday afternoon window shopping that ended with their trip to the video store, pizza, and pajamas, homework coming somewhere between lunch and the pizza. Lizzie concentrated solely on her shake, and shrieked with delight as Todd made a mustache with his french fries. Halfheartedly Daniel tried to make them concentrate on eating their lunch as he flipped through the newspaper.

As much as he dreaded the idea he had to remind Todd that his homework needed to be done after lunch before they headed for the mall and video store. Todd continued his antics, ignoring his father's casual remark.

"Hear me buddy? You have to crack the books before we go out again shopping. We promised Mom, remember?" Again, Todd seemed to have developed a serious case of deafness. He grabbed Todd's hand to get his attention.

"Look at me Todd. Do you hear what I'm saying? We have to go home after lunch and get to the homework. I'll help, OK?"

A stormy look passed over Todd's face. "I don't need you to help. I can do it. It'll only take a few minutes." He sulked for a minute. Lizzie's smile disappeared. She was very attuned to her brother's moods.

"OK, let's just finish our burgers and fries." Daniel kept an eye on Todd as he scanned the newspaper. Eventually, Todd resumed his theatrics for Lizzie who happily returned to shrieking with laughter.

As Daniel flipped the pages of the paper, he stopped at a boxed ad that read, "Dr. Evah Nellsom, renowned child psychologist in the field of learning disorders, will be visiting Lake Wilfred next month. She is an educational researcher who focuses on the impact of learning disabilities on the lives of families. Call now to reserve seats for this seminar." Daniel read on with a guarded interest that stemmed from his own years in school. He remembered reading in the paper last year about Dr. Nellsom's tour through New England. Whenever he read or heard about research in the field of learning disabilities he became anxious, excited, but most of all regretful that his own parents had not had the opportunity to know more, learn more, offer him greater chances for success in school. He worked so hard, and despite the challenge, the sweat and tears, he went to college and was able to build a respectable career for himself in computer technology. He desperately wanted to make the journey more bearable for his son. He tore the ad from the paper and tucked it inside his shirt pocket. He would talk to Lizzie and Todd's mother about it tomorrow.

As Daniel opened the door to his apartment, Todd grabbed his stomach and bent over moaning. "Oh, Dad! I have such a belly ache. Must be the burger and fries. I'm gonna lay down, OK?" Wise to the tactic, Daniel nodded.

He put Lizzie down for her nap and quietly entered the bedroom he shared with Todd. His son was on the bed with his back to his father giggling at a comic book they had picked up on the way home.

"Guess we should have picked up something for your stomachache at the drug store instead of the funny book, huh?"

"I feel better now. I just need to rest."

"OK. You rest for a half hour and then I'll be in to help you start your homework." He saw Todd's back stiffen. "OK. buddy?"

"Yup."

Daniel went into the kitchen and called the phone number listed in the ad to reserve a seat at Dr. Nellsom's seminar series. He learned that the seminar was filling up fast, and he reserved the last two seats for the first of Dr. Nellsom's scheduled visits. If Todd and Lizzie's mother couldn't make it or wasn't interested he would call to inform the organization. Someone who knew and understood learning problems should have the seat! His passion and underlying anger regarding this issue somewhat surprised him. He wasn't prepared for the feelings his son's learning issues were resurrecting.

He again reflected on how stressful his childhood years were in the classroom. Reading was the major culprit, and he remembered that it took him so long, so many years, to feel any sense of mastery! Today, he still found himself reading and rereading instructions, forever questioning his comprehension of written material, and therefore relying on his intuitive talents to keep him feeling as if he were maintaining a leading edge in his field. It was hard work.

Even though Daniel knew his parents couldn't truly understand the private hell he went through each time he sat down with his homework, or when he was called upon to read in front of his peers, they were supportive in their own way. His father would sit in his room with him and help him to prepare for tests. He would read to him and try to help him anticipate the test questions, while Daniel's mother stood in the doorway wringing her hands, riddled with guilt because she herself never learned to read. Daniel's eyes filled with tears from the image he carried of his mother standing in the doorway. He felt determined to do what he could for his son, to break this chain of guilt and shame that constantly enshrouded his life. He was not only a prisoner of his own feelings of inadequacy, but he was helping to foster a sense of secretiveness about his educational history.

Daniel peeked in on Todd, who was chuckling his way through a new comic book. He sat down next to his son, much as his father used to do, and took the comic book away. Todd looked puzzled.

"Hey, I still don't feel good, but it's OK to look at my funny book, isn't it? Huh, Dad?"

"Yup, it's fine. Why don't you read to me. Let's turn back to the first page."

Todd eyed his father with a great deal of suspicion but was willing to take the chance. He loved reading about Red Racer. The pictures made it easier to follow the words, and the boxes kept him moving in the proper sequence. Sequencing information was much more difficult for Todd when looking at only written text.

Daniel laid back and put a pillow under his head, getting comfortable. Todd sat up on the bed, assuming the role of the "teacher."

Todd moved through the pages, sometimes sounding accurate to Daniel, sometimes sounding as if he were making up words to fit the situation or events he was observing from the sequence of illustrations. When he felt stuck he would look at his father and wait for a cue.

"It's OK. Guess at the word for now. You can go back to it later."

Todd continued, and with each page he turned he sounded more confident, more comfortable, more willing to let his father see and hear his mistakes. As Todd finished the last page he said, "That was good Dad, huh? Want me to read you another one? I have *The Great Gorgle* you bought me. There are more words, but I think I can do it for you."

He leaped off the bed and began rummaging through his book bag, returned to the bed, ready to begin again. Daniel didn't want to break the roll they were on and prayed that Lizzie would remain sleeping for a while longer.

As Daniel listened to his son add feeling to the voices of the characters in the story, while struggling with words he could not recognize or sound out, he let himself feel good about the fact that Todd was just simply reading, reading because he wanted to, and reading because he wanted to talk about what he was reading. Maybe this was a step.

Todd stopped in the middle of the story. "Dad, we're still having pizza tonight, right?" Daniel nodded.

"We're still gonna watch a movie before bed tonight, right?" Daniel nodded.

"And we're still gonna see Grandma tomorrow before we go home, right Dad?" Again, Daniel nodded.

"Everything's the same, right Dad?" Daniel grabbed his son and kissed him.

"Of course it is. Now finish The *Great Gorgle* for me. I want to know what happens!"

They basked in the comfort and security of their ritual.

THE SEMINAR

Dr. Nellsom watched the audience file in, carefully choosing their seats. Each setting where she lectured and offered her series of seminars was physically different and seemed to match the overall personality of the group, the community, and the problems the participants were all facing in their families.

This setting was held in a large function hall near a lake. There were large round tables with linen cloths instead of rows of metal chairs like the school she was in last month. This seminar included both urban and suburban families. Despite any difference that might exist in the sociocultural aspect of their lives, they shared common concerns about their children, about their families.

Dr. Nellsom scanned the faces. This was a much more culturally diverse group. She watched as couples and individuals introduced themselves to one another at the refreshment table. She watched the cautious conversations begin, the careful posture of those who weren't sure if they were doing the right thing by being there. She hoped she could quell those feelings of fear and insecurity for people. She was never sure. The anger was often so deeply embedded that it was hard to set it free. Some people needed to keep their anger fueled because they didn't know what to do without it. She knew she couldn't always help those people, and after so many years of doing this work she still felt badly about those whom she couldn't help in some way.

After the group was settled down, the minister from a local church introduced her. He stressed the fact that this was a series of three seminars for parents of children with learning disabilities, and that tonight they would discuss the ways in which families worked together and gathered comfort together.

Dr. Nellsom smiled at her audience. She asked them to take out a piece of blank paper from their packets. Some people were excited about the next move. Others were hesitant about having to write something down, worrying that they would in some way be judged for their responses.

"Crunchy granola. What do you think of when you hear those words? Crunchy granola." She paused for a few seconds. All eyes were upon her.

"Please list your initial thoughts on crunchy granola. This is like free association. What are the things you think about when you see or hear those words? You don't have to show anyone what you wrote, and you don't have to share any of your thoughts if you don't want to. But just try to write down what crunchy granola triggers in your thoughts." They all looked at each other a bit puzzled. Again, some were excited about beginning with an activity. Others remained skeptical.

One by one the participants began to write. Some wrote rapidly. Others were deep in thought while some participants looked around to see what everyone else was doing. Dr. Nellsom gave them about three minutes to respond.

"OK. Do I have any volunteers?"

Louisa, Roberto's mother, shot her hand in the air first. Dr. Nellsom nodded.

"First I thought of cereal. But then thought of something natural, but with substance. Then it felt like something of substance that you can feel that makes you feel better—like healing."

Dr. Nellsom nodded and smiled and pointed to another hand, that of Carrie, Marshall's mother.

"I thought of long skirts, and paintings of women working together, gathering food. I thought of paintings of people that were brown and orange and yellow, that showed the sun—my son is an artist you know. I guess that's how I think." Marshall's art teacher, Ken, patted Carrie on the arm as she spoke. Dr. Nellsom moved on.

Paulette had traveled from the Atlantic Provinces to hear Dr. Nellsom speak. She stood when it was her turn to share her thoughts and faced the audience.

"I run a home school, or really a community school. Crunchy granola is the name of a mixed blend of oats and dried fruits and nuts that our kids package and sell as fund raisers for our school, L'ecole. When I hear the words crunchy granola I visualize our children sitting at a long table in the school's kitchen on Friday mornings, measuring ingredients, filling bags, tying bows. I can smell oats and brown sugar baking in the oven, and I can hear the French music in the background. And laughter—I can hear laughter, children's laughter." Paulette smiled and sat down, so pleased to be here with these people, and anxious to carry what she learned back to her community.

Becky's mother, Martha, raised her hand cautiously. Dr. Nellsom saw the cautiousness with which this woman responded.

"Yes, let's hear from the blonde lady tucked way in the back next to the man with the red plaid shirt." Martha pointed at herself with a questioning look. Dr. Nellsom nodded encouragingly.

"I am a yoga teacher, and when I hear the words crunchy granola I think first of food—food that I recommend my clients eat. Then I think of ways of healing, different ways for different people I guess. But crunchy granola sounds so natural, so real, and so good for you. Hope that makes sense." Martha sat down again hesitantly.

Daniel was sitting next to Martha and congratulated her on her contribution.

"I'm too self-conscious to stand up I guess. I'm afraid that I'll say something way off the mark." He looked ill at ease.

"Don't feel that way!" Martha gushed. "It's just important that we're all here. It's not important whether or not you have anything to say. We're all here to learn from each other and from Dr. Nellsom, and we all do it in our own way, in our own time." She smiled at Daniel. "Relax . . . breathe."

Daniel tried to take a deep breath, but found it difficult to get beyond his own feelings of self-consciousness.

Several more people contributed to the group sharing. Then Dr. Nellsom asked that the larger group of about one-hundred people, break into groups of ten. Most people stayed at the tables where they were already seated, while others began to wander about the room looking for a familiar face, or a better place to hide.

When they were all situated, Dr. Nellsom asked that they appoint a recorder in their group, someone to write down the ideas they would eventually share. After some initial mumblings and further shifting of seats Dr. Nellsom gave her instructions.

"I would like each group to talk about the things they do together with their kids, as families. What are the kinds of things you do together on a regular basis that takes the pressure off of two important issues: (1) your worry as a parent about your child with a learning disability in school, and (2) your child's concerns with school. What are the things you do together that *do not* focus on either or both of these issues?"

Before she could get the last two words out of her mouth, conversation started buzzing. Voices rose, laughter bounced off the walls. People smiled. There was a great clanging of spoons and cups and saucers at each table. Wait staff kept refilling the platters of pastry, bowls of sugar, and pitchers of milk.

Dr. Nellsom found herself intrigued with Daniel. She watched him carefully as he clung to his first connection, Martha. Martha seemed to be pulling him along with her, as she herself began to feel more confident. Dr. Nellsom knew that Daniel would have a great deal to contribute to this first seminar. He knew a lot. She would find a way for him to share his wealth of experience and knowledge so that he would not feel intimidated. He looked up at her from a nearby table and their eyes locked. He smiled tentatively at her. She beckoned to him to come speak with her.

As he sat down with her at a small table he noticed how noisy the large room had become and strained to hear what Dr. Nellsom had to say to him.

"I sense that you have a lot to say about *Crunchy Granola, Intellectualism, and Wisdom for the Family.* Am I right?"

Daniel smiled.

APPENDIX

INTERNET RESOURCES FOR CHILDREN

http://www.americaslibrary.gov
Library of Congress Web site for families

http://www.askjeevesforkids
Info site for kids

http://www.bookwire.com/links/readingroom/echildbooks.html
Presents classics to read on screen or print out

http://forum.swarthmore.edu
Ask Dr. Math answers frequently asked math questions

http://www.funbrain.com
Learning games for kids

http://www.infoplease.com
Encyclopedia, dictionary, almanacs, biographies

http://www.kidsdomain.com
Learning games and activities for kids, information for parents

http://www.libraryspot.com
Access to all kinds of reference materials and tools for children and parents

http://www.magico/math.com
Math activities and answers to math questions

http://www.nosweat.com
Includes Homework Central (grades 1–6 and 7–12) and Encyclopedia Central (college) reference and study site

http://www.onelook.com
Dictionary

http://www.pbskids.org/zoom
Activities for kids; kids can submit ideas

http://www.refdesk.com
Dictionary, encyclopedia

http://www.scholastic.com
Interesting material for children

http://www.schoolwork.org
Reference and homework help

http://www.studyweb.com
Reference and homework help

http://www.wordcentral.com
Merriam-Webster reference site

http://www.Yahooligans.com
Educational activities and homework help for children; information for parents

INTERNET RESOURCES FOR PARENTS

http://www.aap.or
The American Academy of Pediatrics site for information on wide range of topics

http://www.childrenssoftware.com/
Info on technology and family needs, product reviews from Children's Software Revue

htt://www.ericec.org
Eric Clearinghouse on Disabilities and Gifted Education

http://familyeducation.com
Info on education, LD, assistive technology; activities for children

http://familypc.com
Info on technology and family needs, product reviews

http://www.getnetwise.org
Strategies for Protecting Children on the Web

http://www.hood.edu/seri/serihome.htm#learning_disabilities
Lists many Internet resources for information and organizations

http://www.kidsource.com
A commercial site but good resource for material

http://www.ld101.com
Excellent site for LD info and links to other sites

http://ldonline.org
Coordinated Campaign for Learning Disabilities site; excellent source of information

http://www.ldresources.com
Information on learning disabilities and links to other sites

http://www.ncld.org
Site of the National Center for Learning Disabilities

http://www.npin.org
National Parent Information Network site—educational database and links to other sites (sponsored by ERIC and funded by U.S. Department of Education)

http://www.parentsoup.com/onlineguide
Strategies for protecting children on the Web

http://www.rgu.ac.uk/~sim/research/netlearn/web.html
An Internet learning resources directory

http://schwablearning.org
Excellent site for info on education, special needs, technology, etc.

http://www.thegateway.org
Lesson plans and educational resources from ERIC Clearinghouse on Information and Technology

http://www.todaysparent.com
General parenting site based in Canada

http://www.tutor.com/resources
Learning resources for parents and children; help in finding tutors

http://www.ups.edu/community/tofu
Suggestions for helping children learn math

http://www.voicenet.com/~sakossor
Education newsletter

COMPANIES/SUPPLIERS

AlphaSmart
Intelligent Peripheral Devices
20400 Stevens Creek Boulevard, Suite 300
Cupertino, CA 95014
http://www.alphasmart.com
888–274–0680
Portable keyboard

Beyond.com
http://www.beyond.com
Educational software

Broderbund Software
17 Paul Drive
San Rafael, CA 94903
415–492–3200
800–521–6263
Educational software

Cognitive Concepts
1123 Emerson Street
Evanston, IL 60201
888–328–8199
http://www.cogcon.com
Educational software and learning materials

Didax Media
395 Main Street
Rowley, MA 01969
800–458–0024
http://www.didaxinc.com
Educational materials

Dragon Systems
Lernout and Hauspie
52 Third Avenue
Burlington, MA 01803
800–437–2466
http://www.dragonsys.com
Voice-to-text software

Franklin Learning Resources
Franklin Plaza
Burlington, NJ 08016
800–266–5626

http://franklin.com
Electronic speller/thesaurus and e-books

High Noon Books
20 Commercial Blvd.
Novato, CA 94049
800–422–7249
High-interest/low-reading level books

Inspiration Software
7412 SW Beaverton Hillsdale Hwy., Suite 102
Portland, OR 97225
http://www.inspiration.com
Software for organizing ideas

IntelliTools
1720 Corporate Circle
Petaluma, CA 94954
800–899–6687
http://www.intellitools.com
Hardware and software for special needs

Laureate Learning Systems
110 E. Spring Street
Winooski, VT 05404
800–562–6801
http://www.laureatelearning.com
Special needs software

The Learning Company/Mattell
6493 Kaiser Drive
Fremont, CA 94555
415–792–2101
800–852–2255
Educational software
http://www.learningcompany.com

Lernout and Hauspie
52 Third Avenue
Burlington, MA 01803
781–203–5000
http://www.1hs1.com
Text-to-voice software including Kurzweil System and RealSpeak

Scholastic Magazines and Books
50 W. 44th Street
New York, NY 10036

http://www.scholastic.com
Reading materials including high-interest/low-reading level

Smarterkids.com
800–293–9314
http://www.smarterkids.com
Educational software and parent information site

Sunburst Communications
101 Castleton St.
Pleasantville, NY 10570
800–321–7511
Educational software

WizCom Technologies
257 Great Rd.
Acton, MA 01720
888–777–0552
978–635–5357
http://www.wizomtech.com
QuickLink Pen portable scanner, Quicktionary Reading Pen, electronic
    dictionaries

ORGANIZATIONS

Association on Higher Education and Disability (AHEAD)
University of Massachusetts
Morrissey Blvd.
Boston, MA 02125
617–287–3880
http://www.ahead.org

Association of Educational Therapists
14852 Ventura Blvd.
Sherman Oaks, CA 91403
http://www.aetonline.org

CAST
89 Cross Street
Peabody, MA 01960
888–558–9994
http://www.cast.org
Educational organization fostering use of technology for individuals with and
    without disabilities

Children and Adults with Attention Deficit Disorder (CHADD)
8181 Professional Place, Suite 201

Landover, MD 20785
301–306–7070
http://www.chadd.org

Coordinated Campaign for Learning Disabilities (CCLD)
888–478–6463

Council for Exceptional Children (CEC)
Division for Learning Disabilities
1920 Association Drive
Reston, VA 22091
888–CEC–SPED (888–232–7733)
http://www.cec.sped.org

Council for Learning Disabilities
P.O. Box 40303
Overland Park, KS 66204
913–492–8755

Educational Resources Information Center (ERIC)
1920 Association Drive
Reston, VA 22091
703–264–9474
800–328–0272
http://www.ericec.org

Federation for Children with Special Needs
1135 Tremont Street
Boston, MA 02120
617–236–7210
http://www.fcsn.org

HEATH Resource Center
1 Dupont Circle, Suite 800
Washington, DC 20036

International Dyslexia Association (formerly Orton Dyslexia Society)
Chester Building, Suite 382
8600 LaSalle Road
Baltimore, MD 21286–2044
800–222–3123
410–296–0232
http://www.interdys.org

Learning Disabilities Association of America
4156 Library Road
Pittsburgh, PA 15234
412–341–1515

888–300–6710
http://www.ldanatl.org

Learning Disabilities Association of Canada
323 Chapel Street
Ottawa, Ontario, Canada, KIN 7Z2

National Association of Private Schools for Exceptional Children
1522 K Street, NW, Suite 1032
Washington, DC 20005
202–408–3338

National Center for Law and Learning Disabilities (NCLLD)
P.O. Box 368
Cabin John, MD 20818
301–469–8308

National Center for Learning Disabilities (NCLD)
381 Park Avenue South, Suite 1401
New York, NY 10016
212–545–7510
888–575–7373
http://www.ncld.org/

Parents of Gifted/LD Children, Inc.
2420 Eccleston Street
Silver Springs, MD 20902
301–986–1422
e-mail: pgtld@geocities.com

Program for the Advancement of Learning
Curry College
1071 Blue Hill Avenue
Milton, MA 02186
617–333–2250
Support program for college students and adults with LD; diagnostic
   center

Recordings for the Blind and Dyslexic
20 Roszel Road
Princeton, NJ 08540
800–221–4792
http://www.rfbd.org
Textbooks on tape

Schwab Foundation for Learning
1650 South Amphlett Blvd., Suite 300
San Mateo, CA 94402

650–655–2410
800–230–0988
http://www.schwablearning.org
Information source

U.S. Department of Education
Office of Special Education and Rehabilitative Services
The Switzer Building, Rm. 3006
330 C Street, SW
Washington, DC 20202
202–205–5465

BIBLIOGRAPHY

Adelizzi, J. (1996). *The impact of psychological trauma on learning and functioning in women with learning disabilities: Looking at classroom trauma.* Doctoral Dissertation, Lesley College, Cambridge, MA.

Adelizzi, J. (1998). *Shades of trauma: The impact of psychological trauma on learning and functioning in women.* Plymouth, MA: Jones River Press.

Adelizzi, J., and Goss, D. (1995). *A closer look: Perspectives and reflections on college students with learning disabilities.* Milton, MA: Curry College.

American Psychiatric Association. (1994). *Diagnostic and statistical manual of mental disorders (4th ed.).* Washington, DC: American Psychiatric Association.

Ayers, A. J. (1985). *Sensory integration and the child.* Los Angeles: Western Psychological Services.

Brooks, R. B. (1991a). The learning disabled adolescent: A portrait. *Their World,* 27–31. Washington, DC: NCLD.

Brooks, R. B. (1991b). *The self-esteem teacher.* Circle Pines, MN: American Guidance Services.

Caine, G., and Caine, R. (1991). *Teaching and the human brain.* Alexandria, VA: Association for Supervision and Curriculum Development.

Caine, R., and Caine, G. (1994). *Making connections: Teaching and the human brain.* Menlo Park, CA: Addison Wesley.

Coordinated Campaign for Learning Disabilities. (1998). *Learning disabilities: Information, strategies, resources.* Washington, DC: Communication Consortium Media Center.

Elliot, S. (1992). Authentic assessment: An introduction to the neo-behavioral approach to classroom assessment. *School Psychology Quarterly* 6 (4), 62–67.

Fey, M., Windsor, J., and Warren, S. (eds.). (1995). *Language intervention: Pre-school through the elementary years.* Baltimore: Paul H. Brookes.

Fuqua, P. B., M.D. (1993). *A model of the learning process based on self-psychology: Emotions and learning reconsidered.* New York: Gardner Press.

Gaddes, W. H. (1985). *Learning disabilities and brain function: A neuropsychological approach.* New York: Springer-Verlag.

Gardner, H. (1983). *Frames of mind: The theory of multiple intelligences.* New York: Basic Books.

Geary, D. (1994). *Children's mathematical development: Research and practical applications.* Washington, DC: American Psychological Association.

Goleman, D. (1995). *Emotional intelligence.* New York: Bantam Books.

Hart, L. (1983). *Human brain and human learning.* New York: Longman.

Kaufman, A. S. (1990). *Assessing adolescent and adult intelligence.* Boston: Allyn and Bacon.

Lerner, J. (2000). *Learning disabilities: Theories, diagnosis, and teaching strategies* 8th ed. Boston: Houghton Mifflin.

Lewis, R. (1998). Assistive technology and learning disabilities: Today's realities and tomorrow's promises. *Journal of Learning Disabilities* 31 (1), 16–26.

MacArthur, C. (1996). Using technology to enhance the writing process of students with learning disabilities. *Journal of Learning Disabilities* 29, 344–54.

MacLean, P. D. (1973). *A triune concept of brain and behavior.* Toronto: Toronto University Press.

Mercer, C., Jordan, L., Alsop, D., and Mercer, A. (1996). Learning disabilities definitions and criteria used by the state education departments. *Learning Disability Quarterly* 19 (2), 217–32.

Ornstein, R., and Thompson, R. (1984). *The amazing brain.* Boston: Houghton Mifflin.

Osman, B. (1979). *Learning disabilities: A family affair.* New York: Warner Books.

Rourke, B. (1989). *Nonverbal learning disabilities: The syndrome and the model.* New York: Guilford Press.

Rourke, B., and Fuerst, D. R. (1995). *Learning disabilities syndrome of nonverbal learning disabilities: Neurodevelopmental manifestations.* New York: Guilford Press.

Rudel, R. G., with Holmes, J. and Pardes, J. (1988). *Assessment of developmental learning disorders: A neuropsychological approach*. New York: Basic Books.

Sprenger, M. (1999). *Learning and memory: The brain in action*. Alexandria, VA: Association for Supervision and Curriculum Development.

Stahl, N. A. (1983). *Historical analysis of textbook study-systems*. Doctoral dissertation, University of Pittsburgh.

Swanson, H. L. (ed.). (1991). *Handbook on the assessment of learning disabilities: Theory, research, and practice*. Austin, TX: Pro-Ed.

Troia, G., Graham, S., and Harris, H. (1998). Teaching students with learning disabilities to mindfully plan when writing. *Exceptional Children* 65 (2), 235–52.

Ungerleider, D. F. (1985). *Reading, writing, and rage: The terrible price paid by victims of school failure*. Rolling Hills Estates, CA: Jalmar Press.

SUGGESTIONS FOR FURTHER READING

Graves, R. (1987). *The RIF guide to encouraging young readers*. New York: Doubleday.

Greene, L. (1987). *Learning disabilities and your child: A survival handbook*. New York: Fawcett Columbine.

Hurford, D. (1998). *To read or not to read: Answers to all your questions about dyslexia*. New York: Touchstone.

Lauren, J. (1997). *Succeeding with LD: Twenty true stories about real people with LD*. Minneapolis: Free Spirit.

Naparstek, N. (1995). *The learning solution: What to do if your child has trouble with schoolwork*. New York: Avon Books.

Oliver, C., and Bowler, R. (1996). *Learning to learn*. New York: Fireside.

Silver, L. (1998). *The misunderstood child: Understanding and coping with your child's learning disabilities*. New York: Times Books.

Smith, C., and Strick, L. (1997). *Learning disabilities: A to Z: A parent's complete guide to learning disabilities from preschool to adulthood*. New York: Free Press.

Smith, S. (1991). *Succeeding against the odds: How the learning disabled realize their promise*. Los Angeles: Jeremy Tarcher.

Stevens, S. (1996). *The LD child and the ADD child: Ways parents and professionals can help*. Winston-Salem, NC: John F. Blair Publisher.

Tuttle, C., and Paquette, P. (1993). *Parenting a child with a learning disability*. New York: Doubleday.

Weiss, E. (1989). *Mothers talk about learning disabilities*. New York: Prentice-Hall.

INDEX

About the Authors

JANE UTLEY ADELIZZI is a Professor in the Program for the Advancement of Learning and in the Master of Education Program, Curry College, Milton, Massachusetts.

DIANE B. GOSS is a Professor in the Program for the Advancement of Learning and in the Master of Education Program, Curry College, Milton, Massachusetts.